D0908367

Substantial Proofs of Being:
Osip Mandelstam's Literary Prose

Substantial Proofs of Being: Osip Mandelstam's Literary Prose

Charles Isenberg

Slavica Publishers, Inc.
Columbus, Ohio

Slavica publishes a wide variety of books and journals dealing with the peoples, languages, literatures, history, folklore, and culture of the peoples of Eastern Europe and the USSR. For a complete catalog with prices and ordering information, please write to:

Slavica Publishers, Inc.
P.O. Box 14388
Columbus, Ohio 43214
USA

ISBN: 0-89357-169-5.

Text set by Rebecca Wells and Randy Bowlus at the East European Composition Center, supported by the Department of Slavic Languages and Literatures and the Center for Russian and East European Studies at UCLA.

Printed in the United States of America.

ACKNOWLEDGEMENTS

At each stage of work on this study, since its beginnings as a doctoral dissertation, I have been fortunate in finding exemplary readers, for whose criticisms and suggestions I am deeply grateful. It gives me pleasure to acknowledge my indebtedness to Donald Fanger and Kiril Taranovsky, the directors of the dissertation, who gave me my first inkling of what might be involved in an ideal process of scholarly collaboration; to Vida Johnson, J. Marin King, Lena Lencek, Leslie O'Bell, and Valery Petrochenkov for their attentive and helpful readings of the earliest version; and to Sidney Monas, Duffield White, Robert Whitman, and Khachig Tololyan, whose sustained critical attention and support encouraged me to see the project through. I would also like to thank Mrs. Mary Lou Nelles, who patiently typed and retyped the manuscript. Finally, I owe a special debt of gratitude to the AGBU Alex Manoogian Cultural Fund, which provided a subvention for the publication of my research.

CONTENTS

INTRODUCTION

For more than five years, beginning in 1926, the poet Osip Mandelstam wrote not a single poem. This long poetic silence followed upon a four-year period that Mandelstam was later to call the worst in his life. Nadezhda Mandelstam's account, from which the following details are drawn, suggests that her husband's unhappiness, and the loss of his poetic voice, had both external causes and internal, spiritual causes.[1]

One external factor was the social isolation, shading into ostracism, which began as early as 1922. More ominously, in 1923 Mandelstam came under individual investigation by the state security apparatus. The virtual banning of Mandelstam's verse from the Moscow and Leningrad journals was one token of this attention; another was an effort at intimidation that made use of acquaintances of the poet, who were encouraged or instructed by the Cheka to let Mandelstam know of its interest in him. Unable to publish his poetry, Mandelstam was compelled to eke out a living as a translator, a form of labor that drew upon reserves which might otherwise have fed his poetic imagination. His status as an ousider not only gave him little leverage with the publishing houses that commissioned translations, it guaranteed an unsettled existence. Mandelstam's troubled relations with the literary organizations meant that there was no official body that would sponsor him for an apartment or assure him of sufficient work to allow him to remain in one place. As it was, he had to be continually on the move between the capitals, hunting commissions or assistance.

But these are externalities, and external circumstances were to be worse later, after Mandelstam had recovered his equilibrium. Nadezhda Mandelstam conjectures that the true cause of the cessation of his poetry was the loss of "a sense of rightness," a phrase that echoes Mandelstam's youthful article "On the Addressee": "Poetry, after all, is the consciousness of one's own rightness" (II, 326).[2] In the twenties, the demoralized poet was held in a double bind. He was caught between his allegiance to a humanist ethic, shaped by both his Jewish background and the Christian, European culture that drew him, and the moral claims advanced by apologists of the new Soviet order. Appealing to Mandelstam's faith as a Russian *intelligent* in "Revolution with a capital 'R',"[3] these claims were increasingly at variance with his perception of how the Soviet state was changing into a new form of tyranny.

Yet it was not only the moral force vested in the revolutionary ideal that made it difficult for Mandelstam and his contemporaries to see the new order unambiguously. There was also the conviction that, as men and women formed by a world that had passed away, they must free themselves from the burden of outmoded attitudes and values before they might judge the new world. Deny the claims of the past in order to belong to the present, or accept a lack of connection to the age in order to inherit the past: it is not difficult to imagine the inner division that such a choice imposes.

Such was Mandelstam's dilemma until the mid-twenties, after which he gradually regained a larger measure of spiritual freedom. This he accomplished by rejecting the moral pretensions of Bolshevism and by affirming his right to determine his own standards of judgment. From Nadezhda Mandelstam's account, and still more her husband's letters and his "Fourth Prose," it would appear that as the twenties wore on, Mandelstam's poetic silence, whatever the inner conflicts that may have contributed to it originally, was prolonged by pressures from without. As his spiritual dilemma abated, he seems to have been increasingly weighed down by his thralldom to translation, to what he complained of as "constant interruptions, periods of unemployment, searches for a book [to be translated], busywork, and torments."[4]

The literary establishment that refused to acknowledge Mandelstam as a poet also made it increasingly difficult for him to work as a translator. His time was occupied with dunning his publishers, soliciting work, and fighting for professional standards of translation. Then, in 1928, he became the defendant in the so-called Ulenspiegel Affair, a plagiarism controversy that, as it dragged on, developed elements of an antisemitic provocation. All this prevented him, as he put it in "Fourth Prose," from "doing the one thing that could justify [his] existence." Although Mandelstam knew that translating and its attendant cares were suffocating his poetic gift, economic necessity compelled him to expend all his energies just trying to assure the possibility of work that he loathed. This, however, was a bind that admitted of a simpler resolution, which began with Mandelstam's repudiation of the writer's organizations in the wake of the Ulenspiegel scandal. In October of 1930 he began writing verse again.

The contradictions confronting Mandelstam were bound to be displayed in his art, for he was a writer much occupied by his relationship to his times. In all his writings of the twenties and thirties, Mandelstam searches for resolutions to the discords of his world and, ultimately, moves towards his own end, the "teleological cause," as he had once put it, of an artist's work.[5] During the decade and more when he was groping toward a system of values adequate to the world taking shape about him, he transposed his inner uncertainties into the themes of his poetry, his articles and essays, and a series of remarkable prose pieces: The "Noise of Time," *The Egyptian Stamp*, "Fourth Prose," and "Journey to Armenia." In these prose works,

Mandelstam explores new themes, voices, and manners. They can be read as fragments of a longer fiction, at whose heart there lies a confrontation with a series of cultural traditions (e.g., Russian, Jewish, Armenian) to which the narrator's or implicit author's relationship is ambiguous or to which he must earn the right of access. These works, each of which epitomizes some stage in the poet's search for a cultural synthesis, are the subject of the present investigation.

Mandelstam is a brilliant stylist in any genre he assays; yet it is not the brilliance of his writing that gives it a place in world literature but the way in which his style serves a distinctive vision. As he himself foresaw, he has become a writer for our day; in large part, I think, because the dilemmas he faced are our dilemmas also. Our age, after all, is no less ambivalent than his about revolutionary change, about the enterprise of culture, and about our individual connections to the traditions that have formed us.

A writer however, can speak to us only to the extent that he is accessible to us. Every great writer must form his own audience, aided perhaps, by the criticism that grows up around his work. Because the antagonism of the Soviet literary establishment so greatly restricted Mandelstam's opportunities to shape a readership capable of appreciating his achievement, considerably more of this task has devolved upon his critics. In this study I would like to address two groups that ought to constitute an audience for Mandelstam's prose: the first consists of specialists in Russian modernism; the second, of general readers. This second group of readers, who may be confronting either the original texts or translated versions, I hope to serve by providing commentary that goes beyond the tracing of particular allusions to suggest a general approach to Mandelstam's literary prose. This approach will focus on how conflicts that shape the work are displayed through a tension between what Dmitrij Segal has called "the semantics of a text and its formal structure";[6] that is, loosely speaking, between connotative meaning and plot.

Attention to semantics also yields that surest of grounds for deciding which of Mandelstam's writings might best be classed as literary prose. The most superficial reading of Mandelstam's prose cannot fail to make clear to the reader the limited relevance of traditional notions of "fiction"—a term, which, moreover, is narrower in its meaning than the Russian "xudožestvennaja proza," 'literary prose'. Yet the inapplicability of traditional genre distinctions does not imply the disappearance of genre as such; the critic cannot, therefore, follow Mandelstam's own practice of referring to all his prose pieces as simply "proses." But if the problem of how to demarcate literary from nonliterary prose cannot be completely avoided, still there is no need to make heavy weather of it. Since Mandelstam did not single out any of his writings as fiction, there exists no canonical division of his prose according to genre. Any such selection will be a subjective one; the only obligation is to be explicit about the criteria behind the choices.

The following pieces seem to me to represent virtually the entire extent of Mandelstam's literary prose: *The Noise of Time, The Egyptian Stamp,* "Fourth Prose," and "Journey to Armenia." My argument in favor of this selection is that these are texts that are primarily oriented toward language in its aesthetic function,[7] whereas most nonliterary prose is oriented toward the conveyance of information. All nonfiction is "about" its subject, and is judged according to the accuracy or truthfulness with which that subject is encoded in the text. Literary criticism, for example, aims at communicating to its audience something about the properties of literature; a guidebook's message has to do with the places that it describes; a factual biography communicates the history of its subject. In literary prose, on the other hand, the kind of referential meaning that links the text with external reality plays a less all-determining role. In other words, the literariness of fiction or poetry is independent of the ways in which the work may be "about" objects outside itself. If an emphasis on the possibilities of language is what distinguishes literature from nonliterature, the empirical test of truthfulness must be replaced by the semantic criterion of coherence; the appeal to veracity, by density of meaning.

The stylistic affinities that mark all of Mandelstam's writing rule out the possibility of an absolute division between literary and nonliterary forms and necessitate a distinction based upon the relative importance of fictional qualities within each piece. Still, on this basis even such highly metaphorical pieces as *On the Nature of the Word* and the *Conversation About Dante* can be classed as nonfiction. A rule of asymmetry seems to apply here: it takes only a slight degree of willfulness to read and respond to many of Mandelstam's essays and articles as fictions, but to read the literary prose—rich though it may be in autobiographical detail—as nonfiction would lead to an impoverishment of meaning. If the strikingly literary style of the poet's essays subserves utilitarian and didactic ends, it is the aesthetic function which is central to the four works I have classified as literary prose.

The freedom in relation to external structures which is the sign of autonomous fiction is most obviously present in *The Egyptian Stamp,*[8] which the author himself referred to as a *povest',* 'novella' or 'tale'. The essential literariness of *The Noise in Time* is signaled by the ways in which it polemicizes with the confessional and memoiristic tradition in autobiographical prose represented by Aksakov and Tolstoj. In their social remoteness and their fascination with family history, the "epic domestic reminiscences" of these writers are incomprehensible to Mandelstam's narrator, whose stated intent is to distance the past not reproduce it. Yet the attempt, in *The Noise of Time*,[9] to distance and overcome the past by dissolving its real connections and recombining its elements into aesthetic patterns reveals the same, eminently literary impulse that shapes the fictions of childhood created by Mandelstam's great predecessors.

In "Fourth Prose"[10] Mandelstam annihilates his enemies by means of the epithets and similes with which he characterizes them. This use of writing as a symbolic form of retaliation reminds one of Dostoevskij, Rozanov, and Bulgakov. However, for an analogy in Russian literature that is closer in spirit to "Fourth Prose" it is necessary to go further afield, to the Cossacks' reply to the sultan in the Azov Tale, or perhaps to the fulminations of the Archpriest Avvakum, whose *Life* Mandelstam read as a boy. The trait shared by these seventeenth-century works and "Fourth Prose" is their rhetorical quality. As examples of the rhetoric of invective, their dominant orientation would, on the surface, seem to be toward the expressive, and perhaps the hortative functions of language: the Cossacks wish to demonstrate their fighting spirit and loyalty to the faith; Avvakum expresses the strength of his belief and calumniates his enemies; Mandelstam vents his sense of outrage and his hostility towards state-approved "Literature." However, as must be the case with any great piece of invective, the artistic qualities of these works overshadow their expressive or publicistic intentions. The pleasure of reading them has less to do with their historical subjects than with their capacity, as highly organized and complex linguistic performances, to embody a certain incantatory potential of the "word as such." "Fourth Prose" is rancor raised to the level of art.

As for the "Journey to Armenia,"[11] it is an idiosyncratic transformation of the conventions of the literature of travel. While it has its origins in the ostensibly factual journals of early travelers and in the utilitarian type of the modern guidebook, this genre belongs to artistic literature insofar as it is marked by the simultaneous presence of two levels: in addition to the account of places visited, the literature of travel traces some "journey" of the narrator's consciousness. The juxtaposition of these levels has the literary effect of turning the places and people described into images that are correlates for the narrator's state of mind. Mandelstam's "Journey" represents an advanced stage in this process; it is less about Armenia than it is about the faculties of vision and memory.

Because Mandelstam's prose is a poet's prose, these four texts call for the kind of close reading one brings to a poem. The main part of this study is an attempt at such a reading. In the first chapter, however, the focus will be on Mandelstam's verse and criticism as the context in which the prose appears.

CHAPTER ONE

The bare recitation of the circumstances of his birth and death already tells us something of the forces to which Mandelstam responds in his writing: born to a middle-class Jewish family in Warsaw in January 1891 (O.S.), Mandelstam died in a Stalinist transit camp near Vladivostok on or around 27 December 1938 (N.S.). He thus belongs to those newcomers—among them several Jews—who were entering a literary tradition that had been largely a gentry and ethnic-Russian preserve until the last decades of the nineteenth century.[1] In his end, too, he belongs to his literary cohort, decimated by Stalin. The circumstances of Mandelstam's origins are pertinent to more than the sociology of literature, for they help to account for the sense of marginality and the pathos of being torn between potential cultural allegiances that operate in his writing. Moreover, Mandelstam's evolving attitude toward his Jewishness is an important dimension of his growth as a writer. These are threads that will therefore be picked up at several points in this study.

If Mandelstam's Jewishness is unexceptional for a writer of his generation, his being born in Warsaw seems, as Clarence Brown puts it, a "slightly discordant" fact, anomalous in a writer who would be so closely identified with St. Petersburg.[2] Although Osip Mandelstam spent his earliest childhood in the Polish capital, *The Noise of Time* places his family in St. Petersburg by 1894. The poet's only reminiscence of the city of his infancy is found in a half memory, half nightmare that is recalled by the narrator of *The Egyptian Stamp*: "And I was led into a hateful Warsaw room and made to drink water and eat some onion."[3]

What would have happened if the circumstances that brought the Mandelstams to Warsaw had left them there? Might Osip have become a great Polish poet? Or even—given the vitality and historical rootedness of Warsaw's Jewish community—a great Yiddish or Hebrew poet? These absurd might-have-beens may serve to underscore the truth that Mandelstam was born with his gift but had to make himself into a Russian poet.

Central to this enterprise, which we may follow Nadezhda Mandelstam in calling "the growth of the poetic personality," is Mandelstam's attitude toward culture and toward his own place within it. As his widow points out, when Mandelstam uses the term "culture" in a critical, rather than a merely descriptive way, he alternates between two emphases. At times, for example in draft notes pertaining to the "Conversation About Dante," he identifies particular cultures with what he calls their *priličie*, "decorum" or "protocol," which stands for something like E. R. Dodds's "inherited conglomerate," the sum of a society's static and unexamined beliefs and customs. For Mandelstam, it is a task of poetic language to challenge culture-as-decorum, reanimating its frozen forms. Elsewhere (the much earlier "The Word and Culture," for example), "culture" encompasses the sphere of ethics, the aesthetic and other texts that embody its history, and those who seek to safeguard and extend its humanizing influence. It grows out of tradition, but, as the necessary antithesis of culture-decorum, it is also in a perpetual struggle with tradition. "Culture" in this sense is not something one has or belongs to; it is always a matter of volition and contingency, always in a state of becoming. The writer thus acculturates not simply by aligning himself with an authoritative tradition but by reinterpreting it. Sixteen years after this 1921 article, it was along these lines that the exiled and hounded poet was to make a claim for his own achievement, in a letter to the critic and novelist Jurij Tynjanov:

> Please don't think of me as a shadow: I still cast a shadow. But lately I am becoming comprehensible to absolutely everyone. That's ominous. Here it is already a quarter of a century that I, mixing together the important and the trivial, float upon the surface of Russian poetry. *Soon, however, my verses will merge with it, having changed a thing or two in its structure and makeup.* (III, 280-81; my italics)

The young Mandelstam saw in Christianity the principle of authority that underlay and inspired modern Russian and European culture. His youthful Christianity was an ethical and aesthetic resource; beyond a pro forma conversion to Lutheranism to evade St. Petersburg University's numerus clausus, he never adhered to any church. In the style of his apostasy, Mandelstam reflects a belief, shared by many of his assimilationist contemporaries, that Christianity was the gateway to secular Europe. That something like this equation of Christianity with modern secular culture was at one time part of Mandelstam's outlook is suggested by a wonderfully ambiguous passage, also from "The Word and Culture":[4]

> . . . *Culture has become a church.* The separation of this church of culture and the state has taken place. Secular life no longer affects us; we no longer have food, but a monk's repast; not a room, but a cell; not clothing, but vestments. At last we have attained inner freedom, genuine inner mirth. Water in clay jugs we drink as if it were wine, and the sun would sooner shine in a monastery refectory than in a restaurant. Apples, bread, and potatoes henceforth quench not only physical but spiritual hunger. The Christian (*and now every cultured person is a Christian*) knows not only physical hunger, not only spir-

itual sustenance. For him the word is flesh and ordinary bread a joy and a mystery (II, 223; my emphasis).

Elsewhere Mandelstam would broaden the basis of authority to find a place for classical and Jewish influences at the fountainhead of European culture. What remains an invariant feature of his poetic world is a rhetoric that sacralizes the humble artifacts of everyday life, its "water in clay jugs" and "apples, bread, and potatoes." This cherishing of everyday objects as the embodiment of spiritual values gives a peculiar emotional force to Mandelstam's quest for a synthetic culture; his art enshrines a domesticity raised to a metaphysical principle. All of his work might be said to ask the question, how is one to make oneself at home in the face of a condition of perpetual homelessness?

If we want to trace the implications of this problematic, we must be prepared to cast our nets widely. Each of Mandelstam's writings is "open," in the sense that its associations direct the reader outwards. The work discloses its full significance only in relation to what is outside itself. Reading Mandelstam, one senses that any given text is but the tip of an iceberg whose base extends deeply into the currents of history and culture. The intermediate "extratextual structures" (in Jurij Lotman's phrase) that extend between tip and base include the poet's entire body of work. Hence keys to a passage of literary prose may be located in rather remote contexts in his criticism and poetry, not to mention his biography.

Mandelstam's work can be thought of as a single system of global text. What unites the strands of this text is the author's voice: the lyric hero of the verse, the narrator of the literary prose, and the author of the essays and criticism are all recognizable as hypostases of the same poetic personality. Within this system, however, the prose has deeper ties to the verse than to the criticism. The latter may announce a literary project or provide an essential gloss, but the main work of self-construction begins in the verse, continues for a time in the literary prose, and culminates in the later verse. Prose and verse are refractions of the same lyricism, introspection, and inner struggle.

The world of Mandelstam's literary prose takes its origins and horizons from the verse; the lyric hero's history is the prehistory of the prose narrator. A diachronic approach to the authorial persona can enrich our sense of the interconnectedness of Mandelstam's verse and prose, and it cannot but enhance our appreciation of how his model of the world changes as he moves away from his beginnings

STONE

The lyric hero of Mandelstam's early verse (roughly 1908-12) expresses a decorous sadness and an attitude of renunciation. The pleasures he permits himself are quiet and austere ones:

> A suffocating gloom covers the bed,
> And my chest strains for air . . .
> Perhaps what I most prefer
> Is a slender cross and a secret path.
>
> 1910

The quietude and melancholy of this otherwise featureless speaker owe nothing to the conceit of worldweariness often found in the verse of very young Russian poets. Whereas in Pushkin's adolescent verse, for example, the renunciation is motivated by a surfeit of worldly pleasures, the causes of this speaker's malaise are elided.

In general, as Lidija Ginzburg has observed, these early poems are not really *about* the speaker or his emotions.[5] Contemplating hushed, unpopulated landscapes and still lifes, he is mainly a function of the kind of poems with which Mandelstam makes his debut. These show a strong tendency toward minimalism, toward the deletion of everything but the single lyric perception at the poem's center, whether it be of a pregnant silence, an intimation of mortality, or simply of a turquoise veil, evoking summer in a sunlit winter room.

The beginning poet shows himself to be an acolyte of his Symbolist mentors. Symbolist elements include the solipsistic quality, reminiscent of Fedor Sologub, the vaguely despairing mood, and, most important, the contemplation of ambiguous states that may disclose a link between the transcendent world and our fallen world of appearances.

Mandelstam was soon to reject all of this. The intensity of his revolt is suggested by Nadezhda Mandelstam's claim that for this quondam Symbolist "the struggle against Symbolism came to define the whole essence of his life and art."[6] It may be that the seeds of this revolt are to be seen as early as the little quatrain quoted above. In it the motifs of suffocation suggest a barely mastered anxiety underneath the pose of ascetic calm, as if the lyric hero were being suffocated by the role he has selected from the Symbolist repertoire. Another lyric from the same year dramatizes this inner struggle:

> The dark bonds of earthly confinement
> I have found no way of overcoming,
> And I am sheathed from head to toe
> In a heavy armor of contempt.

> At times I am followed by a double,
> Inclined to be kind to me.
> He is as inescapable as myself
> And has studied me attentively.
>
> And, hiding the murky outcome,
> I challenged myself to a joust:
> I tear off my own mask
> And cherish the despicable world.
>
> Of my own sadness I am unworthy,
> And this is my ultimate dream:
> The fateful and momentary clang
> As my patterned shield is smashed
>   through.

This otherwise derivative poem is interesting for its image of the lyric hero totally sheathed (or "imprisoned," a possible figurative meaning of the participle *okovan*) in an "armor of contempt" from which he longs to be released. This longing has an ambiguous quality, however: does the poet wish to drop his pose of fastidious detachment and to accept "the despicable world"? Or is he longing for the liberation from earth's "dark bonds" that only death can bring? The patterned shield gives rise to further ambiguities, for the making of patterns, whatever the medium, is always for Mandelstam an analogue for the making of poems. Does it follow then that the lyric hero is in some sense imprisoned by his gift? Whatever the answers to these questions, the poem sets up a situation in which the claims of art stand against the claims of life—a dilemma which will take a variety of forms in Mandelstam's prose.

The poet's troubled attitude toward "the despicable world" is illuminated from another angle in Nos. 17 and 18, twin poems from 1910. Their central image, a "slough" from which the speaker has emerged but which still draws him to its depths, has been convincingly identified by Omry Ronen as a metaphor for the Jewish background rejected by the young poet.[7] Thus both the Jewish "womb world" (the phrase is from "The Noise of Time") and the broader Russian milieu alternately attract and repel him: the "dear ooze" of the slough is presumably a refuge from the rebuffs of those representatives of a "forbidden life" (17) who humiliate him with their "proud boredom." (18)

Thus the poet's reserve masks a multitude of wounded feelings. In the fourth stanza of No. 18, omitted from the version published in Mandelstam's first collection, *Stone*, he even speaks of revenge:

Neither do I find pleasure in my torments,
Nor do I look to endow them with meaning.
But perhaps in a final victory, soon to be,
I will avenge myself for everything.

For the most part, though, the lyric hero hides his grievances against the world to which he seeks entry; at most, as in "A Body is Given to Me," the famous opening poem of *Stone*, as well as in several other poems, he ends by affirming the value of his own gift. That the poet's ascetic detachment is indeed a role taken upon himself in reaction to the indifference of his environment is suggested by No. 22, a lyric of 1911:

The overcast sky is humid and echoey;
It's pleasant and not at all scary in the woods.
Again I will humbly bear the light
Cross of solitary strolls.

And again to the indifferent fatherland
A reproach, like a wild duck,
Soars sharply aloft:
I do have a place in obscure life,
And my solitude isn't my fault.

A shot rang out. Over the sleepy lake
The ducks' wings are heavy now,
And the trunks of the pines are intoxicated
By their reflected double existence.

The sky is dull, with a strange gleam,
A foggy universal pain;
O let me be just as foggy,
And let me not love you.

It is the atmospherics of the poem, particularly its lighting effects, that are likely to strike the reader first. The air, sky, and life itself are thrown into shadow and obscurity. In the last stanza the narrator speaks of a foggy universal pain of existence and asks to be permitted to participate in that fogginess or vagueness. The lighting, in fact, is part of the poem's dominant semantic field, that of vague, transitional states, e.g., drowsiness or intoxication. But Mandelstam adapts this Symbolist landscape to his own purposes: it is a setting into which an emotional dilemma can be diffused, and thus managed.

The first stanza transforms the "slender cross and secret path" of No. 19 into "the light cross of solitary strolls," a burden of loneliness—humbly taken up perhaps, but not desired. Thereafter the syntax both reveals and conceals. The reproach in Stanza 2 is uttered by the poet, his cry only slightly masked by an oblique introduction through the simile of the soaring duck. There is no other "I" in the poem, and the poet has already alluded to his solitude in Stanza 1. The gunshot that opens Stanza 3 sounds like a sharp retort to the poet's appeal. I take the addressee of the last stanza to be the indifferent fatherland; if it will not accept the poet, let it release him from his devotion to it and let his awareness of his pain be dulled.[8]

Beginning in 1912, the lyrics show a striking shift in the quality of mind that they reveal. As is well known, this shift is associated with Mandelstam's adherence to the new poetic school of Acmeism, whose principal founder was Nikolaj Gumilev. Breaking with the Symbolists, the Acmeists wanted to retain their erstwhile mentors' achievements in the revival of poetic language but to divorce poetry from religion and philosophy; in particular, the Symbolist view of the poet as a priest-theurge seemed like blasphemy to the Acmeists. In place of conjurations of a higher reality through the poetic symbol, the new tendency called for a poetry of this world, attentive to the concrete qualities of things. The Acmeists put the poet-builder, using words as his building materials, in the place of the poet-seer. In place of music, they put architecture and sculpture as the arts that ought to have the dominant analogical influence on poetry.

The precepts of Acmeism gave Mandelstam a metalanguage that helped to stimulate developments that were immanent in his verse, e.g., an ironic attitude toward "other worlds" and a fascination with craft processes as an analogue for poetic production. At the same time, the movement gave Mandelstam a sense of solidarity that created the conditions for a gradual change in the communicative status of his writing. As Nadezhda Mandelstam put it, he had found a "We."[9] The changes in Mandelstam's verse from 1912 can best be registered by comparing an 'Acmeist' poem, No. 33, with a representative early lyric, No. 13:

> The snowy hive is slower,
> The window's crystal more transparent,
> And a turquoise veil
> Has been carelessly tossed upon a chair.
>
> A fabric intoxicated with itself,
> Pampered by the light's caress
> It experiences summer
> As if untouched by winter.

And, if eternity's frosts
Stream in icy diamonds,
Here—a quivering of dragonflies,
Vivaciously ephemeral and blue-eyed.

1910

33. Casino

I do not care for preconceived pleasures;
Sometimes nature is just a smudge of gray.
Feeling a touch euphoric, I am condemned
To explore the colors of a modest life.

The wind plays with a shaggy cloud,
An anchor rests on the sea bottom,
And my soul hangs over the cursed abyss
Like a sail in a flat calm.

But I love the casino in the dunes:
The broad perspective through the foggy window
And the narrow beam on the crumpled tablecloth;

And surrounded by greenish water,
When wine stands in the crystal like a rose,
I love to follow the flight of a gull.

The juxtaposition of the veil, in the earlier poem, with "eternity's frost" is an instance of what several scholars (most notably Clarence Brown and Alexander Zholkovsky) have suggested is an invariant feature in Mandelstam's writings: the opposition between that which is seemingly fragile or ephemeral but vital and that which is massive, threatening and lifeless.[10] Building an aesthetic out of his own precarious situation in life, Mandelstam makes the tension-field to which this opposition gives rise the very locus of his art. The vibratory quality of the image of the veil is produced by a radical condensation and displacement. Lying in its empty room, outside of any concrete history, the veil is suffused by that reverence for artisanship which can be found in all periods of Mandelstam's writing. In this instance, however, the beautiful object has almost occluded the human agents from the poem. The speaker who celebrates the veil remains invisible. So does the veil's owner, although perhaps her qualities are displaced to the veil, which is feminine (*vual'*, "veil," and *tkan'*, "fabric" are feminine nouns and require the feminine form of the personal pronoun) and has the traits of a spoiled beauty, elegant, privileged, and narcissistic.

If in No. 13 the poet seems to reflect upon energies emanating from the veil, in "Casino" there is an "I," which, affirming its likes and dislikes, organizes and valorizes the landscape. The distinctively Mandelstamian opposition of scale and tonality figures here in the images of the soul hanging over the void or the poet surrounded by the waters. But an important mediating term now comes into play: culture as shelter from the inhuman infinite. The room in No. 13 does little more than mark one term in the opposition "inside/outside," but in No. 33 (incidentally Mandelstam's first lyric with a clearly specified, identifiable setting) the casino is charged with significance. As the counterforce to the abyss, it is the source of the positive tonality of the final stanzas. Illimitable space is domesticated by being framed in a window; a threat of ego-dissolution gives way to a view.

It is not only in its use of the materials of a "modest life," e.g., glasses of wine and crumpled tablecloths, as signifiers of a potential at-homeness that "Casino" is a representative poem for its period. It is also typical of Mandelstam's second *Stone* age in representing the world as an open house through which the poet roams freely, but which takes no particular note of him. The lyric hero of *Stone* resembles a more cultivated version of the dreamer-narrator of Dostoevsky's "White Nights," who has substituted an attachment to the world at large for individual human ties. The sustained dialogue in Mandelstam's verse up to 1914 or 1915 is between the poet and his predecessors—especially Tjutčev and Pushkin.

To make the point more generally: in the post-1912 poems, the poet celebrates the human environment and its cultural achievements but does not yet explore the social or cultural significance of his own relationships. The fastidious young aesthete becomes a poet of the city, something of a flaneur, viewing, often with a satirical eye, the imperial capital. He descends to earth: instead of wanting to evanesce, he wants to have his supper. He describes the comings and goings at Carskoe Selo, a Lutheran funeral, a public reading of Poe, a crowd leaving the opera (with "one fool still applauding from the gallery"), a little boy trying to decide which ice cream to buy.

By appropriating the urban scene, the poet is inscribing himself into the "Petersburg text," the fiction and verse centering in the theme of the city. He also claims (in No. 67, "I Never Listened to the Tales of Ossian") to have inherited the "wandering dreams" of poets from remote cultures and times. But his attitude toward the past can also be colored by a sense of belatedness, as in the 1915 poem "I Shall Not See the Famous *Phèdre*," one of the texts that erects the theatre (and concert hall) from a theme into an important symbol in Mandelstam's work.

At the broadest level, Mandelstam's theatre is the Theatrum Mundi, offering a tableau of society that extends from the "heroes and kings" on the tragic stage and the "fashionable motley crowd" in the audience to the coachmen warming themselves around outdoor fires. But the theatre will also become a vehicle for exploring the mode of existence of art and the relations between artist, work, and audience. Part of the poet's fascination with the theatre seems to spring from its capacity to both admit and exclude its audience. And what it offers and withholds is communion with a classical and European cultural tradition. The poet is belated with respect both to the world of Greek tragedy and to its neoclassical continuation: "Heroes and kings! What place can you have in a theater of half-words and half-masks?" For Mandelstam, the theater, like a poem, lives by the spoken word, a point to which he returns in his tribute to the actress Komissarzhevskaya in "The Noise of Time."

In the theater poems the Russian stage is a temple that memorializes the past, a place where the audience participates in the obsequies and resurrection of the "night sun" of art. In *The Egyptian Stamp*, attendance at plays and concerts becomes the defining activity of the pariah-*intelligent*, epitomizing his cultural aspirations.

TRISTIA

Tristia, Mandelstam's second collection, is drawn from his work of 1916-20. If there is no radical break with the later poems of the *Stone* years, the collection does convey a greater complexity of response to its poetic occasions, signified by a growing complexity in semantic organization. Meaning seems to percolate upwards from the deepest strata of language.

Among the constituents of this greater semantic density is an enrichment of contextual meaning. The poems refuse to remain apart, each locked within its own "molecular" world, to borrow Mandelstam's term for an art with too much repose, too little struggle. Not only do the poems group themselves more readily into cycles (e.g., Petersburg poems, poems about theatrical or concert performances, love lyrics), but the great polar themes of *Tristia*—exile and return, death and resurrection, oblivion and memory—are so powerful a presence that they pull everything into their fields of force.

There is also a greater emphasis on motif-structure as a resource for significance; that is, recurrent images, tied together not only by repetition but by their association with words that are their phonological or semantic echoes, crystallize into associative chains that take shape both within individual poems and within larger units of the collection. What is new here is not the use of leitmotifs but the way in which the poet's discourse becomes the arena of a shifting interplay of semantic fields and features. The devices of associative meaning are most obviously at work in such seemingly "obscure" poems as "Salomeja," "The Clock-Cricket's Singing," and "Sisters— Heaviness and Tenderness," but they also operate in more readily accessible lyrics, such as No. 91:

> This night cannot be put to rights,
> Yet for you it is still light.
> At the gates of Jerusalem
> A black sun has risen.
>
> More frightening is the yellow sun—
> Lullaby, lullaby—
> In their bright temple the Jews
> Held my mother's funeral.
>
> Lacking divine grace
> And devoid of holiness,
> In their bright temple the Jews
> Mourned the woman's dust.
>
> And over my mother there resounded
> The voices of the Israelites.
> I awoke in a cradle,
> Illuminated by a black sun.

The articulations of the lyric plot roughly coincide with the poem's stanzaic divisions. There is a movement from effects (omens and other impressions) to their cause, the funeral of the poet's mother. The third stanza interprets the ritual (from an implicitly Christian standpoint; i.e., she is buried under the dispensation of the Law not of Grace) and the last stanza concludes with two lines that summarize and interiorize the poet's response.

This logical movement is in tension with the effects of pattern and variation by means of which the poem attempts to assimilate the experience of death and loss that is its theme. Stated in the second distich of stanza 2, the theme has two repetitions, one following upon the other, in the second distich of stanza 3 and the first of stanza 4, with increasing degrees of deviation from the original wording. The sun, variously black and yellow, also appears three times. Sound repetitions also work to underscore and fuse the elements of the theme: The Russian words for "temple," "mother," and "dust" are *xram*, *mat'*, and *prax*; *xoronili*, the verb in stanza 2, participates in the same paranomastic complex; the stressed /a/ of the three nouns is the most frequently occurring stressed vowel in the poems.

In its semic organization, No. 91 expresses the oppositions 'brightness/
darkness' and 'ascent/descent'. (*Xoronit'*, translated in stanza 2 as "to hold
a funeral," literally means "to bury.") Semantically, the poem emphasizes
the fields "infancy-death." This it accomplishes in part by its allusions to
life's first and last songs (the cradlesong and the mourners' kaddish), in
part by offering itself as a lament cast in the trochees of a Russian lullaby.[11]

As a fusion of lullaby and lament, the poem's dominant trope is oxymoron; hence the black sun of melancholy, borrowed, as Nadezhda Mandelstam observes, from Nerval. The nightmare regression that places the adult
narrator in a child's cradle can also be interpreted as oxymoron. What this
play of associations does is to collapse the spatial and temporal boundary
between cradle and grave, reversing the flow of time and introducing apocalyptic overtones. The mother's death is rendered as a catastrophe that dis-
rupts the ordinary course of the world, and the regression induced by this
catastrophe is all the more frightful to the lyric hero for its associations
with Jewishness.

This next stage in the evolution of Mandelstam's poetics entails a paradoxical shift in the communicative status of his verse: the more allusive and
elliptical the poem, the more it presupposes a community of understanding
that unites author with audience, an audience that requires only hints to
"restore the signs missing from the text," to quote Mandelstam's somewhat
later description of the skill that defines his "poetically literate reader."

In its exploration of the stylistic possibilities of a semantic poetics, the
verse breaks ground that will be extensively cultivated by the prose. However, it is not the style so much as the growth in certain qualities of thought
and feeling that is likely to impress a reader encountering the verse of the
Tristia period for the first time. The "I" of the poems seems a securer presence than the poet of *Stone*. Capable of addressing his own life more
directly, he confronts subjects that include the death of his mother (91),
unhappy love (the poems of the Arbenina cycle), his Jewishness (91, 100,
109), and the Revolution (103, 118). He brings a greater richness of
response to a greater range of experience, a response made possible by new
resources. If the poems of the *Stone* years project chiefly an attitude of
wonder at the aesthetic objects they create, coupled with an impulse toward
self-definition and affirmation in an indifferent or hostile world, the *Tristia*
poems are inhabited by a more reflective consciousness, one which roams
broad reaches of time and space in its search for precedents or parallels
that may serve as intimations of a home.

While many of the poems do have the abundance of vivid sense impressions that led an early and enthusiastic critic to praise their "right-off-the-
street" immediacy,[12] it is the juxtaposition of the sharply-observed moment

with the pressure of the centuries that energizes the lyrics of *Tristia*. The voice that speaks from them addresses his own age by turning to the past, primarily to the world of the Greeks and secondarily to the age of Pushkin, with excursions here and there. This historicist cast of mind is in part an exemplification of what Mandelstam called *preemstvennost'*, a term which in his usage meant something like "legitimacy and continuity of cultural tradition." As such, *preemstvennost'* could function as a counter to the poet's sense of homelessness and to the "eschatological forebodings" that, according to Nadezhda Mandelstam, trace back to the *Tristia* period. At the same time, Mandelstam was very aware that shifts in sensibility always create a new past. It can even be argued that Mandelstam turned to the combinatorial possibilities of synchronic history as a way of escaping what he would call in *The Egyptian Stamp* the "wild parabola" of linear history.[13]

But if allusions to the past imply the continuity of culture and the accessibility of tradition, they also sharpen the perception of difference; indeed, one of the principal effects of the wealth of classical allusion in *Tristia* is to signify pastness as a strongly marked category of otherness. The more vividly the poet summons up the classical world in its sensuous particularity, the more acute the sense of exile from that world. Thus the closing stanzas of two of the finest poems in the collection (92, 105) can be read as threnodies for a lost world of myth and epic:

(92)

Golden Fleece, where are you, Golden Fleece?
The whole way the heavy sea waves resounded.
And, leaving his ship, its sails worn thin on the seas,
Odysseus returned, filled with space and time.

1917

(105)

O where are you, Isles of the Blessed,
Where men do not feed on scraps of bread,
Where there is only honey, wine, and milk;
Where creaking labor does not darken the heavens,
And the wheel turns effortlessly.

1919

For critical purposes, two processes can be distinguished in Mandelstam's approach to the past in *Tristia* and after, one dominated by metonymy, the other by metaphor. When the lyric hero wants to evoke another age, he selects images that summon up its essential qualities, hinting at an underlying complexity of motives and actions only partially revealed by the text. No. 96 illustrates how aesthetic texts—in this case a concert of Schubert Lieder—function for Mandelstam as condensates of their age:

> That evening the organ's spiky forest did not drone.
> Schubert—our own cradle—was sung for us;
> A mill hummed, and in a hurricane's songs
> Music's azure-eyed intoxication laughed.
>
> World of a song from bygone days: brown and green;
> If nothing else, forever young;
> Where the thundering crowns of nightingale-lindens
> Are shaken with mad rage by the forest-king.
>
> And—fearsome force of a nightly recurrence—
> That song as wild as a black wine:
> It is the double, an empty apparition,
> Looking blankly through the cold window!

1917

Recalling the performance, the lyric hero speaks of the associations the songs arouse in him. These associations, e.g., the Erlkonig and the doppelganger, conjure up the world of German Romanticism. Music leads the listener, not to a transcendent harmony à la Symbolism, but to an awareness of the past. With its rush of visual and tactile associations, No. 96 anticipates in this respect the treatment of music in "The Noise of Time" and *The Egyptian Stamp*.

Whenever the poet is intent upon establishing a pattern that includes both past and present, metaphor becomes the dominant trope. Thus the image of Proserpine or Persephone, the goddess of the underworld, who appears in four lyrics (Nos. 89, 93, 112, 116) and is said in the first of them to reign over Petersburg:

> In transparent Petropolis we will die,
> Where Proserpine reigns over us.
> In every breath we imbibe a deadly atmosphere,
> And every hour is for us the anniversary of a death.
> Goddess of the Sea, Dread Athena,
> Remove your mighty stone helm.
> In transparent Petropolis we will die,
> Where it is not you that rules but Proserpine.

1916

If the assertion that Proserpine reigns over Petersburg were to be reduced to a literal paraphrase, it might be expressed as "Petersburg is in a moribund phase." At this level Proserpine is a particularizing synecdoche for the more general concept of moribundity. The goddess is also a metonym, evoking the Greek world that invented her, and the use of the Hellenized poeticism "Petropolis" for Petersburg reinforces the impression that Mandelstam's city is somehow contiguous with the world of classical antiquity. But Proserpine's major functions are metaphorical and metalogical. She provides a metaphoric way of thinking about the main themes of *Tristia* that transforms them from antinomies into complementarities. The intersection of significance that joins her to these themes is 'cyclicity'. Written during the years of war and revolution, *Tristia* is full of portents of the end, of allusions to a funereal, twilit, and decembrish world. But there are also motifs of sunlight and regeneration: just as Persephone only spends half the year in the kingdom of death, the city under her sway can become a place of resurrections as well as obsequies; oblivion may yet yield up the forgotten word; and exiles may, like Odysseus, be restored to their homes.

The workings of the poet's sense of the past may be illustrated by No. 103, "The Twilight of Freedom":

> Brothers, let us hymn the twilight of freedom,
> The great twilit year.
> Into seething night waters
> A weighty forest of snares is lowered.
> You are rising in deaf years,
> O Sun, Judge, People.
>
> Let us hymn the fatal burden
> That the people's leader takes up in tears;
> Let us hymn power's murky burden,
> Its unbearable, oppressive weight.
> He who has a heart must hear, Time,
> How your ship goes to the bottom.
>
> Into battle legions
> We have bound the swallows—and now
> The sun is obscured. All Nature
> Twitters, moves, lives.
> Behind its nets of thick twilight
> The sun is obscured, and the earth sails.
>
> Well, what of it, let's give it a try:
>   a massive, ponderous
> Creaking turn of the rudder.
> The earth sails off. Courage, men!
> Plowing through the ocean waters,
> We will recall, even in Lethe's chills,
> That the earth meant as much to us
>   as ten heavens.

This ambivalent coronation hymn for the Russian Revolution makes hardly any reference to its occasion.[14] The "great twilit year" is surely 1917, but everything else in the poem seems designed to nullify our sense of specific time and place. The first three stanzas join quasiliturgical, quasi-epic formulae to a sequence of apocalyptic omens: the murk of a symbolic twilight and a sun in eclipse, the doomed ship of time, the earth sailing to its unstated destination, the bound swallows coerced into an unnatural servitude, and—seemingly in consequence of this—a loss of clarity and a world without form, instinct with a senseless, twittering life.

The situation of the poem—the poet exhorting his fellow voyagers—invites an allegorical reading that the density of allusion undercuts. The allusion to Lethe is the poem's sole mythological reference, but then *Tristia* is replete with voyages to such famous destinations as the Isles of the Blessed, Hades, Troy, and the homeland of the Golden Fleece. For example, the last stanza of No. 92 alludes to the voyages of Jason and Odysseus. In this wider context, the poet's companions take on something of the aura of the voyagers of epic and myth. While "people's leader" is a Soviet-sounding title, perhaps there is an allusion here to Agamemnon, compelled to the heavy burden of sacrificing his daughter so as to raise a favoring wind; the poem's imagery of nets and snares has its counterpart in Aeschylus's *Agamemnon*.[15] Whatever the actual subtexts involved here, there are buried allusions to a heroic tradition. These support the hortatory intentions declared by the poem, and they do so by implying an exemplary ideal, to which the poet and his contemporaries may subscribe, and which will strengthen their acceptance of the Revolution.

Acceptance of another sort is at issue in No. 109:

> Return to the incestuous nest
> From whence, Leah, you came,
> Because you have preferred
>   the yellow gloom
> To Ilion's sun.
>
> Go—no one will touch you—
> To your father's breast in the dark of night.
> There let her hang her head,
> The incestuous daughter.
>
> But there must take place in you
> A fatal transformation:
> You will be Leah—not Helen,—
> So styled not because

> It is harder for the blood of kings
> To stream through the veins
>   than for other blood;
> No, you will come to love a Jew,
> You will vanish in him—
> And so be it.

Commenting on this lyric, Nadezhda Mandelstam identifies herself as its addressee, going on to explain that her husband viewed marriages between Jews as incestuous unions.[16] Kiril Taranovsky suggests that the poem is also addressed to the poet's muse, and that it images Mandelstam's fear of the Jewish element in himself as a force that might annihilate his gift.[17] But if the poem does imply this composite addressee (Nadezhda Yakovlevna/ Mandelstam's muse), it might also be construed in somewhat less drastic terms, as a rueful and ambiguous acceptance of the predominance of the Jewish over the Hellenic strain in Mandelstam's art.

In its psychological movement the poem would thus suggest one of those periodic descents into the Jewish slough of Nos. 17 and 18. It also offers a curious parallel to No. 91: both poems manage to disparage the rites—burial and marriage respectively—to which they refer. The Jewish funeral service is disparaged as devoid of holiness and grace, while the poet's bride is declared guilty of incest and brutally dismissed. ("So be it," the Russian *Bog s toboj*, literally "God be with you," is actually anything but a benediction.) Whatever other layers of reference the latter poem may contain, this undercurrent of hostility testifies to the intensity of Mandelstam's continuing ambivalence toward the one past whose claims were deepest and most inescapable.

In the twenties, the Jewish theme is displaced to the prose, where it will undergo a substantial evolution. In the poetry it goes underground, leaving faint traces in the form of scattered motifs: a sack of caraway seeds, the poet's perception of himself as a "stepson of the ages," and his characterization of his work as "gathering night herbs for an alien tribe." Yet of these motifs only the first is a specifically Jewish allusion: as a staple of Jewish baking, the caraway seeds crop up again in *The Egyptian Stamp*, where the "native caraway atmosphere" is an emblem of Jewish life.[18] The other motifs allow us to see the tensions of Jewish identity being subsumed in the broader issue of the artist-intellectual as outsider.

VERSES 1921-25

Mandelstam's poetic output for the period preceding the years of silence is his smallest. Only a scant twenty poems are gathered under the heading

"Verses 1921-25," the concluding section of the 1928 *Poems*, the last collection of Mandelstam's verse to appear in his lifetime.

The classical allusions and the consolations of Eternal Return that marked *Tristia* have only weak echoes. In their place stands the lyric hero's attempt to come to terms with a catastrophic disruption of culture. Coursing through the great poems of the Age cycle, the eschatological vision that originates in the *Tristia* period now colors everything the poet writes. For the rest of his career, his work will grapple with the threat of being cut off from its own wellsprings; in the thirties he would even redefine Acmeism as simply "a longing for world culture."

This vision of final things elicits a different tone on the part of the lyric hero. By and large, the rhetoric of these poems moves between lamentation for a dying age of Russian culture and a confessional manner that translates a sense of cultural crisis into the idiom of personal, psychological crisis. While the poet's concern with his own destiny has been present from the beginning, it now rises to a pitch of intensity. If the novice poet felt the necessity of asserting what he would accomplish in the future, the mature poet is doubly vulnerable, for there is now a substantial body of work that must be offered up to fate. It is no wonder, then, that the theme of destiny recurs with such frequency in these lyrics. It takes diverse forms, ranging from the folkloric convention of an evil fate (No. 127), to acceptance of an inescapable conflict between the poetic gift and the course of the world (132), to affirmations of the value of that gift. These affirmations vary from the ambivalent (e.g., though he be a "stepson" of Russian literature or the "sick son" of a moribund age, his poetry will find its place in the tradition) to the very strong (No. 141, a declaration of splendid isolation, which begins, "No, never have I been anyone's contemporary").

The use of recurrent motifs, for example, salt and stars, as a way of creating semantic coherence through the repetition of key words in a wide variety of contexts is a stylistic habit carried over from *Tristia*. At the same time, as the texts quoted below illustrate, a shift has occurred in the overall quality of these key words. "Verses 1921-25" is dominated by a sense of life's insufficiency, of the winding down of creativity in both the human and natural realms. As life is reduced to its essentials, such as the search for warmth and companionship that animates Nos. 127 and 144, so values seem to retract ever more deeply into things: salt, a linen towel, warm chicken droppings, a sulphur match, a clay pot, earth.

The poet's sense of himself and his world can best be illustrated by quoting some texts:

No. 126

I was washing outside at night.
The firmament gleamed with coarse stars:
A starry beam, like salt on an axeblade;
The barrel, brimful, loses its warmth.

The gates are locked shut,
And the earth is guilelessly stern.
A principle purer than the truth
        of a fresh linen towel
Is unlikely to be found.

A star dissolves in the barrel, like salt,
And the icy water is blacker,
Death is purer, misfortune saltier,
And the earth more truthful and more frightening.

                                              1921

No. 127

For some, winter, arak, and blue-eyed punch;
For some, wine fragrant with cinnamon;
For some, it is given to bear the salty commands
        of the cruel stars
Into a smoky peasant hut.

Some warm chicken droppings
And muddled, sheeplike warmth:
I will surrender everything for life—
        so in need am I of solicitude—
And a sulphur match could warm me.

Look: in my hand there is only a clay pot,
And the stars' chirping tickles my weak
        hearing.
But it is impossible not to come to love
The yellowness of the grass and the topsoil's warmth
        through this meager fluff.

To softly stroke a furry hide and turn the straw;
To starve like an apple tree in winter, under its matting;
To reach out to a stranger with pointless tenderness;
And to fumble about in the void, and patiently to wait.

Let conspirators hurry through the snow
Like a flock of sheep, while the fragile crust crunches.
For some, winter means wormwood and acrid smoke
        for their night's lodging;
For some, it is the stinging salt of solemn wrongs.

Oh if I could only lift a lantern on a long pole,
Walk, my dog before me, beneath the salt grains
        of the stars,
And bring a rooster in a sack to a fortune-teller's
        place.
But the white, white snow eats painfully at my eyes.

                                                        1922

No. 144

I will rush through the dark street's gypsy camp
After a bird-cherry branch in a black sprung carriage,
After a snowy bonnet and a ceaseless, milling hum . . .

I have only managed to memorize the misfire of chestnut
        braids,
With a smoky, bitter taste—no, with an acid overtaste;
They leave on the lips an amber dryness.

At such moments even the air seems chestnut-brown to me,
And her pupils are arrayed in rings of bright edging,
And, as for what I know about her apple-smooth, rosy skin . . .
But, all the same, the runners scraped on a sleigh-for-hire,
The barbed stars glanced through openweave mats,
And hooves spaced out their beats along the frozen keyboards.

And the only light comes from the stars' barbed lies,
While life will sail by like the foamy lace of an actress's
        bonnet,
And there is no one to whom I can say: "Out of
the dark street's gypsy camp . . .

                                                        1925

These homely objects and unelaborated natural materials belong to that
tendency in Mandelstam's writing whereby the poet uses not only master-
works from the arts and crafts but also the everyday and familiar as emblems of a human-centered universe. What is remarkable about the uses to
which these images are put in the verse of the early twenties is the suppression of the strong modal aura that surrounded them earlier. There has been

a shift in registers, from cathedrals to clay pots, and the images, for the most part, no longer offer themselves to the poet as subjects for celebration but stand as mute emblems. However, in an encoding process that will also figure in the prose, these homely images can become signifiers for complex moral situations. The coarse towel of No. 126, with its capacity for awakening the poet to elemental truths of existence, may serve as an example.

The encipherment of an ideal that had been openly proclaimed in the earlier verse is a token of a threatened loss of memory, of the drying-up of the past as a vitalizing resource for the present. This rift makes itself felt most strongly in the meaning of silence in these poems. In Mandelstam's early verse, silence represented an ontological music of endless creative potential:

> The cautious and muffled sound
> Of a fruit fallen from the tree
> Amid the unceasing melody
> Of a forest silence profound.
>
>   1908

This silent music is now transformed into an inert silence, a background for the weakening reverberations of the past, as in these lines from No. 136, "The Horseshoe Finder":

> The sound still rings out, although its cause has vanished.
> The horse lies in the dust, lathered and snorting,
> But the steep turn of its neck still preserves the memory
>   of galloping with outflung legs

But the silence of the twenties is also associated with the poet's growing sense of isolation from his contemporaries, of being condemned to "fumble about in the void." The ring construction of No. 144, which, by denying the possibility of a listener, seems to fold the poem back upon itself, is another adumbration of a lost sense of community.

It is all too easy to see in the lyric hero's dilemmas the etiology of the condition that was to silence the poet in Mandelstam from the mid-twenties. Yet it should be stressed that the silence that overtakes the poetry is not a symptom of radical subjectivity. The "I" of these lyrics refracts a crisis of values not merely of his own status. He is supremely adequate to the historical circumstances—the aftermath of revolution—to which the poems bear such powerful witness.

FROM POETRY TO PROSE

The development of the lyric hero may be summarized as follows: The young Mandelstam begins by contemplating a world of objects and impressions that gradually coalesce into a network of cultural associations. He begins to explore and to complicate the "I" positioned within this network. To be complete, this observing consciousness must define itself in relation to a community, and the poet moves between more abstract and more concrete conceptions of community as he seeks to find a refuge in his age for the values he champions.

Much of this order of creation is recapitulated and amplified in the literary prose. Thus just as Mandelstam begins with poems that construct an image of the poet while they focus on their own genesis, so he experiments with a prose that creates an authorial persona by thematizing its own processes of composition.

The consciousness that constructs itself in Mandelstam's verse expands its resources, first by incorporating more of the world, then more of the self. Mandelstam shows an abiding concern with finding an equilibrium between a subjective, lyric perception of life and a perspective that seeks to embody the "objective" experience of his times. As his poems evolve from single lyric perceptions to structures of greater thematic and narrative complexity, the authorial persona gradually abandons the abstract and attitudinizing "Poet" for a distinctive and idiosyncratic voice. The turn to literary prose will provide Mandelstam with a medium for the further evolution of his language, ideology, and themes.

Several scholars have remarked upon the role of the prose in providing Mandelstam with a "democratized" language, capable of bringing more of the postrevolutionary world into his writings.[19] According to Nadezhda Mandelstam, prose also served as a laboratory for the generation of values to live and write by: "Working on prose, O. M. defined his own place in life; in affirming a position, he was discovering his own ground."[20] But there is also another dimension to this process, whereby Mandelstam was able, via his experiments in prose, to overcome a limitation in his poetic model of the world. It seems to me highly significant that whereas the poetry and criticism of the twenties is haunted by a fear of cultural amnesia, that is, the silence of memory, Mandelstam's first published literary prose begins with the phrase "I remember."

What the narrator of "The Noise of Time" remembers is his childhood; this is also true, to a considerable extent, of the narrator of *The Egyptian Stamp*. The theme of the poet's childhood had been only implicit in the verse, evoked through such metaphors as the slough of Nos. 17 and 18 and the cradle illuminated by a black sun in No. 91, both of which are associated with the poet's Jewish origins. Jane Gary Harris has suggested that Mandelstam turns to autobiography in his prose as a way of overcoming the stylistic constraints that operate in his criticism and lyrics;[21] I would add that it also serves to bring together his history-laden intellectual perspective and his poetic practice. This is demonstrably true with respect to the uses made of the poet's childhood. The verse that precedes the prose treats only the adult dilemmas of sonship, both actual (the death of the poet's mother) and metaphorical (the lyric hero's relationship to the Age-father); the verse of the early thirties will contain several allusions to the stream of childhood recollections that wells up in the prose.

The evolution of the Jewish theme may serve as a benchmark here. In the earlier verse, the lyric hero manages the conflicts aroused in him by his background by encoding it into allegory, e.g., the slough of Jewishness (Nos. 17 and 18), the poet as a young Levite (No. 100). Now it provides material for detailed reminiscences and becomes a positive artistic and moral resource. In this shift, the Jewish theme epitomizes more general changes wrought by the prose in the poet's structure of thought and feel-ling.[22] While Mandelstam's work always combines a sense of the forces of fragmentation and a longing for a principle of unity, this dialectic threatened to break down in the early twenties; hence his turn to his own past as a new locus of positive associations, capable of affirming life. But he needed to do this in such a way as to uphold the connectedness of self and world, past and present. Mandelstam's rejection of radical subjectivity is a constant in his outlook; as late as 1935 he warned: "Lyrical self-absorption [liričeskoe samoljubie], even in its very best forms, is deadening. It always impoverishes the poet" (OM, IV, p. 165). In his prose, Mandelstam turns his past into a thematic resource by endowing it with a universal significance.

After tracing the main lines in Mandelstam's construction of a poetic identity, I am now in a position to return to the question of how this self-construction is specifically a *Russian* identity. Mandelstam's attempt to make his work merge with Russian poetry (to paraphrase the letter to Tynjanov, quoted on page 15) involves several interlinked strategies. In his early work, Mandelstam claims a place in Russian literature chiefly through the assertion of his rights as a poetic inheritor. He does this by emphasizing the links between his verse and that of such predecessor-poets as Pushkin, Tjutčev, and Baratynskij. Beginning in 1912, two new emphases appear: the poet's assimilation of his work to a contemporary poetic trend, Acmeism, and to a thematic current, the Petersburg Text.

Another way in which Mandelstam makes a place for himself in Russian letters is to appropriate the literary language by the invention of a distinctively Mandelstamian variant. While the syntactic and semantic rules of this reconstruction can be said to have been worked out, in the main, by the end of the *Tristia* period, the experimental prose would yield a more flexible and expansive diction and lexicon.

Finally, Mandelstam would have to create a Russian literary identity that would incorporate his Jewishness. I have already suggested the reasons why this became a literary necessity; it was also a psychological one: as is argued by the intensity both of his early aversion and his subsequent affirmation, Mandelstam's sense of his Jewishness was not vestigial. In making Russian-Jewish experience a part of Russian literature Mandelstam resembles his friend Isaac Babel. More distinctive is a trend that appears in the poetry of the twenties[23] and develops in the literary prose: the fusion of two varieties of outsiders, the Jew and the *raznochinets*, which enables a Jewish identity to blend into a Russian identity.

THE END OF THE NOVEL

Mandelstam's prose becomes an arena for the display of tensions that are deeply rooted in his verse. His criticism provides us with explicit formulations of his sympathies and antipathies and of the project he sought to realize in his experimental prose.

Mandelstam's criticism contains parallels, not only to the ideas of the Russian formalist school but also to the concerns of other linguistically-oriented writers, such as Baxtin and the psycholinguist Vygotskij. (Nadezhda Mandelstam mentions that Vygotskij became friendly with her husband in the thirties.) Points of contact may be gathered under the rubric of the nature of the "word as such." They include such issues as the form/content distinction, the relationship of writer and reader, the distinctive qualities of poetic language, the complementarity of poetry and prose, the alternation of dominant literary forms, and the relationship between thought and speech. However, despite the common line of descent from the philologist Potebnja, Mandelstam was no more a "poetician formaliste"[24] than were Baxtin or Vygotskij. Despite the tribute he pays to the "new muse" of Russian poetics, "summoned to life by Potebnja and Andrej Belyj and grown mature in the formalist school of Ejxenbaum, Žirmunskij, and Šklovskij," his own criticism owes as much to the brilliant impressionism of Annenskij as it does to the exponents of the "formal method." Mandelstam is not, in the last analysis, concerned with *literaturnost'*, i.e., the aesthetic excellence of literature, but with ethics and the continuity of culture. For him the dynamism and free play of transformations within the literary text has its macrocosmic counterpart in the free transformation and renewal of the traditions of high culture.

Mandelstam never explicitly discusses his own writings in his criticism. Indeed, his whole aesthetic orientation excludes such aids to the reader. What he offers instead is a vision of the nature and direction of literature. Hence, in order to arrive at a conception of Mandelstam's aims as a writer, it is necessary to extrapolate from his comments on other writers and on the trends they exemplify. In the comments on prose scattered throughout his works, the following themes emerge: the opposition, not between one prose genre and another, but between prose and poetry; the cyclical succession of prose forms; and the conflict, manifest throughout Western culture and not just in prose, between what Mandelstam calls "Buddhist" and "European" tendencies.

When he talks about particular genres, Mandelstam's comments tend to be descriptive rather than critical. His remarks on fiction in the articles "The End of the Novel"[25] and "The Birth of Plot"[26] constitute an exception, of sorts, to this rule. It is the first of these two pieces that has the clearest programmatic significance for his own literary prose. In "The End of the Novel" he takes up the question of the novel in relation to other prose forms: "The novel is distinguished from the tale, the chronicle, memoirs or any other prose form by its being a composed, closed, extended narrative, complete in itself, about the fate of a single character or of an entire group of characters." (II, 266). Since "composed" (*kompozicionnoe*) in Russian usage can refer to the process or result of composition in music, the graphic arts, or literature, the novel is "composed" in the sense that it is constructed according to a unified design. To characterize the novel further as "closed" (*zamknutoe*) and "complete in itself" (*zakončennoe v sebe*) is to define it as a fiction that is not, in the final analysis, dependent upon external reality for its authentication and that may be read as an independent work even if it forms part of a larger narrative cycle. To describe the novel as an "extended" (*protjažennoe*) form seems to imply a contrast between it and more compact fictions, such as the short story or the novella.

It is the final attribute of the novel—its stress on the fate of a central character or characters—that is most stressed by Mandelstam. In his view, it is this emphasis that is responsible for the emergence of the novel from its origins in folklore, and on this basis he associates himself with the opinion that Longus's *Daphnis and Chloe* deserves to be considered the first European novel.[27] The focus on the biography of the hero or heroes is said to permit an expansion of the *fabula*, the story line. The development of the folk tale into a more compendious narrative can take place because biography, in Mandelstam's sense of the term, includes the whole web of relationships linking the central characters to their social and historical environment.

Mandelstam uses the metaphor of a planetary system to illustrate the conditions associated, respectively, with the novel's flowering and with its decline. In the novels of Goethe, Stendhal, or Tolstoj, to name some of the authors whose works exemplify for Mandelstam the great age of the novel, there is said to be a balance of centrifugal and centripetal forces between the work's center—the individual or group of individuals with whose fate the narrative is concerned—and its sociohistorical periphery. The planetary imagery in "The End of the Novel" is another instance of that human-centered world which first makes its appearance in the later poems of *Stone*. Placing individual destinies at the center of its universe, the "biographical" novel illustrates for Mandelstam one of the ways in which literary art has embodied this ideal.

Mandelstam sees the career of Napoleon as the model for the *fabula* of the nineteenth-century novel. Through its pages parade a succession of would-be Napoleons, attempting to rise from the lower to the upper rungs of the social ladder. The swan song of this novelistic tradition, in Mandelstam's opinion, is Romain Rolland's *Jean Christophe* (published 1908-09). The next stage in the evolution of the novel is characterized by the "destruction" of biography. Unlike the formalist Ejxenbaum, who posited an immanent "law," according to which dominant prose forms are continually ossifying and being replaced by "peripheral" forms, Mandelstam emphasizes the manner in which the alternation of prose forms reflects the trend of social history. In particular, the fortunes of the novel are for him somehow associated with shifts in society's perception of the role of the individual in history. He seems to argue that the shape of prose must follow the perceived shape of life. Thus if the epic narrative of the nineteenth century novel reflects the belief in its own significance of a landed upper class or rising bourgeoisie, the prose of an epoch in which life is fragmented and the individual has been "evicted from his own biography"[28] must display that sense of fragmentation and personal insignificance. For prose, in Mandelstam's view, always holds up a mirror to society.

The rise of what Mandelstam calls variously the "psychological" or "analytic" novel is for him an essentially degenerative development. If the writer's "sense of personal significance" has been swept away by revolution, psychologism (*psixologičeskie motivirovka*), which has its beginnings as a complement to the narration of events, cannot be an authoritative substitute for "biography" in Mandelstam's sense. Psychological motivation is "discredited and impotent before the real forces whose bloody reckoning with psychologism becomes fiercer from hour to hour . . . psychology no longer determines actions of any kind." These "real forces" are not specified, but since "The End of the Novel" was written in the early twenties, the reference to the turmoil of the first years of the revolution is clear.

Mandelstam's argument, i.e., that psychology cannot be a substitute for biography since neither can determine events if the individual is simply the victim of history, has some curious points of contact with the critique of modernist literature put forward by Georg Lukács.[29] The great Marxist critic takes over a Hegelian distinction between "concrete potentiality," the actual possibilities that a social environment holds out to an individual's wishes and dreams without regard to the objective possibility of their realization. In Lukác's view, if the literary character is represented as quarantined within the limits of his own subjective experience, concrete potentiality (which is equivalent to Mandelstam's balance of centrifugal forces) gives way to abstract potentiality, which corresponds to the danger of centripetal collapse implied by Mandelstam's planetary analogy.

Lukács decries a strange paradox that results from the replacement of concrete by abstract potentiality in modern literature: the exaltation of subjectivity in a solipsistic universe leads to the impoverishment and ultimate disintegration of the literary character's personality. Mandelstam points to the same danger, warning that the mere fact of a human life does not constitute a biography and cannot serve as what he calls the "backbone" of the novel. He holds that the novel must reflect conflict and adjustment between the individual hero and his social and natural environment. Thus the key to the classic novel's construction—its "backbone"—is not the isolated hero but the hero in his trajectory through a series of confrontations with the surrounding world.

Unlike Lukács, however, Mandelstam does not seem to believe in an imminent revival of the realist tradition. In a sense his most "fictional" work amounts to a comment on the novel as excluded possibility. Poor Parnok is repeatedly contrasted with the "Napoleonic" heroes of the novel's past. They conquered Paris, while he cannot even hold on to his morning coat and dress shirts. *The Egyptian Stamp* thus offers a literary demonstration of the end of the novel.

WESTERNIZING BUDDHISM

Commenting on narrative prose, Mandelstam is not only concerned with its specificity within the totality of literature and the history of its leading forms but also with the cultural perspective that it embodies. This latter concern emerges clearly in connection with the theme denominated by the opposition of so-called "Buddhist" and "European" tendencies. In a draft for the "Journey to Armenia" Mandelstam wrote that reality has an uninterrupted character. The prose that corresponds to reality, no matter how clearly and minutely, no matter how straightforwardly and faithfully, always forms an intermittent series (III, 166).

A subsequent definition of prose narrative as "the discontinuous sign of a continuity" emphasizes a clear distinction between prose and non-textual reality, *dejstvitel'nost'*. This distinction stresses the nature of literature as an artifact, a conscious construction, rather than a direct imitation of nature. It also implies a prose that is self-conscious about its own place in literary tradition and about presenting the problematic of its writing as one of its constituent themes.

Mandelstam tended to equate any writing that attempted to mimic the flow of reality with the passive, tyrannical, mechanistic complex which he metaphorized as "Westernizing Buddhism," a theme developed most fully in his 1922 essay "The Nineteenth Century."[30] There he views the past century as the conductor of a Buddhist undercurrent in European culture. The "European principle," an active dialectical struggle of "mutually fructifying forces," is contrasted with a "Buddhist" nirvana that excludes any attempt at active knowledge of the world. This "hidden Buddhism" is said to take the form of evolutionism in science and theosophical tendencies in religion. Mandelstam, at this point in his career, seems to have understood both evolutionism and theosophy as expressions of a blind positivism which, in effect, denied any God-given freedom of initiative to Man and Nature alike.

In the criticism he wrote during the early twenties, Mandelstam argues that even the greatest writers can undermine the European literary tradition if they are infected by the complex of values and tastes that he calls "hidden" (or "Westernizing") Buddhism." He singles out Gustave Flaubert and, in Russia, the Symbolist Andrej Belyj as the great exemplars of the "Buddhist tendency" in prose. What it is that he objects to in these writers is not obvious; certainly he does not dispute their great literary powers. When he speaks of *Madame Bovary* or *Petersburg*, Mandelstam is not concerned with judgments of aesthetic qualities but with the relationship of those works to the ethical traditions of European letters. Moreover, his attitude toward Flaubert and Belyj involves elements of attraction as well as repulsion. One senses, in fact, that they represent for Mandelstam an unconstrained subjectivism or an art-for-art's sake tendency that is not wholly alien to his own writing, whatever opinions he may have expressed about the social nature of prose. Thus his allusions to Flaubert and Belyj can illuminate his own artistic ambivalence.

Mandelstam's most extended attack on Flaubert is to be found in his essay "The Nineteenth Century." An abundance of shared motifs suggests that the polemical subtext may well be not so much *Bovary* as Flaubert's famous letter to Louise Colet[31] in which he voices his ambition to write

> " . . . a book about nothing at all, a book which would exist by virtue of the mere internal strength of its style as the earth holds itself unsupported in the air—a book which would have almost no subject, or in which, at least, the subject would be almost imperceptible, if such a thing is possible . . .
>
> Form becomes attenuated as it becomes more adroit, abandoning all liturgy, all rule, all measure, abandoning the epic for the novel, verse for prose, denying all orthodoxy, and being as free as the will of each of its creators. It is for this reason that it would almost be possible to establish an axiom—speaking from the point of view of pure art—that there are no such things as subjects at all, style being in itself an absolute way of seeing things."

Mandelstam drew his own implications from the Flaubertian ideal of style regnant:

> There is nothing accidental, it seems to me, in the attraction of the Goncourts and their allies the first French Impressionists to Japanese art, to the engravings of Hokusai, and to the form of the *tanka* in all its varieties; that is, to a finished, hermetic, and immobile composition. All of *Madame Bovary* is written according to the *tanka* system. Flaubert wrote it so slowly and with such agony, because he was obliged to begin anew every five words.
>
> The *tanka* is the favorite form of molecular art. It is not a miniature, and to confuse the *tanka* with the miniature because of its brevity would be a gross error. It is itself a world and the constant inner vortical movement of molecules.
>
> The cherry branch and the snowy cone of the beloved mountain, the patronesses of the Japanese engravers, are reflected in the gleaming lacquer of every sentence of the burnished Flaubertian novel. Everything here is covered by the lacquer of pure contemplation, and, like a rosewood surface, the style of the novel can reflect any object. If such works did not frighten contemporaries, this ought to be attributed to the latter's striking insensitivity and lack of aesthetic perception.
>
> (II, 281)

Mandelstam's main criticism has to do with what he takes to be a disjunction and disproportion between the text and the extratextual reality, an idea that he condenses into a pun in a passing reference to Flaubert as a "Simon Stylites of style." Flaubert's ideally polished style and his professed hatred of reality seem to have represented for Mandelstam the antithesis of his own humanism, and especially of his hope that art might exemplify a human-centered universe. At the same time, the circumstances under which Mandelstam was writing also ought to be kept in view. His attacks on

Flaubert date from the period of his own attempt at a "transvaluation of values," that is, to a time when his aspiration toward solidarity with the Revolution would have made it especially difficult to espouse the Flaubertian rejection of any obligation to society on the writer's part—or at least on the prose writer's part: the "blessed senseless word" Mandelstam reserved to poetry. While he seems to have wanted the writer to be free to interpret such claims in any way he wished, Mandelstam also seems to have believed—or perhaps feared—that any prose which utterly ignored them would be barren.

Comments on Belyj have many motifs in common with comments on Flaubert. Once again Mandelstam's basic concern is with what he considers to be an imbalance between world and text. He attributes this imbalance, in Belyj's case, to an overburdening of the text with abstractions that are so private and gnomic that the reader may be lectured to; he may even be put into a trance; but he cannot enter into a dialogue with the work. Like Flaubert, Belyj is held up as a danger, "an unhealthy and negative phenomenon" that runs counter to the "Hellenistic" ideal. Part of this danger has to do with Belyj's association with the tradition of psychological or analytic prose. For Mandelstam, the analytic novel is inherently antisocial, isolating man from his web of relationships and reducing character to the analysis of conflicting psychological impulses. Belyj, like Flaubert, is said to represent a dead end: "Russian prose will move forward when the first prose writer who is independent of Andrej Belyj appears.[32] (II, 335)

Mandelstam views Flaubert and Belyj, for all the distance that separates their fictional worlds, as carriers of the same threat to the European cultural tradition. Their writings are emanations from nirvana. On this point the literary prose illustrates what the criticism declares:

> Books melt like chunks of ice brought into a room. Everything grows smaller. Everything seems like a book to me. Where is the difference between a book and a thing? I do not know life; they switched it on me as long ago as the time when I recognized the crunch of arsenic between the teeth of the amorous French brunette, the younger sister of our proud Anna. (II, 34)

In this passage from the *The Egyptian Stamp*, which concentrates many of the tensions operative in Mandelstam's life and art in the twenties, Flaubert's Emma is presented as a fatefully attractive succuba, who draws the narrator/reader away from life as active cognition.

THE NATURE OF THE WORD

The clash of "Buddhist" and "European" tendencies within language is one manifestation of a dialectical contradiction that is as fundamental for

Mandelstam as the concept of class struggle is for Marx.[33] In Mandelstam's view, the various forms taken by this opposition at any given time are reflected not only in art but in all essential cultural values. It should be emphasized that he does not treat this conflict as a temporary crisis of culture but as something immanent in human and even natural history. Culture is always threatened with catastrophic breaks, and the fear of catastrophe becomes—at least in part—something positive for Mandelstam: the irritant that produces the pearl of poetry: "Poetic culture arises from the striving to halt catastrophe, to subordinate it to the central sun of an entire system, whether that sun be love, of which Dante talked, or music, to which, in the end, came Blok." (II, 275)

The commemoration of Blok from which this passage is drawn highlights those concerns of the late poet which are close to Mandelstam's own. In particular, Mandelstam is close to Blok in his concern with culture as tradition and with the conditions that facilitate or disrupt the dissemination of this tradition. In the hierarchy of values that informs Mandelstam's conception of literature, his views on prose are governed by his thinking on the nature of language, while his idea of language is itself rooted in a moral vision. This vision achieves its fullest expression in the essay *On the Nature of the Word*.[34] Although it is concerned with the Russian literary language generally and not just with prose, this essay sets forth positions that illuminate Mandelstam's whole oeuvre, including the prose that was his major creative outlet during the mid to late twenties.

Setting forth his views on the nature and destiny of the Russian language, Mandelstam couches the issue in characteristically modernist terms: in the face of what he calls "accelerated time"—the maelstrom of war and revolution—is it still possible to speak of an unbroken tradition, connecting contemporary writing with the Russian literary past? Mandelstam's answer is that language itself provides this unifying core. As Clarence Brown points out, this observation is saved from banality by the striking manner in which Mandelstam goes on to render the vital qualities of the Russian language.[35] Everything valuable in the nature of Russian tends for him to become a proof of what he calls its "Hellenistic" essence, and this concept of Hellenism is basic to Mandelstam's artistic credo.[36]

At the most general level, Mandelstam's "Hellenism" participates in that yearning for the south, particularly the Mediterranean world, which runs through the poet's life and work. Part of this yearning is surely attributable to Mandelstam's own "southern," that is, Jewish, heritage. Nadezhda Mandelstam writes of the peculiar nature of her husband's "racial memory," which preserved a sense of kinship with the Jews of the medieval Mediterranean diaspora but retained no record of the much more recent movement across central Europe into the Russian Empire.[37] In fact, *On the Nature of the Word* is explicit about the Jewish element in Mandelstam's Hellenism. As one definition of the latter, Mandelstam describes it as "a system in the Bergsonian sense" (II, 254), having earlier stated that Bergsonism, according to which phenomena are linked through internal connections determined by the recording consciousness rather than by temporal or causal sequence, is the product of a "profoundly Judaistic mind" (II, 241-42). In a theater article of 1927, he writes of the Jewish people as the bearers of the tradition of Greek tragedy. These disconnected hints linking Bergsonism, Hellenism, and Judaism make it tempting to speculate that Mandelstam's insistence on the Hellenistic nature of the Russian language represents in part an unconscious attempt to rationalize his own status as a Jew, capable of mediating the Russian and Greek classical traditions, and thus to legitimize his own contribution to Russian literature. Such claims, however, play no conscious part in Mandelstam's Hellenism; what is paramount is the ostensible preservation of the Greek worldview within Russian culture through the Russian language.

Within Mandelstam's discussion of Hellenism, two vantage points can be discerned. One might be called classicist; the other, Christian. From the classicist perspective the essential legacy of pagan Greece seems to be a characteristic outlook, defined by a joyful acceptance of the world. This outlook, which hallows and consecrates the relationship of man to his surroundings, is somehow mirrored in language, where it takes the form of a predisposition toward nominalism. Mandelstam's linguistic nominalism, as the acceptance of reality—almost physicality—of words seems, by analogy, to entail an acceptance of the concreteness and specificity of the whole objective world.

The Christian perspective operates only beneath the surface of *On the Nature of the Word*. That it nonetheless does operate is suggested by a comparison with "Pushkin and Skrjabin," a 1913 address to the Religious and Philosophical Society. Only a large fragment of this paper has survived. Speaking of it much later as his "basic article," Mandelstam expressed regret over the loss of the complete manuscript. The surviving part connects Hellenism and Christianity through the assertion of a Hellenic, that is, tragic, element in Christian art. Greek tragedy is viewed as a precursor in meaning of the crucifixion: "Hellenism, made fruitful (*oplodotvorennoe*) by death, is Christianity" (II, 318).

Hellenism as a "nominalist" tendency in language and Hellenism as the thesis of a Christianized tragic vision would seem to be rather disparate ideas. Yet Mandelstam brings these senses of Hellenism together through what recent structuralism would call a "modeling system" or "cultural paradigm." These expressions refer to the projection into the linguistic sphere of the essential values held by writer or speaker, values which may be either idiosyncratically individual or reflections of the beliefs of a given society. Such a linguistic model does not operate conceptually, that is, by simply naming these values. Rather it models or mimics the worldview that they imply, and it does this chiefly through language's associative potential.

In the prison novels of Solzhenitsyn, for example, the language of prisoners and the narrator is saturated with irony. The pervasive irony models their fundamental attitude toward a world in which normative and norm are a state of complete dissociation. The language of the poet Velemir Xlebnikov, a writer much admired by Mandelstam, models a different world. A writer with a taste for archaisms and rare words, Xlebnikov is particularly praised by Mandelstam for his remarkable neologisms. He invents words, but words that respect the principles of Russian etymology and word-formation. Hence Xlebnikov's neologisms can be thought of as an attempt to model the unity of culture. In his poetry and prose, the endless productivity of roots and suffixes forges a continuity between what is archaic and what is yet to be.

In parallel fashion, Mandelstam's "Hellenistic" Russian models that human-centered world which appears as the ideal in "The End of the Novel." In *The Nature of the Word* this ideal is associated with the capacity of language to evoke man's calling as master of the created world. For Mandelstam, words can do this if they are used in such a way as to affirm man's freedom of choice. Language can play a role in preserving these humanistic values by means of its possession of what he calls the "secret," or perhaps—because of the religious connotation—"mystery" of free embodiment. This inner freedom of language is closely associated with a polysemantic conception of meaning. Mandelstam's position seems to be that in respecting the poetic word's wealth of connotation, its freedom from slavery to the thing it denominates, artist and audience are respecting their own spiritual freedom.

This ideal, for which Mandelstam found the metaphor of "Hellenism," has broad implications for both his verse and his prose. The general problem of the connection between language and freedom, in particular with regard to freedom of speech and of the press, is a traditional concern of that branch of the "fourth estate," the democratic intelligentsia, from whom Mandelstam claimed descent. The link between the corruption of language and the diminution of freedom is a frequent theme in his writing. Moreover, Mandelstam's conception of the interrelatedness of language, freedom, and tradition provides the key to the reconstructed literary language that he created. His elliptical, fragmented style is at once a reflection of his belief in a humanistic tradition of respect for the reader and a sign of what Blok called "the crisis of Humanism."

In his regard for a central cultural tradition and his apprehension that the center cannot hold, Mandelstam is a typical modernist, whose work compasses these contraries of affirmation and doubt. His contention that poetry is the product of an eternal struggle against the threat of catastrophe implies that these contraries admit of no final resolution. Yet there is also the implication that the tension they generate is a productive tension. Some extrapolating from hints is required here, but Mandelstam seems to believe that in periods when Western culture is threatened with disruption, the very processes that seem to turn life and art into a series of unrelated fragments also intensify the drive to affirm continuity and significance. At such times, it is the capacity of art to model the core values of the cultural legacy (e.g., the Hellenistic potential of the word) that must become paramount, because it is this core on which continuity depends. Hence the persistence in Mandelstam's work of such motifs as cores, kernels, seeds, buried currency—even flies trapped in amber. For Russian culture, it is only this core that can be posited in more than a conditional way: "We have no acropolis. Our culture wanders about and cannot find its own walls. On the other hand, every word in Dal's dictionary is the kernel of an acropolis; a little kremlin; a winged fortress of nominalism, provisioned by the Hellenic spirit for an unwearying struggle with formlessness, with nonexistence that threatens our history from all sides" (II, 251).

In this passage the acropolis becomes a metaphor for an all-inclusive cultural synthesis such as Mandelstam supposes to have existed in classical or medieval Europe but not in Russia. Each entry in Dal' is described as a "kernel" or "little kremlin" to suggest an ever-present potential for the emergence of such a synthesis. Language is represented as being caught up in an endless struggle against an eternal adversary, which Mandelstam elsewhere calls the "antiphilological spirit."

Mandelstam's comments on the "nature of the word" are normative as well as descriptive. All sins against the "Hellenistic" nature of Russian have in common the attempt to suppress the implicit freedom of the language by flattening words out so that they can express only one or a few aspects of their system of constituent meanings. Mandelstam calls this reductionist tendency "utilitarianism." It includes any "exploitative" use of language, whether in the interests of mundane practicality (e.g., acronyms and contractions), literary attempts to forecast the future (Futurism), or of the sacrifice of language to either "mystical intuition" or any system of thought that is "hungry for words." This "higher utilitarianism" is said to be symptomatic of Andrej Belyj's prose and of Symbolism generally.

The critique of Russian Symbolism that is presented in *On the Nature of the Word* focuses on the arbitrary nature of its symbols. If the Hellenistic spirit in Russian can convert any utensil into a symbol of the unity of man with his surroundings, what need is there for explicit symbols, "assigned exclusively for liturgical use?" In Mandelstam's view, the Symbolists have hypostatized figurative meaning. Tending to exclude all other aspects of meaning, especially literal, referential meaning, this hypostasis is said to represent another form of coercion of language.

Mandelstam warns that, taken in the aggregate, such sins against the language could lead, within a few generations, to a "falling mute." Since language, in his view, provides Russia's claim to true historicity, such a lapse into silence would be equivalent to "historical death" (II, 248). He wanted to see in the Russian literary language the repository of the humane tradition and the guarantor of its survival through the "Soviet night." This was a faith that was to be put sorely to the test: Mandelstam knew that the life of the word depended upon the welfare of the language community. Were that community to be corrupted, the word would become a mute cipher, which might, in the best case, be resurrected in some unknown future. This is the impending catastrophe confronted by his writing. The main aesthetic problem that Mandelstam confronts in his prose can now be formulated as follows: in the face of a threatened rift with the past, what is to replace realism, in which the "biographically" engendered plot is the organizing center of gravity, and psychologism, which represents for Mandelstam an extreme subjectivism centering in the implicit author? The evidence of Mandelstam's literary prose and criticism suggests that he sought the answer in the creation of a prose in which language itself, informed by "Hellenism," would become the unifying center.

CHAPTER TWO

THE NOISE OF TIME

Mandelstam wrote *The Noise of Time* mainly during the fall of 1923, while he was staying at Gaspra in the Crimea. I. Ležnev, who had commissioned the piece for his journal *Rossija*, rejected the manuscript on ideological grounds. As Nadezhda Mandelstam comments, Ležnev was looking for a different type of memoir, "the story of a Jewish youth from a *mestečko* [a Ukrainian and Byelorussian term for 'town'] who discovers Marxism for himself."[1]

The Noise of Time was eventually published in two different versions, the first of which was brought out by Georgij Blok (a cousin of the poet Aleksandr Blok) in 1925. The 1925 version included the chapters that treat the civil war period rather than the narrator's childhood. When *The Noise of Time* was republished in 1928, its unity of theme was increased by separating out these chapters as a distinct piece with its own title, "Feodosija." According to Nadezhda Mandelstam's account, the "Feodosija" chapters, together with "V ne po činu barstvennoj šube" ("In an Overly Grand Fur Coat"), the conclusion of the 1928 version, were written later, after an interval of more than a year and a half.[2] However, in spite of "being made from different material" as Nadezhda Mandelstam contends, "In an Overly Grand Fur Coat" is an integral part of *The Noise of Time*, for it recapitulates and brings to their culmination the main themes of the work as a whole. Hence the 1928 text will be used as the basis for discussion in this chapter.

The Noise of Time has in common with the rest of Mandelstam's literary prose an acute and polemical awareness of the literary tradition that stands behind it. The most important strand of this tradition is that which we may call the *detstvo*, promoting a Russian common noun meaning "childhood" into a quasi-genre: the literary reminiscence of childhood. It is against the background of this genre that Mandelstam's piece comes into contrastive focus. There are grounds for juxtaposing *The Noise of Time* with the memoiristic works of S. T. Aksakov, with Tolstoj's trilogy, with the childhood sections of Herzen's *Byloe i dumy* (*Past and Thoughts*), and with Belyj's *Kotik Letaev*. While this brief list can hardly be said to exhaust the literary context of Mandelstam's work, these authors seem to have influenced its shape insofar as it reflects the *detstvo* tradition. Mandelstam himself refers to Aksakov and Tolstoj in a passage of central significance. Hence their memoirs of childhood can be considered as subtexts. They signify for Mandelstam a possibility that he considers closed to contemporary prose: the nineteenth century novel, realistic in mode, and "biographical" (in the sense used in "The End of The Novel" and "The Birth of Plot") in design.

While Mandelstam makes no explicit reference to Herzen, Nadezhda Jakovlevna's claim that the spirit of Herzen's work informs *The Noise of Time* seems well-founded.[3] There is no noticeable polemic with *Past and Thoughts* as a representative work of prose Realism; there is instead, an affinity in the respective attempts of Herzen and Mandelstam to fix the broad historical meaning of the ages which produced them.

Where Herzen, to a certain extent, serves as an ideological model, Belyj, like Tolstoj and Aksakov, can be considered as a polemical target. Like his criticism, Mandelstam's literary prose confronts not only the heritage of Realism, but also what he calls "psychological prose." Although there is no mention of Belyj in *The Noise of Time*, the fact that Mandelstam considered Belyj's prose the summit of the psychological style suggests that *Kotik Letaev*, a work published only a few years earlier than Mandelstam's, can reasonably be considered as a negative influence.[4] As an important contemporary example of a *detstvo* in the psychological and Symbolist manner, *Kotik Letaev* typifies two aspects of Modernist prose towards which Mandelstam was antagonistic.

The programmatic statement which opens "Komissarževskaja," the penultimate chapter of Mandelstam's text, reveals something of his attitude towards the conventions of the *detstvo* and related biographical genres:

> I do not wish to speak about myself but to follow after the age, the noise and germination of time. My memory is hostile to everything personal. If it depended on me, I would only wince, recollecting the past. Never have I been able to understand the Tolstojs and Aksakovs, the Bagrov grandsons in love with their family archives containing epic domestic reminiscences. I repeat: My memory is not fond but hostile, and it works not at reproducing the past but at distancing it. A *raznočinec* needs no memory; all he needs is to tell about the books he has read, and his biography is finished. In the place where, for fortunate generations, the epic speaks in hexameters and chronicles, for me there is a hiatus sign; and between me and the age stands a gulf, a trench, filled with reverberating time: that is the place set aside for my family and my domestic archive. What was it my family wanted to say? I do not know. It was congenitally tongue-tied. Yet it did have something to say all the same. I and many of my contemporaries are oppressed by the burden of hereditary tongue-tie. We did not learn how to speak but to babble. And only

by listening attentively to the swelling sound of the age, and by being
bleached in the foam of its crest, did we acquire a language. (II, 99)

Mandelstam's claim, in this deeply autobiographical work, that his
memory is inimical to everything personal and that it works to distance the
past rather than to reproduce it, takes on meaning when *The Noise of Time*
is juxtaposed to the *detstva* mentioned above. In Tolstoj's trilogy, for
example, the focus rarely strays from the narrator-hero and his perceptions
of his family, teachers, relatives, and friends, all of whom collectively form
the environment for his evolution through successive stages of moral consciousness. The dialectical clash between young Nikolaj's ideals of physical
attractiveness, social acceptability, and moral perfection on the one hand,
and his frequently critical image of himself on the other gives the work its
dynamism. The process of growing up is presented in terms of the hero's
experiencing of various states of mind and feeling: grief at his mother's
death, shame and guilt induced by his alternating sense of superiority to
others and of rejection by them, hatred (the episode with St. Jerome the
tutor), the onset of adolescent sexuality, and so forth.

It is this focus on subjective emotions that imbues Tolstoj's work with
the 'personal' and 'domestic' qualities against which Mandelstam's narrator
reacts. But an equally important gauge of the difference in perspective
which divides these two writers is the extent to which they view the social
landscape from opposite ends of the telescope. In Tolstoj's world, Mandelstam's narrator could hardly have hoped for more than the social status of
poor Il'inka Grap, the victim of the aristocratic boys' bullying. Put more
abstractly, the narrator of *The Noise of Time* not only objects to the 'personal' in Tolstoj and Aksakov but feels his own distance from the aristocratic family circumstances under which the habit of such introspection is
formed.

In Tolstoj the narrative traces a growth in self-awareness which culminates in a degree of withdrawal by Nikolaj from his *comme il faut* milieu.
Engendered by the friendship with Nexljudov, the episode of Baron Z's
party, and the hero's exposure to the plebeian Zuxin and his circle, this
final phase does not transcend the conflict between Irtenev's youthful
altruism and the social conditioning inherent in his family status.

There is no such estrangement in the world of Aksakov's narrator—at
least not on the surface. *A Family Chronicle* and *The Childhood Years of
Bagrov-Grandson* are saturated with a pride of place that is unique among
the works under consideration. Aksakov represents the extreme example of
fascination with one's family history, with being "in love with family

archives." This fascination is demonstrated most obviously by the fact that the entirety of *A Family Chronicle* is devoted to the familial prehistory of Bagrov's grandson. This sense of rootedness, of continuity within a family tradition, contrasts sharply with the attitude expressed by Mandelstam's narrator. For him Aksakov's memoirs are incomprehensible, not simply because they dwell at such length upon the writer's family, but because they assume that the lives of such characters as Grandfather Bagrov and his daughter-in-law Sofija Nikolaevna yield an important moral legacy for succeeding generations. For Aksakov, the legacy of his family is clear, whereas the legacy of Mandelstam's "tongue-tied" family is rendered ambiguous by the "noise of time."

In the case of Aksakov, one might take Mandelstam's objection to the 'personal' even further. The strongly 'personal' intonation of Aksakov's family memoirs has as much to do with a highly partisan use of the biographical material as it does with the presence of biographical elements in the first place: both works on the Bagrov family can be read as documents which represent the point of view of one faction within a perennial family quarrel. Yet for all the idealization of the exemplary qualities of Grandfather and Mother and of their love for each other, the reader is at times uncomfortably aware of how short a distance it is from Bagrovo to Saltykov-Shchedrin's Golovlevo, with its similar cast of characters, including a dictatorial family head, scheming children who lack their parents' vitality, and a general atmosphere of coarseness.

Neither Tolstoj nor Aksakov gives much attention to the impingement of history upon the process of character formation; the influence of the times upon the narrator's early development is taken more or less for granted. By contrast, Herzen's *Past and Thoughts* is infused by a concern to demonstrate the interweaving of personal fate with the course of history. It is in this respect that Herzen can be said to provide a model for Mandelstam. The opening of Herzen's work, which correlates the author's infancy with Napoleon's presence in Moscow, is emblematic of this impulse. Herzen presents his younger self as representative of a particular generation of Russian youth. This concept of generations whose leading characteristics are somehow called forth by the specific historical configuration of their age informs *The Noise of Time* as well.

With respect to the relationship between the child and his age, *Kotik Letaev* stands at the other extreme. Partly because Kotik is glimpsed only between the ages of three and five, and partly because of the work's Symbolist and Anthroposophical orientation, the focus remains fixed throughout on the development of the isolated self, not on its interactions with the history of the times. Through the kind of global solipsism deplored by Mandelstam as "the extraction of a pyramid from the depths of one's own soul," the external world is reduced to a set of mere coordinates for subjective feelings.

The problem of self-consciousness is central to *Kotik Letaev*, yet the frame of reference is not moral, as it is in Tolstoj, but purely epistemological: "Impressions are the records of Eternity. If, at that time, I could have tied together my impressions of the world, a cosmogony would have resulted."[5] The truly historical imagination can have no place within this framework. History dissolves into recapitulation of archetypes, treated as cultural universals. Mandelstam, too, is concerned with archetypal patterns, but his patterns operate in history. Indeed such patterns, as the expression of what he calls *preemstvennost'*, the living spirit of tradition, are a necessary condition for the very existence of history; they impart meaning to its otherwise purely local and accidental content. But where Belyj, in *Kotik Letaev*, is mesmerized by the archetypal "Eternal," Mandelstam respects the local content of history as the sign of human free will.

History, for Mandelstam, is not merely a static cycle; it is a dialectical and teleological process, a "Jacob's ladder by which angels descend from heaven to earth," as he puts it in "Čaadaev" (II, 286). It is the "sacred link and alternation of events," and the individual human life only receives its full meaning in relation to its historical context. However, for the narrator of *The Noise of Time* his personal and family history is not something self-evident, a meaning to be affectionately reproduced. Rather, it is something which must be restored as if it were the original of a highly defective text. However distant Mandelstam's anti-'personal' and historiosophic approach to his childhood and to the age that formed him may seem from the clinical framework of Freudian theory, one senses a similarity in intent between what his narrator is attempting and the psychoanalytic method: the past must be understood in order to be free of it; in order to "distance" it, in Mandelstam's phrase.

"We did not learn how to speak but to babble": for Mandelstam, there can be no inner meaning to life until one's relationship to one's time is made clear. Speech and babble stand here for that clash of opposing principles which figures in Mandelstam's criticism, and especially in *On the Nature of the Word*. "Speech" belongs to the same conceptual field as Hellenism and the philological spirit. It connotes a full consciousness of cultural tradition, of the legacy of ethical values inherited from the past. "Babble," on the other hand, correlates with the mindless adaptation to unexamined and shifting social imperatives. It is the discourse of the antiphilological spirit. The transmutation of "babble" to "speech" is a constant goal of Mandelstam's art.[6] In *The Noise of Time*, what was babble for the child must retroactively become speech for the adult.

The web of relationships that unites Mandelstam's narrator with his world, past and present, bears a markedly different character from that found in the other *detstva*. He is not simply estranged from his surroundings like Kolja Irtenev or young Herzen. In his claim that his sense of identity owes far more to the books he has read than to his family, he is that contemporary European, posited by Mandelstam in "The End of the Novel" who has been "evicted from his own biography."

However, the claim that the *raznočinec* has no need of a memory is hyperbolic and ironic. The narrator of *The Noise of Time* does not in fact represent himself as a deracinated figure, formed by books alone. His search for identity reflects a twofold cultural displacement. Not only must he somehow come to terms with the cataclysmic disruption of pre-revolutionary Russian culture, but he must also come to terms with the fact of his Jewish descent. The conflicting claims put forward by these two traditions put his identity under tension from two directions. The dislocating stresses that they create underlie the theme of the outsider with divided loyalties which pervades both *The Noise of Time* and Mandelstam's verse of the same period.

Within *The Noise of Time* the search for an integrative identity is complicated by questions of social class and ideological perspective as well as by considerations of ethnic identity. First of all, the narrator is remembering himself as a Jewish child seeking to be assimilated to Russian culture. But there is also a tension in the inherently ironic fact that the literary legacy ultimately championed by the *raznočinec*-Jewish narrator is so largely the product of an alien aristocratic class. Moreover, whatever resolution of these conflicts might have been achieved by the child must be reevaluated by the narrator in the light of the Revolution and its critique of the past.

The setting in which all these divisions of the self must be overcome is also an important factor in determining the direction of the narrator's growth. St. Petersburg, home of the dreamers and outcasts of Russian literature since Pushkin's day, accommodates all the strands in the identity of the author's spokesman, just as its emblematic colors, yellow and black, merge, for Mandelstam, the colors of Jewish ritual and eschatological forebodings of the end of the age.[7]

In *The Noise of Time* as in other *detstva* discussed here it is the family which is the primary mediator between the child and the broader social environment. The narrator's attempt, in "The Bookcase," to understand "what it was that his family wanted to say" is central to his efforts to situate himself within the currents of history and culture.

The commingling of these currents is complex. To begin with, the narrator opposes the "Judaic chaos" of his family's apartment to Russian Petersburg. Within the family circle, however, the Jewish influence is associated with the paternal line, while the mother is acculturated to the tradition of the Russian intelligentsia. Looked at from a slightly different angle, the parents represent two stages in the history of Russian Jewish secularization. The father, whose world view and language are formed by his youthful intoxication with German philosophical literature of the Enlightenment, is a throwback to the *Maskilim*, the first advocates of secular enlightenment, who emerged in the eighteen forties. As with Mandelstam's father, the *Maskilim* came from the Baltic regions, wanted the Jews to participate in German culture, and were characterized by an anachronistic eighteenth century outlook.[8]

Where Mandelstam's father is portrayed as an autodidact of German thought, his mother's pride in her Russian schooling reflects the assimilationist hopes of the seventies and early eighties. Mandelstam deepens the perspective on this process of secularization and assimilation by carrying it back another generation. The real locus of the "Judaic chaos" which is so frightening and repellent to the narrator as a child is the household of his paternal grandparents. It is aesthetically appropriate that these unassimilated and incomprehensible old Jews live in Riga, for this intensifies the little boy's sense of Jewishness as something spectral, a ghostly influence from without upon Petersburg.[9]

Turning towards the past in order to turn away from it, Mandelstam does seem, however, to want to retain at least a few positive images associated with his Jewish legacy. Negative evaluations of Judaism are found mainly in the earlier chapters, which tend to treat the period of early childhood. Later chapters, which tend to deal with memories of the boundary of adolescence, show Jews and their culture in a more positive light. One example of this more positive treatment is the chapter devoted to Julij Matveič, the rather affectionately portrayed "Jewish general." There is also the admiring characterization of S. A. Anskij, a major Yiddish author, whose stories captivate the narrator. Anskij is described as a "Gleb Uspenskij out of the Talmud Torah," that is, a figure in whom Russian populism coexists with Jewishness. In another characteristically anomalous juxtaposition, Anskij's presence suggests a "gentle [*nežnyj*] hemorrhoidal Psyche" (II, 95), a phrase worth attending to not only because of its paradoxical combination of positive and negative associations, but because its positive terms (*nežnyj, psixeja*) have an important place in Mandelstam's lexicon.

Nežnyj is one of Mandelstam's favorite epithets: the *Concordance to the Poems of Osip Mandelstam* cites 48 occurrences in the poetry alone.[10] As for Psyche, the first of the 1920 twin-poems "Kogda Psixeja-žizn' spuskaetsja k tenjam" ("When Psyche-Life Descends to the Shades") and "Ja slovo pozabyl, čto ja xotel skazat'" ("I Have Forgotten the Word I wanted to Say") freely reworks that episode in Apuleius's version of the Cupid and Psyche myth when the outcast and wretched Psyche is sent by Venus, her implacable mother-in-law, on an errand to Persephone. In the second twin-poem, the Psyche-soul is replaced by the poetic word, which descends into the Tartarus of unconsciousness. This equation of Psyche with the poetic imagination is made explicit in the 1921 essay "Slovo i kuľtura" ("The Word and Culture"): "Can it be that the object is master of the word? The word is Psyche. The living word does not designate an object but freely chooses, as though it were selecting an abode, this or that referential meaning, thing-ness, or beloved body" (II, 226).

Like Psyche in her wanderings, Anskij is homeless, sojourning in a Petersburg study "bez prava žiteľstva," 'without a residence permit,' an allusion to the civil disabilities placed upon Jews. But Anskij also resembles Psyche in her association with the poetic word, capable of disclosing the record of its descents into time and the unconscious. He is for Mandelstam the Psyche of the Jewish folk imagination, who "has preserved everything, remembered everything."

The other formative influence on the child—Russian culture of the late tsarist period—must also be reevaluated. Much of it, beginning with the "infantile imperialism" inspired by the very architecture of Petersburg, is rejected. The political and social atmosphere of the period is metaphorized as a long winter night and as Russia's "remote and desolate years" (II, 45). The fact that the child felt himself to be an outsider to this world, too, is also a kind of judgment upon the age which preceded the Revolution. However, it is the substitution of spectacle for real engagement with life which is implicitly presented as the chief sickness of the Silver Age. For Mandelstam, this tendency cuts across all ethnic and social divisions. The same spirit which manifests itself in Imperial pomp and display also characterizes the intelligentsia, with its ineffectual demonstrations and "political" literary gatherings.

In *The Noise of Time* the legacy of the previous age for the Soviet period is an ambivalent one. Even the fascination of Petersburg is always qualified by a negative, sometimes apocalyptic, note. One locus of positive associations is the Tenišev School. Another is the household of Mandelstam's school friend Boris Sinani. Writing of his classmates and teachers, Mandelstam emphasizes their enthusiastic idealism. The same trait is praised in the schoolboys' older counterparts in the left intelligentsia, whose spiritual qualities (*duxovnost*) are pointedly preferred by the narrator to the cheap philosophizing of the Symbolist literati (II, 90, 98).

Mandelstam characteristically authenticates the behavior of his friends by presenting it as a repetition of the gatherings of young people in the *divannaja* (drawing room) in *War and Peace* (II, 94), or by drawing a parallel between the atmosphere in the Tenišev School in the 1905 period and that in Pushkin's Lycee in 1812 (II, 86). This attribution of historical precedent, of *preemstvennost'*, removes the actors from the sphere of the accidental in the same way as does Mandelstam's association of his teacher V. V. Gippius with the figures on Old Russian icons (II, 103).

In the figures of Gippius and of Boris Sinani, Mandelstam portrays those qualities of mind and spirit which partly redeem the "deaf years" for him. While both exemplify the moral fervor of the *raznočinec*, Sinani's ardor is directed towards politics while Gippius' is directed towards the preservation and dissemination of the Russian literary tradition. "In an Overly Grand Fur Coat," the chapter devoted to Gippius, echoes several of the motifs of Mandelstam's criticism. It pays tribute to the qualities of the Russian language, affirms the unity of the Russian literary tradition, and pictures literature as a family to which the ardent reader is admitted:

> Starting with Radiščev and Novikov, V. V. had what was already a personal relationship with Russian authors, a bilious and affectionate acquaintanceship that included noble envy, jealousy, facetious disrespect, and profound unfairness—as is to be expected within a family. (II, 106)

This is surely the most appropriate complex of 'familial' emotions in a "servitor" or "retainer" (*domočadec*) in the house of literature, who asserts his kinship with a family in which "not friends, not dear ones, but alien, distant people" constitute the main line (II, 104). It is a claim that does not expect to go unchallenged, perhaps, but it is a claim. Hence in *The Noise of Time* as in *On the Nature of the Word*, literature becomes a model of Man's potential to be at home in culture and history.

Of the other motifs from Mandelstam's poetry and criticism that reappear in *The Noise of Time*, the most striking is the image of the narrator's age as moribund. This image of the dying age is also central to the "Vek" cycle of lyrics (Nos. 135-140). The differences are illuminating. The poetry differs from the prose especially in that the sense of loss, of lamentation for the past, is much more open. The dying age is called both "beautiful" (*prekrasnyj*) and "pitiable" (*žalkij*), and the attitude towards the present is highly ambivalent.

This contrast is suggestive of the differing functions which, in Mandelstam's view, are fulfilled by prose and poetry. The more open expression, in the lyrics, of emotional ties to the age which formed him points up the corresponding "avoidance of the personal" in Mandelstam's prose. It is accordingly easier to extrapolate a critique of the past from *The Noise of Time* than it is to establish the narrator's feelings about the society which was taking form after 1917, or—more narrowly—to get a sense of his views on the role of the past in forming the Soviet present.

Nadezhda Mandelstam sees *The Noise of Time* as an attempt by her husband to overcome a sweepingly negative view of his own situation during the early and mid-twenties, the period he was to look back on as the worst years of his life.[11] She sees a strong eschatological undertow in his work, evident as early as the poems collected in *Tristia* and continuing through the twenties. This vision of the end of a cultural order complemented a sense of isolation from the present. It may be that *The Noise of Time* displaces both the eschatological current and the sense of isolation to Mandelstam's childhood. However, the past is also used as a screen to criticize the present indirectly. Evidence of his dissatisfaction with this present is easy enough to find, given the permeabililty of Mandelstam's writings to each other.

The image of the implicit author in Mandelstam's verse which emerges from Stephen Broyde's study agrees with the picture built up by Nadezhda Jakovlevna.[12] Their studies indicate that, in the "growth of the poetic personality," Mandelstam evolved from a sense of himself as an outcast, at odds with an age which appeared inimical to his art, to an affirmation of his own truth in the face of that hostility and a belief in the potential for survival of humane values modeled by aesthetic culture.

As concerns Mandelstam's response to the new age, it is significant that there is a tendency for images of negative tonality, associated with the past in *The Noise of Time*, to appear as traits of the present in his lyrics. In No. 127, "Komu zima, arak, i punš goluboglazyj" ("For Some There is Winter, *Arak*, and Azure-Eyed Punch") (1922), for example, the poet appears as an outsider in a dark, shaggy wintry world. This imagery parallels the characterization of the nineteenth century in "In an Overly Grand Fur Coat" but in the lyric it is the Revolutionary present that is depicted in such threatening terms. Images of night and winter, in association with rough and shaggy textures, also crop up in Nos. 114 and 118, lyrics that have theatrical performances as their immediate subjects. These motifs conjure up a hostile universe which threatens to overcome the flame of culture. Here again, it is the "Soviet night," not the tsarist one, which carries the threat of "universal emptiness."

There is also a link between "In an Overly Grand Fur Coat" and No. 132, "Ja po lesenke pristavnoj." As Kiril Taranovsky points out, the image of the poet who "tunes his lyre as if hastening to grow a shaggy fleece" is connected both with Pushkin's portrayal of Ovid in exile and with the theme of the nineteenth century literary legacy as developed in *The Noise of Time*:[13] in a wintry and hostile environment, art must acquire a shaggy protective covering in order to survive. Yet in the lyrics, this hostile environment is part of the present, not the pre-Revolutionary past.

Ležnev was presumably the first reader to react to an implicit critique of the present in the piece he had commissioned. He rejected it, after all, because his own sense of the present required a different kind of past, one that would extol the new 'Soviet reality' by emphasizing its role as a latent presence and inexorable moral force within the old social order. Mandelstam's narrator does discover Marxism, it is true, but for him it is more of a cosmic metaphor than an instrument of social change. And even this turns out to be a transitory infatuation that gives way before the agrarian Socialism of Boris Sinani and his circle.

In Mandelstam's view, the treatment of the role of the individual in history in literary prose is a barometer of the state of society. The sense of life as spectacle in *The Noise of Time*, and of the age as moribund, is expressive of how Mandelstam saw the contemporary status both of prose and of the individual as an actor on the historical stage.

What possibilities are held open for individual engagement with life in this work? One such possible role is that of witness to history. The chief examples are V. V. Gippius and, by implication, the narrator himself. In different ways, each seeks to stress the value of the past for the present. Claiming that figures on Novgorodian and Pskovian icons contain the archetype of his teacher's "literary spite," Mandelstam describes them as "dragged by the hair to be witnesses in the Byzantine court of history" (II, 103); their *raznočinec*-descended Gippius bears zealous and partisan witness to literary history. Gippius' ardent assertion of the significance of literature thus exemplifies a form of that victory over the "noise of time" which the narrator also seeks.

But the narrator bears witness to a broader range of phenomena than does his eccentric teacher. It seems fair to say that in the characterization of Gippius, books have indeed replaced a personal biography. In the case of the narrator, however, one would have to say that he is not so much preoccupied with literature as such; instead there is a tendency for everything in his world to be incorporated into the same order of experience as literature, to be viewed through literary screens. This process will go much further in *The Egyptian Stamp*, but its seeds are present in *The Noise of Time.*

The Petersburg setting seems to have much to do with inducing this process of turning life into a text. Mandelstam includes many details of the life of his city, such as the Pavlovsk concerts, the formal decorum of the children at play in the Summer Garden, the gloomy crowds that are the subject of the narrator's earliest clear memory, the military parades and the student demonstrations. Yet at the same time the actual city is assimilated to the "Petersburg text," that is, to the city as it exists in literary tradition. Part of this perception of the city as a literary phenomenon is signaled by the use of explicit literary echoes, an important one being the identification of Petersburg with Tjutčev's veil over the abyss. But the most important ways in which the physical and literary cities are merged are more diffuse. The very fact of a literary work which is set in the imperial capital and which accommodates the theme of an outsider-hero who is estranged by the grandeur of his architectural surroundings cannot help but conjure up the literary image of the city.

Another implicit measure of the significance of the individual 'biography' is the manner in which the characters embody their personal fates; i.e., whether or not they reach the limits prescribed by what Lukacs calls "concrete potentiality." In the light of Mandelstam's emphasis on the interpersonal, societal, determination of biography, one might expect some kind of congruence between the quality of the times and the careers of its representatives. This congruence is evident in Mandelstam's portrayal of his mentor Sergej Ivanyč (II, 79-82) and of his friend Boris Sinani (II, 89-98). The gravitational influence of a dying world is discernible in both their life trajectories.

In each case the character's career is deflected from its apparent course and the hopes lodged in him are disappointed. Sergej Ivanyč's apostasy at the critical moment is implicit in his image from the first: part student revolutionary, part gendarme. Mandelstam presents him as a young man who is doomed to express an allegiance to the upper-middle class even in his very hatred of it. His radical credentials are undercut by his rootedness in the service nobility, and Sergej Ivnayč fades like the memory of 1905 itself.

By contrast, Boris is a true *raznočinec.* Uncompromised by life, his revolutionary potential is anulled by early death. There is a play of religious imagery about his figure; he is described as looking "something between a Russian boy playing the game of *svajka* and an Italian John the Baptist" (II, 89). He is portrayed as a unity of opposites that have a recurring fascination for Mandelstam: North and South, Russian and non-Russian, and secular and religious motifs. The narrator's friendship with Boris is that of a disciple with a teacher. Even in comparison with the treatment of Gippius—also a teacher—the image of Boris Sinani carries the strongest and most open emotional charge of any character who appears in the work.

Boris is represented as the forerunner (*predteča*, the title of John the Baptist) of the Revolution, not of a new religious teaching, yet what he has to convey is not so much the theory of S. R. populism as its spiritual cast (*duševnyj stroj*). While the revolutionary impulse is somehow doubtful and compromised in Sergej Ivanyč, in Boris it takes on an almost hagiographic purity and intensity. That which is best in the social ethic of the narrator's youth, everything which is not "dull and deadening" (*ploskoe i mertvjaščee*) (II, 90), is represented in the person of Boris.

In the characterization of Boris Sinani, Mandelstam infuses his feelings about his childhood friend with the broader thematics of the dying age. Loyalty to the best qualities of the time of his childhood, together with regret for their loss, enters into the portrait. The narrator renders the image of the dying Boris prototypical and literary by juxtaposing it with the image of the dying Andrej Bolkonskij. There follows a rare instance of a personal emotional response: "I was upset and anxious. All the turmoil of the times affected me" (II, 98).

The context suggests that this sense of uneasiness is called forth by the fatal illness of his friend, yet it comes to be attached to all of the "strange currents" of the times. The question arises as to why Mandelstam makes this connection.

Clues to the solution of this question are dispersed throughout the chapter "The Sinani Family," which deals with the period of Mandelstam's school days. Reconstructing the atmosphere of his adolescence, the narrator mentions a variety of personal styles open to the youth of his day. These alternatives form the background to the portrait of Boris. Whether they are "young suicides" or—in the sarcastic expression of Boris himself—S. R. "Christlets" (*Xristosiki*), there is something distinctly negative about all these roles and players. Hence they contribute to the aura of exceptionality which surrounds him.

Boris' genuine idealism contrasts with the fin-de-siècle perversity of such types as poor Natasha, whose hair turns prematurely grey from the frequency with which she changes her convictions: "Natasha was by turns a Social Democrat, Socialist Revolutionary, a member of the Orthodox Church, a Roman Catholic, a Hellenist, and a Theosophist, with various intermissions" (II, 94). In a world where the question of "the role of the individual in history" has been cheapened by becoming the subject of partisan polemics, Boris is the most fully developed sketch for contemporary version of the "Napoleonic" hero described in "The End of the Novel." The desire for glory and sacrifice, shared by Boris and the other Teniŝev students, makes him akin to the heroes of Stendhal and Tolstoj; hence the recurrent references to *War and Peace* in connection with him.[14]

There is, then, a fatal link between Boris Sinani's death and the narrator's intense perception of the anxiety of the age. In the absence of the potentially heroic model represented by Boris, the stage is left to those who have been swept away by the "strange currents" of the day.

Mandelstam's narrator also bears comparison with narrators of other *detstva* insofar as the role possibilities which he himself represents are concerned. The most far-reaching distinction which emerges from such comparisons has to do with the fact that Mandelstam's narrator functions as a synthesizing consciousness almost exclusively; as an actor in the recounted events, hardly at all. His narrator sees, thinks, and feels, but does not act. At the same time, unlike Belyj's Kotik, whose confusing welter of impressions is the primary vantage-point for viewing the untrustworthy external world, Mandelstam's narrator neither sees not is seen through the screen of "psychological motivation." In *The Noise of Time* the focus is resolutely fixed upon other people, upon places, objects and events. In seeking the general significance of the age that formed him, Mandelstam is much less concerned than his predecessors in the *detstvo* tradition with the growth of his own moral and intellectual awareness.

Like so much else in *The Noise of Time*, the detached synthesizing consciousness of the narrator takes on part of its significance from the Petersburg setting, which itself promotes the idea of life as a spectacle to be observed rather than as an arena that invites direct participation. Mandelstam's narrator seems destined to his role as an observer, both as an adult who is reconstructing the outlook of a child and as a Petersburger who is a literary descendant of Pushkin's poor Evgenij, Gogol's clerks and minor functionaries, and Dostoevskij's dreamers.

The theme of social and civic life as a *zreliŝĉe*, a spectacle, is only one dimension of the broader theme of life in which "symbolic action" (in Kenneth Burke's sense) has overweighted direct personal experience: "A raznoĉinec needs no memory . . . ." The Petersburg of the narrator's childhood exists as a world of intertextuality, a book to be interpreted in the light of other books. These texts, inscribed in the consciousness of the interpreter, leave little room for other ways of being in the world. To the extent that books become replacement for 'biography,' language becomes a metonym for character. It is strongly indicative of Mandelstam's relationship to the *detstvo* tradition that in his central discussion of his parents' influence upon him, the latter are represented by their book collections (II, 57-61), and that he points to the significance of parents in forming the child's language rather than his character as such (II, 66). Yet for Mandelstam one's language is more than an index of tastes and attitudes; respect for language is equivalent, in *On the Nature of the Word* elsewhere, to respect for human beings.

MUSIC AND MEMORY

To discuss the role of the narrator of a literary work inevitably leads back to the problem of the narrative point of view. The fact that an adult narrator, with adult values, is describing the world of a child strongly conditions the vantage point afforded to the reader for understanding the narrated events in the *detstvo*. In *The Noise of Time*, moreover, the shifting perspectives created by changes between the speech event—usually attributable to the adult narrator—and the narrated event also help to give a culture-modeling capability to the language of the work.

In this respect, the opening chapter, "Music in Pavlovsk" ("Muzyka v Pavlovske"), serves the function of establishing the initial perspectives. It introduces a set of analogies, all of which are somehow bound up with the work's angle of vision:

$$\frac{E_n}{E_s} = \frac{\text{past}}{\text{present}} = \frac{\text{province}}{\text{metropolis}} = \frac{\text{child}}{\text{adult}} = \frac{\text{binary logic}}{\text{synthesizing memory}}$$

Forming two dichotomous series, these terms are kept apart by "the noise of time," insofar as they belong to temporally discrete categories: the narrator's childhood belongs to a vanished age; his adulthood to the Soviet present. From the "cosmopolitan" perspective of this present, the past age is recalled as a time of moribund provinciality.

It is part of Mandelstam's stategy that these oppositions are set up in order to be overcome. There are two forces within this remembrance of childhood that have the potential to bridge these discontinuities: music and memory—memory that brings about an imaginative reconstruction of the past. The importance of music as an explicit theme in *The Noise of Time*, as well as the implicit 'musicality' of its play of leitmotifs, suggests that these two forms of artistic production are closely connected for Mandelstam. This connection already figures in the opening section of the work, which is an act of memory concerned with musical phenomena, the concerts at the Pavlovsk Station.

The opening paragraph of "Music in Pavlovsk" establishes a retrospective view of the nineties as a provincial backwater:

> I well remember Russia's deaf years, the nineties, with their crawling pace, morbid calm, and deep provincialism; they were the quiet haven and final refuge of a dying age. (II, 45)

By starting with the polemical use of a subtext from Blok—a lyric in which the latter claimed that members of Mandelstam's generation had no historical memory—this opening immediately establishes the narrator's propensity for viewing life in literary terms. The submerged image of the age as a dying, crawling creature suggests the close connection between *The Noise of Time* and the poems of the "Age" cycle. It also illustrates Mandelstam's manner of implying metaphorical analogies between Culture, Nature, and History: The age as a dying beast; the past viewed from the present as if it were provincial life viewed from some metropolis.

A different angle of vision is soon introduced:

> Here, in a few words, is the essence of the nineties: Ladies' bouffant sleeves and music in Pavlovsk. The spheres of these sleeves, along with everything else, revolve around the glass-walled Pavlovsk railroad station, and the orchestra conductor Galkin is at the center of the world. (II, 45)

This passage begins with an attempt to capture the essential quality of the nineties through a paradoxical bipartite formula: "Ladies' bouffant sleeves and music in Pavlovsk." The narrator goes on to provide the associative chain that underlies this formula. The ladies' sleeves serve as metonyms, first for the ladies themselves; second, for the concert audience in general; and finally for the whole culture of the period. Their roundness makes it plausible to picture them as "spheres" whose center of rotation is the conductor Galkin. In this imagery of orbiting spheres, Mandelstam again draws upon the metaphor of a planetary system, which elsewhere in his work seems to signal the theme of art as the model of a potential harmony in human existence.[15]

As is true of all the important passages dealing with the theme of music, "Music in Pavlovsk" combines both visual and aural codes. To the extent that the musical performance is rendered as a visual experience, it becomes a constituent of the idea of life as spectacle, which is part of the thematics of Petersburg in literary tradition. At the same time, the image of the puffed sleeves is repeated in varying contexts in the manner of a musical leitmotif, reinforcing their connection with the theme of music. But this connection is also suggestive of the characteristically Acmeist device of presenting something concrete, or even trivial, as a correlate for something important, or even profound.

The formula itself illustrates Mandelstam's love of apparent paradox, and his penchant—pointed out by Berkovskij—for naming and defining things.[16] It also hints at the reductionist logic of a young child, the tendency to explain the world in exhaustive oversimplifications, which often have a binary form. Thus it serves as a signal to the reader that there has been a shift to the child's point of view. From this vantage point, the surrounding world of the nineties does not appear in the form of a dying provincial civilization. On the contrary, there is a sense of being at "the center of the world." It is the double perspective of the adult narrator which makes this merely the center of a peripheral "provincial" cultural period.

While Mandelstam's description of the Pavlovsk concert is very vivid, it also implies the idea of music as a synecdoche for art in general. Hence the appropriateness of music as an analogue for artistic memory. The representation of music as a unifying center in *Šum vremeni* suggests a parallel with Mandelstam's comment (in "The Badger Hole") that poetry is created out of the need to avoid catastrophe and to subordinate phenomena to the "sun" of the writer's poetic system. A similar impulse is at work in *The Noise of Time*, where music, poetry, and even political theory are presented as variants in the attempt to impose an aesthetic meaning and harmony upon primeval chaos.[17]

The power of music is an important theme in two other chapters: "The Judaic Chaos" and its sequel, "The Concerts of Hofmann and Kubelik." In "The Judaic Chaos" the noise of time becomes noise of the most literal kind. The tongue-tied quality which Mandelstam ascribes to his father's speech and thought and to his family generally is revealed here as the product of the clash of cultural strains, not a lack of culture. The uneasy mixture of German, Jewish, and Russian elements in the senior Mandelstam is spatialized in the image of ethnically divided Riga with its warring orchestras: the German orchestra plays Strauss, while Čajkovskij is the favorite in the Jewish sector.

But Jewish Dubbeln (now Dubulti) is itself a cacaphonous chaos surrounding the orchestral harmony: "I picked out the fragments of powerful violin music out of the barbaric gramophone of discords coming from the *dachas*" (II, 70). The intensity of the narrator's early passion for Čajkovskij is a measure of his need to escape from the "dirty Jewish sewer" into which the violin voices penetrate. The emotional impact upon the narrator of these performances at a coastal resort area near Riga in the nineties connects them with the "Petersburg concerts" in the grand style in the 1903 and 1904 seasons which are the subject of the following chapter.

The image of Skrjabin, seemingly about to be crushed by the surrounding singers and strings, which appears at the end of "The Judaic Chaos," effects this transition. There is a similar tonality and even a similar disposition of figures in the description of the performers in "The Concerts of Hofman and Kubelik." Pictured as frail demigods who seem to be in danger of being torn to pieces by their perfervid admirers, the two virtuosi are further described as the conquerors of a savage dionysiac element in their audience. But the "alpine cold" that is said to characterize their playing has a paradoxical effect: ". . .But what was clear and sober in their performance only served all the more to madden and incite to new acts of frenzy the crowd that thronged about the marble columns, hung in bunches over the galleries, covered the flowerbeds of the stalls, and packed the stage hotly." (II, 73).

Sweeping the reader by degrees from the crowd's periphery to its leading edge, this seems more a description of a mob—the lynch mob in *The Egyptian Stamp*, for example—than of a concert audience. The paradox here is that this seething crowd, which threatens to inundate the entire space, has a potential for violence which, far from being soothed by the purity and rationality of the music, is increased by it. The passage seems to connote that the artists' articulation of the surrounding chaos into order results in a balance which is at the same time fragile and tenacious. The atmosphere of the concert hall seems to carry the threat of some kind of mob violence, yet this threat is contained, and the artists repeatedly triumph.

The particular hysteria surrounding the concerts of Hofmann and Kubelik is offered as a portent of the approaching Revolution of 1905. The description of these concerts therefore implies something of Mandelstam's view of the relationship between art and politics. Revolution is one form of that periodic threat of catastrophe which he considered to be inherent in human history because human history belongs to natural history. In "Komissarževskaja" he even goes so far as to equate Nature and Revolution: "Nature is revolution, an eternal hunger, a state of inflammable excitement . . ." (II, 99). Both art and political theory are treated by Mandelstam as responses to this "hunger." Where revolutionary theory seeks to understand and harness forces with catastrophic potential, art seeks to affirm the continuity of culture against the threat of a catastrophic break.

If the three chapters in which the theme of music is elaborated are compared, an evolution in emphasis is disclosed. In "Music in Pavlovsk" Mandelstam abstracts chiefly visual details from his memory of the concerts at the railway station. The immediacy engendered by this focus on sights and (to a lesser extent) sounds and smells is suggestive of the fresh perceptions of a young child. In "The Judaic Chaos" the personal, emotional response of the narrator is stressed more, and there is more description of those qualities in the music that produce this response. There are also strong—in part ominous—emotional overtones in the description of the concerts of Hofmann and Kubelik. In fact, it is the atmosphere of these concerts, combining the "peculiarly Dionysian element" (*svoeobrazno-dionijskaja stixija*) animating the audience with the purity and clarity of the soloists' performances, which makes them such an indelible memory. Yet there is also a more intellectual quality to the discussion of these performances. The narrator's distance from the events described shows in his generalization of their significance as an expression of contemporary social undercurrents.

The modulations of the music theme are illustrative of the special quality of Mandelstam's memory. His cognition of the past is not static and uniform; rather, his artistic memory hints at the evolution in logic and judgment which is part of the cognitive development of every child. But he also stands outside of this development, long since completed; the capacity for distancing the past which he attributes to his memory reveals itself in the superimposition of an adult perspective on the child's evolving perspective.

This evolution is conveyed primarily through subtle hints, such as the change in semantic perspective implied by the abandonment of binary logic in favor of more complex forms of understanding as the text progresses.[18] There is also the more positive treatment of the Jewish theme in later chapters, as well as the movement away from the sense of oneself as an outsider and towards an affirmation of "one's own truth" which is completed in the final chapter. There is, perhaps, also some movement away from the perception of life as a passively observed spectacle and toward an approach to life as a text that must be mastered.

To the extent that it does occur, this change is more a subtle shift than a radical transformation. Life, whether it presents itself as spectacle or text, is still at one remove from the narrator's direct involvement. While this sense of life accords well with the feelings of powerlessness which are a part of childhood, it may also reflect a displacement of Mandelstam's deep feelings of estrangement during the period when he was writing *The Noise of Time.*

Thus the evolution of perspective in *The Noise of Time* is not so much an explicit subject of the narrator's discourse as it is a process that is reflected in the connotative qualities of his language. Moreover, it is not always an easy matter to distinguish between simulacra of a child's outlook and manifestations of a broader tendency in Mandelstam's writings; at times the extremes of naivete and sophistication—of the child and the poet—seem to shade into each other.

The classic studies of child logic by Vygotskij and Piaget indicate that its most general characteristic is an obliviousness to the boundaries that adults impose upon experience. Very young children neither differentiate between semantics and phonetics nor draw a distinction between the word and the object or concept which it denotes. Child thought is highly syncretic; it does not recognize barriers between different conceptual orders and it translates experience freely and spontaneously from one cognitive or sensory code into another. Because it transcends conventional distinctions between entities, child logic constructs a world which is highly metaphoric. The world of nature and the world of human culture freely exchange attributes with each other; the same object may be treated as animate (anthropomorphic or zoomorphic) or inanimate. An abstract concept or emotional orientation can be metaphorically represented by an olfactory or tactile sensation.

Like myth and its literary descendants, child logic effects the mediation of discontinuities and affirms the unity of the world. But where these other logics seek to restore a lost harmony, child thought takes this unity for granted. Despite these different starting points, the results are similar. Of course this description of child logic is a gross compression of a genetically complex process; with this reservation in mind, however, it is possible to point to parallels to child logic in Mandelstam's work, and to describe how they function there as a means for modeling the world of childhood and as an approach to mythical wholeness.

One such parallel is to be found in Mandelstam's use of what Bakhtin called the "alien word" (*čužoe slovo*). In an article on the semantic structure of *The Egyptian Stamp*, Dmitrij Segal points out the tendency of the narrator and of Parnok to recollect certain abstract concepts acquired in childhood and to treat certain situations as signifying these concepts. In the mind of the narrator/protagonist, the expression "little man" (*malen'kij čelovek*), for example, is a code word, a magical formula which conjures up a complex set of emotional associations rather than a concrete denotative meaning.[19]

The same tendency to take over what Vygotskij calls "non-spontaneous concepts"[20] from the speech of adults operates in *The Noise of Time*. Such code words are found especially in "The Bookcase." They have a special appropriateness here, because in this chapter the narrator sets out to reconstruct the world views of his parents. Terms from their lexicon become abstract labels that cover a whole world of emotional and ideological associations as that world is understood by a member of the next generation.

The narrator's response to his parents' characterization of Dostoevskij as "heavy" (*tjaželyj*) (II, 59) illustrates this process. As a description of the works of an author he is forbidden to read, the abstract ideas of 'heaviness' can have no concrete significance for the child. He therefore fills it with his own content; *tjaželyj* becomes a vague connotative term with strong negative overtones, which the child associates with the weight of tombstones.[21]

As Segal points out, not only words but also sensory experiences of any type can be the coded signifier of an abstract concept for Mandelstam. Something as complicated as the concept of the Judaic chaos, for example, can be represented by an olfactory sensation: "As a bit of musk fills a whole house, so the slightest influence of Judaism overfills one's whole life" (II, 56). In a similar fashion the abstract idea of human labor is signified for the narrator by the smell of leather that was a constant of his childhood world, since his father was a leather merchant (II, 56). In another example, the juxtaposition of an abstraction and an odor emphasizes the narrator's judgment of value on the abstraction: "At the end of an era of history abstract concepts always stink like rotten fish" (II, 104). The concepts alluded to here belong to Symbolism. Since this phrase clearly represents the thinking of an adult, it indicates that Mandelstam's use of this device is not restricted to contexts in which he is modeling the thinking of a child.

While the interchange of attributes between nature and culture which is characteristic of Mandelstam's writing is much more complex than the simple obliviousness to such distinctions found among young children, it nonetheless suggests another parallel—albeit a remote one—between the child's world and that of the poet. The sustained simile (in "The Bookcase") which compares his parents' bookcase to a geological formation is perhaps the outstanding example in *The Noise of Time* of Mandelstam's tendency to create connections between literary culture and natural history. While this transposition of cultural experience into a 'geological' code is only one variant of the fusion of nature and culture in his prose and poetry, it seems to me to be a particularly idiosyncratic and unprecedented trait.

There are three such geological images in "In an Overly Grand Fur Coat," the final chapter. V. V. Gippius' books are described as "[threatening] to avalanche, like the crumbling walls of a ravine" (II, 102); his concern for literary history determines his sense of the present: "Thus does one enter the present, the modern day, as if it were a dried-up river bed" (II, 103). Speaking of Leont'ev as a writer with a highly developed aware-ness of tradition, Mandelstam comments that "of all the Russian writers he is most inclined to build with clumps of time" (II, 108).

The book/avalanche simile, based on a readily apparent visual and kinetic resemblance, also fits in with the imagery of the nineteenth century as a wintry cave-world in this chapter. The latter two passages are richer in significance. Linking literary culture and geology as parallel processes, both involve a substitution of a spatial image for a temporal concept: the present as a dried-up river bed, a time of cultural drought in comparison with the resources of the past; clods of earth substituted for blocks of time. What these images do is to give to the process of literary history something of the scale of geological time. Such analogies work in both directions. Not only is human culture assimilated to longer-term natural processes, but—in keeping with one of the central ideas of *On the Nature of the Word*—man understands and domesticates nature by seeing its activity as akin to his own.

In *The Noise of Time* this can take the form of animating nature or the world of cultural objects. The representation of the age as a beast illustrates this tendency. A related example is the animation of Petersburg, the em-blem of the age. Thus at one point the narrator speaks of "the gentle heart of the city" (II, 50). Elsewhere the process of animation takes on an anthropomorphic cast: "Prerevolutionary Petersburg, from Vladimir Solo-v'ev to Blok, was pervaded by Finland, pouring the Finnish sand from one hand to the other and rubbing the light Finnish snow on its granite fore-head, listening, in its heavy delirium to the harness bells of the undersized Finnish horses" (II, 62). Here the image of the city is animated by stages. What begins as a conventional metonymy ("prerevolutionary Petersburg"; i.e., the inhabitants of the city) develops into a metaphor of the city as a living giant with features, gestures, and a state of consciousness (delirium) which are recognizably human.

Childlike and mythical traits come together in this picture of Petersburg as a delirious giant, attempting to slake its fever with the Finnish snow. The act of personification, and especially the implied difference in scale between this giant and the narrator, are suggestive of the world of child-hood. The logic of myth and of poetry is implied by the transformation of the city into a totemic emblem of its own culture, and also by the transposi-tion of an historical situation—the prerevolutionary agitation—into a metaphor with allegorical overtones: the details of this picture of Petersburg rubbing Finnish snow on its granite forehead are motivated by geographical proximity, but its import is chiefly political. Finland is treated in *The Noise of Time* as the place for anti-tsarist plans to be developed; for "thinking through that which it was impossible to think through in Petersburg" (II, 62), an idea which also crops up in the description of a terrorist meeting in a *dača* near Raivolo (II, 97).

In addition to animating the inanimate, Mandelstam also at times pictures the human in terms of the animate non-human and *vice-versa*. Examples include the description of Julij Matveič as a "pinniped" (II, 83) and the animal-like behavior of V. V. Gippius, whose "hibernation" (*spjačka*) and feral shagginess are represented as consequences of his having been a foundling of literature, which is itself described as a "beast" (*zver'*), a "bear," and a "she-wolf" (II, 105-106). There is also the image of Petersburgers as a type of small fish (*plotva*) (II, 71), and the division of humanity into "people-books" and "people-newspapers" (II, 79).

The last two examples require little comment. The comparison of concert-goers to a teeming mass of fish is typical of Mandelstam's tendency to present the human world in terms of the animal kingdom and to make use of the characteristic contrasts in scale between people and city which is a component of the Petersburg tradition from Pushkin to Eisenstein. The witticism about people-books, attributed by the narrator to a friend, is a simple instance of Mandelstam's inclination to see people as texts.

The use of animal imagery which is part of the characterization of Julij Matveič and of V. V. Gippius is more complex. On one level, Julij Matveič's fin feet and the traits of a wild animal ascribed to V. V. Gippius can be seen as adaptive responses to the respective socio-historical environments of these characters. In this respect, they foreshadow Mandelstam's discussion years later in "Journey to Armenia" of the free interplay between organism and environment (II, 164). The Lamarckian motifs in the portrait of Julij Matveič are there mainly as a comic device, while the mood in the final chapter is more serious. However both examples share in the broad tendency in Mandelstam's writing to refer human experience to the model of natural history. Yet here too, behind the adult world view and the adult narrator's love of paradox, there is something which looks very like a child's propensity for spontaneously applying concepts; i.e., one version or another of evolutionary theory, in 'inappropriate' contexts.

A similar playfully deliberate confusion of conceptual orders can be found in "The Erfurt Program." This chapter is concerned with the discovery of a common ground shared by Marxist theory and poetry; the emblem of this common ground is the unlikely union of the German Marxist Karl Kautsky and the politically conservative poet Tjutčev.

"The Erfurt Program" refers back to the ambience of "The Tenišev School." This connection underscores the fact that the young adolescent's sense of his own unfolding is the basis for his awareness of how the same image-reservoir—that of organic growth and decay—is shared by lyric poetry and contemporary political thought: "Everything that smacked of a worldview was greedily devoured" (II, 87). The imperative need of these schoolboys to develop an understanding of themselves in relation to the surrounding world makes them tolerant of any world view which can satisfy their thirst for "unity and harmoniousness."

This paradoxical homology of political theory, poetry, and the teleology of growth is basic to "The Erfurt Program." It also fills in the semantic link with the preceding chapter, "Julij Matveič," for these two move from example to explanation. The comic mix of natural history ("pinniped") and politics ("Bismarck") in the affectionate caricature of Julij Matveič becomes, in the light of the next chapter, an illustration of the application of a schoolboy world outlook (*miirooščuščenie*).

The theme of growth—in this case intellectual growth—through a natural cycle is present from the beginning of "The Erfurt Program": "A brochure plants a larva—that is its function. From the larva a thought is born" (II, 86). In the discussion that follows upon this claim, the 1891 German S. D. Party Congress report is the pamphlet which gives rise to this "larval" stage of thought.

The narrator's reading of the *Erfurt Program*, his observing of the grain ripening in the Kurland fields, and his reflections on Tjutčev and on the early Symbolist Konevskoj are all presented as strands of a single harmonious experience. Accidents of contiguity facilitate this harmony. Konevskoj lived and drowned nearby, and these fields are in a neighborhood where the peasants, caught up in the ferment of 1905, have recently burned out the masters and have themselves been repressed by the authorities.

These facts conduce to a simultaneous awareness of poetry, politics, and the agricultural cycle. At the same time, the narrator's meditation illustrates the extent to which literary categories mark experience for Mandelstam. In addition to its other associations, the Kurland landscape is described in terms that echo a line of Tjutčev's ("And the spider web's slender hair trembles in the idle furrow") ("I pautiny tonkij volos drožit na prazdnoj borozde"), cited as evidence of the latter's power to evoke "cosmic sensations": "That year, in Segewold, in Courland, on the River Aa, there was a clear, autumn *with spider webs in the barley fields*. The barons had just been burned out . . . ["V tot god, v Zegevoľde, na kurljandskoj reke Aa, stojala jasnaja osen' *s pautinkoj na jačmennyx poljax.* Toľko čto požgli baronov . . ."] (II, 87).

All of this is the sign of a special receptiveness of the surrounding 'text' on the teleology of growth. This disposition also underlies the implicit juxtaposition between Konevskoj's poetry, with its level of meaning beneath the surface (". . .his difficult verse had a sonorousness like that of a forest with the wind blowing through it right down to the roots." (II, 88)) and the Marxist claim to be able to see beneath superstructure to base. Reading the *Erfurt Program* makes the narrator feel like a kindred spirit to Konevskoj because it enables him to see beneath the "visible world," with its "barley fields, country lanes, castles, and sun-drenched spiderwebs" to the underlying relations of production.

There is a certain retrospective irony in this recreation of an adolescent vision that mingles Tjutčev, Konevskoj, and the ripening and impending fall of capitalism. However, "The Erfurt Program" also has overtones connected with the literary atmosphere of the early nineteen twenties. The narrator comments on how his adolescent ideology made it possible for him to "populate and socialize" the surrounding pastoral landscape. In this vision, poetry and political theory meet in the common aim of making man at home in the world. Apart from its schoolboy schematism, it is not fundamentally different from Mandelstam's adult views on the relationship between art and politics, as these views are expressed in his criticism. For all its ironic distance, "The Erfurt Program," is another instance of Mandelstam's championing of poetry as a significant social activity.

THEMATIC PATTERNS

Beyond the obvious fact of a single narrator who is engaged in the same enterprise throughout and whose memories are arranged in a loose temporal sequence, what gives aesthetic coherence to *The Noise of Time*?

For one thing, there is the use of various types of foreshadowing. The repetition of motifs from chapter to chapter is one sign to the reader of the presence of an overall design. Thus for example the sixth chapter, "The Judaic Chaos," ends by asserting a connection between the shabby concerts in Dubbeln and the brilliant occasion of a performance of Skriabin's *Prometheus* at the Hall of the Nobility in St. Petersburg. This ending does more than prefigure the "concerts in the grand style" in that same hall which will be the subject of the next chapter, "The Concerts of Hofmann and Kubelik": In the image of the composer, seemingly about to be crushed

by the orchestra and chorus that surrounds him from all sides, it anticipates the main theme of the seventh chapter, which is the capacity of art to
hold catastrophe at bay.

The concert motif foreshadows a thematic development which follows
immediately, but this is not always the case. The phrase "Judaic chaos"
first appears in the third chapter, but receives its elaboration only in the
sixth; the leitmotif of the family bookcase first appears in passing in a
description of the narrator's father's study in the third chapter, serves as
the main image of the fourth, and departs, as it were, in the opening lines
of the fifth, where its travels metonymically represent the peregrinations of
the Mandelstam family.

In the same way, Boris Sinani is first mentioned in a few lines in the
chapter on the Tenišev School, and then reappears as the center of attention
in the twelfth chapter, "The Sinani Family." Likewise, there is a passing
reference to Mandelstam's Tenišev teacher, V. V. Gippius, at the beginning
of "The Erfurt Program," which foreshadows his reappearance as the hero
of the final chapter, "In an Overly Grand Fur Coat."

The enumeration of such motifs illustrates one way in which chapters are
made to cohere with each other. However, the separate chapters also show
structural affinities with each other, for they disclose signs of being cut to
the same pattern. There is, for example, a tendency for passages, or even
whole chapters, to be built around a single controlling field of imagery and
to end with a judgment or generalization, frequently in the form of a concluding reversal. Not unexpectedly, many of these controlling images or
image complexes are drawn from the realm of nature. Several have been
already mentioned: the bookcase, which is the controlling image of the
fourth chapter is translated into a geological 'code.' Natural history, this
time in a Lamarckian variant, is the controlling complex in "Julij Matveič."
Similarly, the images of growth in "The Erfurt Program" have their source
in the agricultural cycle, while the round of the seasons and the alternation
of day and night underlies the representation of the nineteenth century as a
long winter in the last chapter.

The imagery of combustibility dominates two passages concerned, broadly speaking, with political themes. In the characterization of Mandelstam's
mother's generation of *intelligenty* and, in particular, in connection with
the phenomenon of Nadsonism which caught up the youth of the eighties,
the imagery of fire, of various literal and figurative forms of combustion, is
pervasive.

A book of Nadson's verse is described as "glowing hot from handling
(*raskalivšajasja ot prikosnovenij*)"; the portrait of the poet which serves as the

frontispiece is a paradoxical combination of "genuine fieriness" (*ognennost'*) and complete lack of expression. Candles and "burning faces" (*gorjaščie lica*) figure prominently among the details in an evocation of Nadson's public readings; the youth of the eighties is compared to insects circling a lamp fire: "As summer insects beneath the hot glass of a lamp, so the whole generation was charred and burned in the flame of literary celebrations ["kak letnie nasekomie pod nakalennym lampovym steklom, tak vse pokolen'e obuglivalos' na ogne literaturnyx prazdnikov . . ."]."The whole intelligentsia is said to have turned to self-immolation (*samosožženie*). The revolutionary populists of the People's Will movement are said to have burned "like high torches coated with pitch ["Kak vysokie prosmolennye fakely"]" while their supporters "smoldered sympathetically ["sočuvstvenno tleli"]." Finally, there is the daguerrotype of Uncle Miša, of whom the family says that "he did not simply go insane but 'burnt up' [*sgorel*]" (II, 59-61).

"To burn up," in the sense of "perishing from the exhaustion of one's energies in the course of some powerful experience or in the service of some obsession," is a common figurative meaning of *sgoret'*. However, the enclosure of *sgoret'* in quotation marks indicates its thematic connection with the complex of fire imagery. This verb is presented as one of those code words, taken over by the child from the older generation, and signifying not only some situation but also a value judgment on that situation. What runs through this series of fire images is an association with the idea of ritual (torches and candles) and especially with the idea of sacrificial ritual. Mandelstam in fact emphasizes the ritualistic and cultic aspects of the public ceremonies of the eighties. In describing and judging the sacrifice of this generation, it seems to be the consuming, rather than the purifying power of fire that he stresses. The eighties remain an enigma for the narrator because, with the exception of a few "ikons" (the likenesses of Nadson and of Uncle Miša), there is nothing left. Nadson's appeal remains an incomprehensible riddle, and the political terrorism of the day led to the destruction of the terrorists themselves.

The imagery of another attribute of fire plays an important role in the chapter on Sergej Ivanyč. The main theme of this chapter is the ambivalent, transitional nature of the events of 1905. Sergej Ivanyč, whose dualistic nature is an uncertain fusion of revolutionary and reactionary currents, serves as Mandelstam's emblem for 1905. His portrait is one of the products of that special aesthetic working of memory which is the motivating force behind *The Noise of Time* as a whole: "Memory loves hunting in the dark . . ." (II, 79). *Tma*, 'pitch darkness,' is another expression of that chaotic element whose noise and babble the narrator must overcome in order to come to terms with and to distance the past.

Both 1905 and Sergej Ivanyč, its representative, are repeatedly described as "chimerical" (II, 79, 82). Semantically dominated by images of opacity, transience, and evanescence, the chapter follows a dynamic that moves from thickening or coalescing to dispersion, from coming into focus to a final fading of outlines. The significance of 1905 is presented as hidden behind two kinds of opacity. First memory must dredge the events up from the blackness of the unconscious. But, even when this is accomplished, the meaning of events remains inherently ambiguous because of the complex mixture of social currents which fed into them.

The theme of the 1905 Revolution as a brief, chimerical foreshadowing of 1917 is reinforced throughout by the use of smoke imagery. The aesthetic appropriateness of this pattern of imagery is determined, first of all, by the action of smoke when it coalesces over a fire and then disperses. As mentioned, the events of 1905 are said to exhibit this same pattern, and the analogy with smoke is suggested in the recurrent use of the root GUST, ('thick,' 'dense') to connote the first part of this process. Thus memory must retrieve its contents from "the very thick of the murk" ("v samoj *gušče* mraka"), and Sergej Ivanyč first appears in memory in the distance, "out of the dense shaggy murk" ("iz *gustogo* kosmatogo mraka"), on a Nevskij Prospekt which has been suddenly plunged into a Biblical outer darkness ("pogruzilsja v kromešnuju noč") (II, 79). Visiting Sergej Ivanyč's apartment, the narrator shudders from the "dense, acrid odor ("ja sodrognulsja ot *gustogo* i edkogo zapaxa")" (II, 80). The stuffy and odoriferous atmosphere of the room is suggestive of the artificial environment in which Sergej Ivanyč operates. Here the idea of 'thickness' or 'density' shades into that of 'closeness' and lack of air. Airlessness is always a strongly negative concept in Mandelstam's work, one which evokes coercion and oppression. This makes the next appearance of 'thickness' and odor—this time in a positive context—all the more paradoxical: the ambivalence of Sergej Ivanyč's character is suggested by his passion for unusually "thick and aromatic hot chocolate ("*gustoj* i aromatnyj šokolad")" (II, 81). Finally, as the Revolution approaches, Sergej Ivanyč's air of mystery "thickens" in the sense of becoming more and more marked: "The closer the arrival of 1905 and of the appointed hour, the denser became his air of mystery and the more his gloomy authority increased ("Po mere približenija devjat'sot pjatogo goda i časa *sguščalas'* ego tainstvennost' i narastal mračnyj avtoritet")" (II, 82).

Dispersion and blurring—the second part of the action of smoke—begins at this same point: "Like a chimera he dissolved at the light of the historic day ("Kak ximera, on rassypalsja pri svete istoričeskogo dnja.")." This dispersion—the counterpart of his failure, in the eyes of the narrator, to maintain an uncompromisingly revolutionary stance—is presented as an augmentative process: "He had faded completely. He no longer had a face, his features had been so much erased and drained of color ("on vylinjal okončateľno, na nem ne bylo lica, do togo sterliś i obescvetiliś ego čerty . . .")" (II, 82). This description comes from a post-1905 glimpse of Sergej Ivanyč and leads to the narrator's final evaluation of him: " . . . he ought to have departed this life, he was such a chimera (" . . . on dolžen byl ujti iz žizni, do togo on byl ximera.")" (II, 82).

Neither a personality so ambiguous nor the historical situation whose embodiment Sergej Ivanyč is can be understood by precise acts of cognition. Both from the point of view of anticipation, and the point of view of recollection, the shadowy aureole that surrounds Sergej Ivanyč and the first Russian Revolution requires acts of perception which are closer to being sensory than to being intellectual. Hence the subject is approached through verbs (*čujat', ulavlivat', lovit'*) that denote intuitive groping, sensing, or grasping (II, 70).

The initial sighting of Sergej Ivanyč on Nevskij Prospekt evokes for the reader a part of the Petersburg literary tradition which traces back to Gogol's "Nevskij Prospekt," and to several of Dostoevskij's Petersburg works, such as *The Double*, "White Nights," *Notes From Underground*, and *Crime and Punishment*. This is the tradition of the capital as a place of deceptive shapes and shadows, the setting of vague fantasies created and lived out by a race of dreamers in stuffy rooms, and of demonic materializations out of the darkness.

The image of smoke is not merely a critical analogy for the pattern of action and mode of perception in "Sergej Ivanyč." His cigarette and its effects are an explicit and recurrent motif both for the metonymical representation of Sergej Ivanyč and for the larger historical forces he represents. For example:

> Interlinear translations of the revolution poured out of him; they rustled like cigarette paper in his head, stuffed with headcolds, he shook out an ethereally light illegal literature from the cuffs of his cavalry jacket, the color of seawater, and his cigarette gave off a forbidden smoke, as if its wrapper were rolled from illegal paper. (II, 79-80)

This passage creates a fusion between the sounds, actions, and results of smoking a cigarette (the scattering of ashes, the rustles of paper, the "ethereal lightness" of smoke, and the shaking out of ashes caught in cuff-pockets) and the action of distributing and speaking revolutionary propaganda. On the one hand, the impression is created of Sergej Ivanyč's activity as an unrestrained, rather messy outpouring; on the other hand, the revolutionary posture expressed in his pamphleteering is extended even to his manner of smoking.

The analogy between Sergej's intellectual style and his habit of smoking recurs twice more. Wondering at his tutor's gift for improvisation and his disregard for sources while working on a long and "magnificently useless" article on the fall of the Roman Emire, the narrator conjectures as to whether Sergej Ivanyč might be spinning the material out of the smoke of his cigarette. The closeness of the atmosphere in the tutor's room (his usual workplace) is also the result of his habitual smoking: "A room made stuffy and acrid with years of smoking . . ." ("Komnata, nadyšennaja i nakurennaja godami . . .") (II, 80). The overall effect of this pattern of imagery is to make the cigarette a synecdoche for Sergej Ivanyč and, indirectly, to reinforce the value judgment implied by the description of both Sergej and the 1905 Revolution as "chimerical." If fire is a conventional symbol for destruction and renewal, smoke connotes the insubstantial and the indecisive.

"Sergej Ivanyč" is also illustrative of another principle of coherence which figures in *The Noise of Time*. Together with several other chapters, it makes use of the plot device of a reversal near the end: at the narrative level, Sergej is presented as a revolutionary figure who unexpectedly ceases to be a revolutionary at the moment of truth. Thus, while appearances seem to support one view of him, the reality, i.e., that he was "only a rehearsal director of the Revolution," turns out to be different. Of course, this final judgment is implicit all along at the semantic level, with its hints of something hazy about Sergej, and the recurrent presence of the epithets *žandarmskoe . . . studenčeskoe* ('policeman-[like]', 'student') in connection with his image. The manner in which the pattern of imagery only discloses its full meaning at the point where the narrative line reverses itself gives the chapter a logical structure like that of a riddle: the artistic memory (and subsequently the imagination of the reader) must resolve the riddle of Sergej Ivanyč's true historical identity.

Concluding reversals are also used in the second and third chapters. In both instances they serve to open up a distance between the narrator and the surrounding late Petersburg culture. The conclusion of the second chapter, "Infantile Imperialism," juxtaposes the narrator's own family with that of a hypothetical corps commander to suggest the utter inappropriateness of the child's taste for imperial pomp. This conclusion has been prepared for by repetitions of the motif of the "Petersburg street," with its power to insinuate a "craving for spectacle" which—as it turns out—is completely at odds with the boy's Jewish family environment.

The next chapter, "Revolts and Frenchwomen," reiterates the idea of the narrator's marginality in relation to his Petersburg surroundings. This time the reversal takes on a stronger personal note:

> What concern of mine were the celebrations of the guards' regiments, the monotonous prettiness of the hosts of infantry and the horses, the stony-faced battalions, streaming with booming steps along Millionaja, a street grey with granite and marble? (II, 55)[22]

The opening phrase intones more emphatically a question which has been raised a page earlier, in connection with the narrator's impression of the ceremonial lying-in-state of the Italian ambassador. The whole concluding passage serves as a transition to the theme of the Judaic chaos, which is developed in the fourth and sixth chapters.

"Finland," the fifth chapter, also contains a concluding reversal that points up the narrator's ambivalent attitude towards tsarist Petersburg. Throughout the chapter the focus is on "the special meaning that Finland held for Petersburgers." In the last few sentences, the focus shifts, and a glimpse is offered of the significance of "Petersburg" for the Finns: they are a colony, subject to the "yoke of Russian militarism" (II, 64). The final image—an allegorical picture of the maiden Suomi (Finland), threatened by the imperial double eagle, which is said to hang in every Finnish home—contrasts sharply with the earlier image of Finland as a place for vacationing Petersburgers to breathe more freely, or as the location for typical garrison-town romances.

In "The Sinani Family," as mentioned earlier, the concluding reversal takes the form of praise for the moral qualities of the SR's, whose intellectual narrowness, together with the pomposity of their leadership and the affectation of some of their youthful adherents, has been ironically treated up to this point.

Mandelstam's tribute to Komissarževskaja concludes with a more elliptical kind of reversal. More than any other part of *The Noise of Time*, "Komissarževskaja," the penultimate chapter, brings to mind the later prose and poetry in its use of a sudden and apparently 'unmotivated' thematic shift. It begins with the long programmatic statement on the workings of Mandelstam's artistic memory and his relationship to the *detstvo* tradition. From this he turns to the theme of the Revolution, which he elevates to a principle of existence by equating it with Nature. In speaking of the inimical quality of his memory and in addressing himself to the need of the Revolution to see itself as a radical break with the "sources of being" (*istočniki bytija*); that is, cultural tradition, it may be that he is responding to an anticipated misunderstanding of the intent behind *The Noise of Time*. After all, why write about a middle-class childhood in 1923?

At this point, without any apparent logical transition, he begins his discussion of Komissarževskaja and her theater. The main point of this critique is a paradoxical one: Komissarževskaja's greatness is said to reside in her turning away from all the "cheap trappings" of the Russian theatrical tradition, but as a result, "the heart of the theater was coming to a stop." Yet Mandelstam concludes by crediting her with the creation of "the illusory and impossible oxygen of a theatrical miracle" (II, 101). This judgment is consistent with the idea of the artistic performance as a fragile miracle in the face of catastrophe—an idea that is also implied by "The Concerts of Hofmann and Kubelik."

Representing her as a champion of the human voice, which in his view has always been the life of the theater, Mandelstam reverses his earlier, negative, estimate of Komissarževskaja's legacy. There is a parallel in meaning here between the opposition of the human voice to the "hog's maw of declamation" (II, 101) and the opposition of speech to babble earlier in the chapter.

He had addressed the same point in "The Moscow Art Theater and the Word" ("Xudožestvennyj teatr i slovo"). In this 1923 article Mandelstam criticizes the intelligentsia of the preceding generation for the antiphilological spirit evident in its "hostile inarticulateness" ("kosnojazyčie," 'inarticulateness' or 'tongue-tie': the same trait he ascribes in "Komissarževskaja" to his family and contemporaries). In MXAT's reliance on what the article terms "the crutch of declamation," Mandelstam sees the consequences of the intelligentsia's "distrust of the word" (III, 100-01).

The implications of Mandelstam's discussion of Komissarževskaja become clearer in relation to its point of departure: the revolutionary principle and its refusal to "accept so much as a drop of moisture from alien hands." Mandelstam seems to be making an indirect plea for the Soviet theater not to break with the humane tradition exemplified in Komissarževskaja's career.

In addition to symmetries produced by repetition of motifs and of compositional devices, *The Noise of Time* depends for its overall design on the 'musical' concatenation of its themes. The major constituent themes whose modulations and culminations give shape to this work are: music and memory; the quest for personal identity; and the theme of Petersburg.

As two forms of aesthetic activity, music and memory function as analogues for each other. However, each has its own culminating point in the text. Music is presented in the first chapter as an object of memory, as a figure for the essence of the past age. Subsequently it comes to represent an escape from various forms of disorder: in the sixth chapter, the Judaic chaos; in the seventh, the prerevolutionary hysteria of the period just before 1905.

The musical theme as such culminates in "The Concerts of Hofmann and Kubelik," which occupies the midpoint of the work as a whole (ch. 7 of 14 chs.). Aesthetic memory as a means for imposing an order on the chaotic 'noise of time' has its thematic culmination in the last two chapters. The late introduction of a programmatic statement on the workings of the narrator's memory in the next to last chapter serves two functions. In the first place, the placement of this statement in the penultimate position underscores its significance. The last chapter is a reckoning with the cultural legacy of the prerevolutionary past, and the conscious articulation of the workings of the narrator's memory is a final prerequisite for the recovery of the meaning of the past. What it does is to authenticate this achievement. At the point at which he claims an objective, non-apologetic role for his own memory, the memoirist is able to recapture that "feeling of one's own rightness": which Nadezhda Mandelstam sees as the product of her husband's work on *The Noise of Time* and which permeates the last chapter.[23] If the work is viewed as the expression of an ascendant process of self-awareness on the part of the implicit author, the narrator's consciousness of his own relationship to the age that produced him in "Komissarževskaja" can be viewed as a discovery arising out of the efforts of memory in the preceding chapters. At the same time, the year-and-a-half delay before the writing of the last chapter makes one wonder about the evolution in outlook that was transpiring in the explicit author. Perhaps the cumulative effect of the act of writing, up to the point of having completed the next-to-last chapter, could not be realized without a long gestation period.

The Jewish theme modulates and alternates with others in a similarly musical manner. It is most markedly present in the earlier chapters (especially the second, third, fourth, and sixth), and it is presented there in a predominantly negative light. As a central concern, the Jewish theme is supplanted by music in the sixth and seventh chapters. In the seventh chapter, with its playing-off of the concert performances and the prerevolutionary agitation of the period, music forms a counterpoint to political motifs. What may be broadly labeled the political theme dominates the ninth, eleventh, and twelfth chapters: "Sergej Ivanyč" is about 1905; "The Erfurt Program" touches upon the narrator's Social Democratic phase; and "The Sinani Family" offers a view of Socialist Revolutionary circles. Literary

references are everywhere, but literature first appears as an explicit theme
in the fourth chapter, in the discussion of the family bookcase. It serves as
a counterpoint to the political theme in the eleventh chapter, and it is the
central theme of the last chapter.

The biographical and literary space in which the narrator's conflict over
his cultural identity is played out is St. Petersburg. As an explicit presence,
the city figures most importantly in the earlier chapters. The Petersburg
theme has an early culminating point in the third chapter, when the narrator draws his Tjutčevian metaphysical analogy between the imperial capital
and a veil cast over the abyss. The details of place that open the final
chapter could be treated as a reprise of the Petersburg theme.

The complex of themes which are associated with the image of the city
include the idea of life as a spectacle (chs. 1, 2, and 3; to a lesser extent, 7
and 8) and the theme of the self as an outcast. The narrator first reveals a
sense of himself as a Jewish outsider in a gentile environment (second and
third chapters) and then as an outcast from Judaism (fourth and sixth
chapters). The city presents him with another kind of outcast identity, that
of the *raznočinec*. The narrator's identification with this tradition begins
through his exposure to the intelligentsia tradition assimilated by his
mother. This identification is deepened by his immersion in the current of
political opposition which dominates the TeniševSchool. His school ties
seem to provide the most important models of the *raznočinec* for Mandelstam. First (in the narrative sequence at least) there is the influence of the
Sinani family and their circle, and then there is the figure of V. V. Gippius,
whose déclassé identity is insisted upon by the description of him as a *raznočinec* three times in the course of a few paragraphs.

Thus in the development of the ousider theme, there is a movement from
negative tonality (the ousider-Jew) to positive (the ousider-*raznočinec*). This
change holds out the possibility of reconciliation with Jewish identity also,
for to be a Jew participating in Russian culture means to be a *raznočinec*.
Identification with this tradition also makes it possible to accept the literary legacy of the alien and aristocratic nineteenth century, for this legacy is
guarded by the fierce 'familial' protectiveness of the *raznočinec* writer
Gippius.

The manner in which the Jewish theme is sublated in the theme of the
artist-outcast, itself suggested by the literary and political possibilities given
by the Petersburg context, is illustrative of the workings of the most over-
arching structural principle operating in *The Noise of Time*: the development of what Vygotskij calls "superordinate structures." Motifs and themes
which initially seem to be in conflict with each other—Jewish and Russian

cultural identities, for example, or art and politics—tend to become linked through association with some more comprehensive theme that points the way towards their unification in a harmonious order.

The theme of natural history is the most important of these superordinate structures. The imagery of natural growth, development, and decay is present from the opening mention of the "dying age." In "The Bookcase" it reappears in connection with the family books, and it establishes a link between family traditions and literary history. Interpreted in Lamarckian terms in "Julij Matveič," the natural cycle lends a comic mock-general significance to the subject's life. In "The Erfurt Program," politics, poetry, and agriculture are all brought under the workings of the round of Nature. The imagery of this round also casts a penumbra over "The Sinani Family," where its traces can be detected in the motifs of cyclical repetition (the "divannaja") and interrupted growth. In the penultimate chapter, the workings of literary memory are made explicit within the context of an identification of nature and revolution ("Nature is revolution"). Finally, a homologous series of nature, culture, and the self enters into the understanding of the nineteenth century in the concluding chapter.

In this last chapter, the Jew is implicitly identified with the figure of the *raznočinec*, while the latter is assimilated to the figure of the writer in exile. As mentioned earlier, the image of the literary exile, covered in shaggy furs as protection against a hostile environment, is also found in Mandelstam's poetry of the same period. In the poetry, he draws on a tradition tracing back to Pushkin by taking Ovid as the prototype of the literary exile. In *The Noise of Time* motifs of shagginess are associated not only with the writer-outcast but—through the image of the *šuba*, or fur coat—with the literary tradition that he professes. Thus Ovid-Literature's "furry hide" (*pušnaja škura*) (II, 108), i.e., its alien aristocratic trappings, take on the quality of a Lamarckian response to an alternation in the natural climatic cycle, and, as in Mandelstam's criticism, literary history is incorporated into a vision of natural history.

CHAPTER THREE

THE EGYPTIAN STAMP

The Egyptian Stamp, published in 1928, is as close as Mandelstam ever came to conventional narrative fiction.[1] Unlike *The Noise of Time*, it has elements of a plot (the Parnok episodes) and a hero (Parnok) who is, if not altogether fictitious, at least partly so. However, the center of gravity of this fiction is far from either the plot or the characters, the two elements identified in Mandelstam's criticism as fiction's traditional centers.

For all its experimental quality, *The Egyptian Stamp* shows several marks of kinship with *The Noise of Time*. Both pieces concern themselves with time and with the workings of imaginative memory as a counterforce to time. Both juxtapose the time sense of the human individual to the longer rhythms of historical and natural epochs. The theme of Petersburg as the cultural-historical space in which conflicts of personal identity must be resolved is as important in the novella[2] as it was in the earlier work; the problem of the significance of the Petersburg legacy for a declasse outsider is again the dominant aspect of this theme.

In both works, the atmosphere of the city influences the consciousness of its residents. In *The Egyptian Stamp*, however, what the city itself has to communicate is considerably more ominous than the "childish imperialism" taught by the imperial architecture to the narrator of *The Noise of Time*. Devices such as metonymically transferred epithets, animation of the inanimate world, and the juxtaposition of contrasting scale and emotional tonality played an important part in the memoiristic piece; they are met with even more frequency in the narrative fiction. Accordingly, the tendency to organize the meaning of the text around its figurative level, rather than its narrative level, is intensified. In light of Mandelstam's views on the nature of prose, it is reasonable to see this focus on figuration as an attempt to solve the problem of a new organizing center for prose—one capable of replacing the old discredited "biographical" and "psychological" dominants discussed by Mandelstam in "The End of the Novel" and "The Birth of Plot."

To find new compositional principles for a new prose, Mandelstam turned to the aesthetics of his own poetry. Respecting the autonomy and complementarity of prose and verse, he took from his lyrics only the manner of building meaning through patterns of association; as his attack on the style of Belyj's *Notes of An Eccentric* makes clear, he had no use for 'poetic' prose which attempted to mimic the rhythmic regularities of verse.

Two kinds of evidence indicate the state to which Mandelstam's experiment with prose had evolved during the writing of *The Egyptian Stamp*. One is the greater emphasis on varieties of associative meaning. The other is the intensification of the 'personal' emotionally-charged overtones in the voice of the narrator, which may reflect a displacement into the prose of poetic resources. Since this highly personal tone is even more evident in "Journey to Armenia" and "Fourth Prose," it is reasonable to assume that by the mid-twenties Mandelstam had abandoned his earlier opinion, stated in "The Birth of Plot," that the "personal, accidental, and catastrophic" belonged in lyric poetry, not in prose (II, 234).

In this connection, *The Noise of Time* and *The Egyptian Stamp* represent complementary possibilities for the intertwining of life and literature. If *The Noise of Time* is 'impersonal' autobiography, *The Egyptian Stamp* is an 'autobiographical' fiction that imbeds biographical materials in an invented narrative. Whatever their other purposes might be, the fictional framework and ornamental prose style of the later piece also serve as screens through which Mandelstam could speak his deepest concerns without falling into the confessional mode which he had attacked in the earlier one.

A small but interesting body of criticism has formed around *The Egyptian Stamp*. If it has drawn more attention than the other "proses," the reasons are partly to be sought in its relatively greater conformance to what we expect fiction to look like and in its place as a turning point in the evolution of Mandelstam's prose style: *The Noise of Time* will be comprehensible to any reader of Russian literature, but the rules for reading "Fourth Prose" and "Journey to Armenia" are first exemplified in *The Egyptian Stamp*. However, the critical interest evoked by Mandelstam's tale is most of all a tribute to the work's excellence.[3] Of the poet's literary prose pieces, the novella, with its haunting thematization of the condition of inner division and cultural homelessness, most deserves a place, not just in Russian, but in world literature.

N. Berkovskij's "On Mandelstam's Prose" ("O proze Mandelstama") provides the first significant commentary on the story. Berkovskij's argument moves back and forth between the style of the prose and the historically-conscious world view that is said to inform it. Discussing Mandelstam's style, Berkovskij fixes his attention on the use of figurative language. He notes that the dominant feature of Mandelstam's metaphors and similes is not the assimilation of tenor and vehicle but their differentiation from each other: "incompatibility is the motive principle of Mandelstam's style."[4] Hence, Mandelstam's metaphors are seen as more "playful" than "expressive" or "communicative." This playful style, however, is presented as the expression of a highly serious world view.

Asserting that the thing with which the concrete term is juxtaposed always provides clues to the author's outlook (*mirovozzrenie*), Berkovskij comments that in Mandelstam's writing, this second term tends to be drawn from the fields of culture and history, and that this "historiosophic" perspective implies an underlying unity among apparently unrelated images. Mandelstam, in Berkovskij's view, brings about the agreement of incommensurables both by research into the history of his subjects and by their association through contiguity. Thus the "oaty voice" (ovsjanyj golos) of a Petersburg cab driver is an attribute bestowed upon him thanks to the proximity of his horse, who is otherwise unmentioned; and a complex of biographical associations connecting childhood illnesses and pharmacies is chiefly represented by the pharmacy telephone.

Berkovskij uses this insight into Mandelstam's imagery to characterize such stylistic devices in *The Egyptian Stamp* as the transferred epithet (association through contiguity) and what he calls the "generic perception" (*rodovoe vosprijatie*) of objects (association through 'biography'). Parnok is offered as the prime target of the 'generic' approach. Berkovskij goes so far as to contend that there are no original elements entering into the portrait of Parnok, and that he "summarizes" the classical nineteenth century image of the *raznočinec*, with attributes drawn from Pushkin's poor Evgenij, Gogol's Popriščin, and Dostoevskij's Goljadkin.

Berkovskij calls the novella "a stylization in the form of a manuscript containing two texts." These two texts are the Parnok narrative, which is assumed to be the basic element, and the author's marginal comments, consisting of various asides and of biographical fragments which Berkovskij sees as a continuation of *The Noise of Time*. The two constituent texts are said to be linked by the recurrence of certain motifs, now in one fragment, now in another, according to the play of associations. Thus the motif of *draže*, which can mean either a kind of candy or a sugar-coated pill, appears in one aside as a "homeopathic pill" (*gomeopatičeskoe draže*) that signifies the lost conception of personal honor (II, 27), and then reappears in another as a piece of "dragee" candy (*krupinka "draže"*) in a girl student's paper sack (II, 30).[5]

This observation anticipates later research on the semantic coherence of Mandelstam's prose, yet it is also suggestive of the limitations of Berkovskij's article. For one thing this play on image and variation is preeminently a poetic technique, and Berkovskij makes a principle of ignoring the manifold connections of Mandelstam's prose with his verse. For another, many of the motifs used in this way serve to establish a similarity between the narrator and Parnok. They point to original elements contributed by Mandelstam to Parnok's makeup. There is, for example no residue of literary tradition to account for one of the most curious aspects of Parnok: the story has a Jewish ambience which issues from the narrator and seems to tinge Parnok because of the strange bond between narrator and protagonist; yet, within the work itself, only Parnok's surname identifies him as specifically Jewish. Parnok is, in other respects, ethnically opaque.

While he largely ignores the ethnic motifs, Berkovskij does recognize that the story is saturated by that same sense of '*prišlost'*,' the consciousness of the perennial outsider, which permeates *The Noise of Time*.[6] Perhaps the publicistic aim of Berkovskij's article dictated its choice of emphasis. This aim was to uphold Mandelstam's example as a desirable guide for the direction of Soviet prose, which now (in the late twenties) should be concerned with what Berkovskij called "the problematic of cultural revolution": the problem of assessing and integrating the past.

Clarence Brown's introductory essay, published as a preface to his translations of *The Noise of Time* and *The Egyptian Stamp*, takes up some of Berkovskij's themes.[7] Of Professor Brown's own insights into Mandelstam's prose style, the most interesting is his idea that there is a pattern to Mandelstam's selection of images that involves contrasts in scale and emotional tonality and that spreads through the text from its base in the conflict between Parnok (fragile, positive) and Kržižanovskij (powerful, threatening, negative).[8] This notion can be reconciled with Berkovskij's observation on the cultural and historical saturation of Mandelstam's abstract terms, since it is culture which is threatened in *The Egyptian Stamp*.

In his interpretation of the meaning of the tale, however, Professor Brown's emphasis is not on style but on the attempt to disclose the literary and biographical sources that account for the plot and for the character types of Parnok, Kržižanovskij, and Mervis. This attempt can be viewed in part as an amplification of Berkovskij's comment on the "summarizing" quality of Parnok. But Brown also goes beyond the earlier critic in his discovery of a real-life model for Parnok in the writer Valentin Parnax, and in his hypothesis that the Parnok story reflects an episode in Mandelstam's life—his altercation with the Chekist Bljumkin.

Professor Brown views Dostoevskij's *Double* with its echoes from Gogol's story "The Nose," as the principal subtext: ". . .the hero, a helpless little man, finds his identity split in two, the second half being endowed with all those attributes of power and invulnerable knowledge of the world lacking in the first . . ."[9] The fact that Parnok claims Captain Goljadkin as his ancestor lends plausibility to this interpretation. The evidence that follows, however, points to resemblances that are undeniable but formal in character. True, Parnok shares a great fear of social disgrace with his ancestor, but is this not a generic feature found in all the *raznočincy* in the "Petersburg text"? Both have a tendency to be reduced to "irrelevant" thoughts during moments of stress, but the coordinates of this tendency to non sequiturs are different in each case. As Brown notes, Goljadkin is falling into a psychotic state; at times Parnok's mumblings might suggest a reversion to child logic, but not impending madness.

The similarity in gait between Parnok and Goljadkin mentioned by Brown is also purely formal. Dostoevskij emphasizes that Goljadkin's walk is mechanical in fashion, as if he were on springs. This odd mechaincal walk is another sign of the impending split in his personality. Parnok's gait is also emblematic, but it is sheepish and timid rather than mechanical.

The second most important subtext, in Professor Brown's view, is Gogol's "Overcoat," and here too I would like to extend the interpretation by stressing differences between the source and target texts. Thus Gogol's text shares with Mandelstam's the motif of the stolen coat, in each case too grand for its owner; but Akakij Akakievič's *šinel'* is presented as the fulfillment of his dreams, whereas Parnok's *vizitka* (morning coat) is only a starting point, somehting he needs in order to make a career.

Brown sees the tailor Mervis as another borrowing from "The Overcoat." There is a Gogolian intonation to the first description of Mervis in Ch. 1 when the narrator raises the none-too-relevant question as to whether the tailor had been employed by the lycee students: "Mervis the tailor lived on Monetnaja, right next to the lycee, but whether he did any tailoring for the students is much in question. Most likely this was taken for granted, as it is assumed that a fisherman on the Rhine catches trout and not just any kind of trash" (II, 8).

Yet to extract Mervis only from Petrovič is to miss an important point about the tailor's genealogy. Mervis, after all, is a Jewish tailor, who has several literary cousins in the literature and theater of the twenties.[10] It is worth keeping in mind that during the period when *The Egyptian Stamp* was being conceived, Mandelstam was an admiring spectator at the performances of the State Jewish Theater, which he reviewed in a 1926 article, "Mixoèls." There are interesting parallels between the language in which Mervis is described and the language of this article. This is particularly true of the description of the brilliant leading actor Mixoèls—whom Mandelstam saw (among other roles) as the tailor Soroker in Šolom Alejxem's *The Big Prize*.

In both the article and the fiction, what is basic in Mandelstam's portrayal of traditional Jewish types is the ascription to them of an impressive seriousness of manner. This seriousness is presented as the impress of the Jewish experience, going back to antiquity.

In "Mixoèls," Mandelstam describes a traditionally-attired Jew as an "endlessly refined porcelain pedestrian ("beskonečno izjaščnyj farforovyj pešexod")" (III, 106). 'Refinement' and 'porcelain' enter into the description of Mervis also. In Ch. VII, Mervis is characterized as "a most refined porcelain tailor ("izjaščnejšij farforovyj portnoj")" (II, 33).

A commentary to this description is found in "Mixoèls," where the troupe of GOSET (the State Jewish Theater, *Gosudarstvennyj evrejskij teatr*, also known as the Jewish Chamber Theater, *Evrejskij kamernyj teatr*) is said to "profess and justify the conviction that at no time or place can a Jew cease to be a piece of fragile porcelain ("ispovedovat' i opravdyvat' uverennost', čto evreju nikogda i nigde ne perestat' byt' lomkim farforom . . .")" (III, 107). Hence this image combines the ideas of fragility and durability—a link which is not out of place in *The Egyptian Stamp*.

Both the article and the story indicate that Mandelstam no longer chose to represent Jewish identity as wholly antithetical to other forms of cultural identity. On the contrary, Mervis and Mixoèls incorporate traces of the cultures in which Jews have lived. Both, for example, are described in terms that unite the Jewish and Hellenistic traditions. A character played by Mixoèls is dancing at a wedding: "Here the dancing Jew resembles the leader of a classical chorus (*antičnyj xor*)" (III, 108). Mervis gives rise to more explicit classical associations, including "a Greek satyr, the unfortunate singer Kytharedes, at times the mask of a Euripedean actor . . ." (II, 33).

This motif of the actor's mask is of special interest. Whether it is Mervis or a role from the repertoire of the *Evrejskij kamernyj* that is being described, the representation of the Jewish experience is not verbal, but is expressed through the appearance and gestures of the face, hands, and body (Nadezhda Mandelstam points out that her husband did not understand Yiddish;[11] the gestural side of Mixoèls' acting would therefore have made an especially strong impression.). For example: "during the dance, Mixoèls' face takes on an expression of sagacious weariness and sorrowful ecstasy; it seems to become a *mask* of the Jewish people" (III, 108). (All emphases are mine unless otherwise noted). And it is Mervis' face which draws the attention of the narrator of *The Egyptian Stamp*. It, too, expresses a mute wisdom: "I must admit that I love Mervis; I love his blind face, furrowed by wrinkles that see. (II, 33). (These "seeing wrinkles," incidentally, are paralleled by Mixoèls' "thinking fingers as inspired as articulated speech.")

Mervis and Mixoèls both conjure up the image of epileptics, an association which seems to combine the ideas of vision, ecstasy, and suffering as parts of the Jewish legacy.[12] In the case of Mervis, the motif of epilepsy also has a Dostoevskian ring, and reinforces the notion of Jewish identity as containing echoes of other cultures.

Dmitrij Segal's "Problems in the Poetic Organization of Semantics in Mandelstam's Prose" provides the closest reading to date of *The Egyptian Stamp*.[13] Despite differences in critical vocabulary, Segal's study, too, can be read as a more systematic exploration of territory first charted by Berkovskij. Where the earlier critic proceeded from the "incompatibility" (*nesoobraznost'*) of the imagery to the underlying unity of the author's philosophical outlook, Segal takes asymmetry (*asimmetrija*) "the absence of balance among the constructive elements," as the principle on which Mandelstam's prose is built, and finds a compensatory unifying principle at the semantic level.[14]

Segal hypothesizes that Mandelstam turned to prose in order to overcome a split in his earlier poetry between the rather restricted and uniform poetic persona and what Segal calls "everyday experience." Thus *The Egyptian Stamp*, in Segal's view, is part of a search for new linguistic resources necessary for an adequate literary response to post-revolutionary social and cultural currents.

In his search for the principles of semantic coherence that operate in Mandelstam's tale, Segal carries the inquiry into the pattern of selection of images further than Berkovskij or Brown. He notes that the appearance of imagery from one semantic group in a wide variety of contexts tends to turn this imagery—which may appear on the surface to be merely arbitrary or contingent (*neobjazatel'nyj*)—into distinctive subcodes that convey the major themes of the work. It is the discovery and analysis of these subcodes (and of other, more restricted, semantic patterns) which is Segal's main contribution to the understanding of the tale and of Mandelstam's later prose generally.

Segal's main example is what he calls the 'geographical-national' subcode. The story's first page alone would yield the following terms that signify either a geographical territory or the peoples that inhabit it: "Polish serving girl"; "Church of Guarenghi"; "Chinaman"; "American duel";[15] "Petersburg water"; "Viennese chairs and Dutch plates"; "Valhalla." Segal suggests that the density of such references in the first chapter is so great that it shifts the emphasis from the narrative to the semantic level and, consequently, to the narrator who is the source of all this material, and for whom the Parnok story is only part of what he has to say. In effect, the 'geographical' code becomes the message. It introduces a theme which is not yet present at the surface of the discourse: the theme of "geographical diversity, space, ethnic and national identity and specificity," all of which ultimately belong to the theme of Petersburg.[16]

Other subcodes mentioned by Segal are those of 'music' and 'illness.' This list could certainly be extended, as could the list of "pervasive motifs" (*skvoznye motivy*). These motifs ('coffee' and 'boiling water' are Segal's examples) operate in the same way as the subcodes, but are intermediate in their extent and significance between fully realized subcodes and ordinary leitmotifs ('dentist,' for example).

In his conclusion, Segal attempts to extrapolate from various kinds of semantic linkages to the theme of language, speech, and writing. For Segal, this seems to be the central theme of *The Egyptian Stamp*. He describes it as being made up of two major components: the gradual disclosure of how the story itself is being written, and the (self) characterization of the writer. He contends that the first part of the language theme actually modulates into the second, and ". . . the process of textual creation merges on a description of the awareness of self of the text's creator, and this awareness, in its turn, is presented as a feature inherent in the city and its history."[17]

At first glance this may seem merely a rebarbative way of stating the homely truth that we know the narrator through his language. There is more, however, to Segal's interpretation. He implies that the implicit author's growing absorption in the writing process and in the 'text' of Petersburg life culminates at the end of the work in a liberating epiphany. The narrator ends up with a new perspective and a new self-confidence. This idea is buttressed by an outline of how the themes of the language-complex are developed. Initially submerged in asides (such as the narrator's comment on the mastery of the German Gothic alphabet in Ch. I), the language-complex comes to include the use of words quoted from the speech of other persons and of literary references; the idea of life and Petersburg as texts, and a corollary, the theme of the interchangeability of different communicative codes, such as writing, speech, painting, drawing, musical notation, sign language and semaphore.[18] Segal notes that the theme of literature and of ambivalence towards literature as a social institution only becomes explicit at the end of the fifth chapter in the passage beginning "Scandal is the name of the devil . . .". He also points out that allusions to the writing process first appear in Ch. IV, in the passage which describes the writer's marginal sketches.

To show how the description of the writing process merges into the dawning self-awareness of the implicit author, Segal establishes a number of connections between these subjects. For one thing, the perception of the 'text' of life 'read' by Parnok and by the narrator is always in some way a perception associated with Petersburg. The city has the status of a part of the implicit author's biography at the same time as his work can be read as part of the "Petersburg text." Moreover, towards the end of the work there is a heightening of the text's 'personal' intonation. This takes the form of appeals to the reader, greater fragmentation of the narrative, and a corresponding increase in emphasis on narrative asides. These phenomena, according to Segal, are anticipated by the references to the processes of writing and drawing in Chs. IV and V. This is writing and drawing which aims at capturing the marginal and the "accidental," and which also attempts to substitute one aesthetic code for another. Thus, for example, the visual experience of looking at paintings is translated into verbal equivalents, while music is transformed from an aural to a visual/verbal code through the description of the associations which the musical scores suggest to the narrator.

These passages hint at the manner in which *The Egyptian Stamp* itself is being composed by the narrator who is its ostensible author. Thus what Professor Brown calls the story's "mosaic" quality is a sign of its dynamic character: the fragments of this mosaic construction are to be read as traces left by the progress of the writing process. Segal calls this process one of "increasing degrees of freedom" as the text moves towards its conclusion. This increase in freedom is presented as both a theme which intrudes upon the consciousness of the implicit author and as a movement within his style.

From this it could be inferred that, with *The Egyptian Stamp*, Mandelstam's prose attains that ability to model a realm of freedom which has been taken away from the narrative level of prose fiction. In other words, in this story it is not love or ambition which grows and evolves, but language.

It is doubtful, however, that such an achievement would have fully satisfied the requirements of Mandelstam's anthropocentric vision. Nadezhda Mandelstam's criticisms of *The Egyptian Stamp* are instructive on this point. In her judgment, the novella is one of her husband's rare failures. Those of her comments which do not merely explicate a particular passage betray a sense of discomfort, having its immediate source in the question of the extent to which Mandelstam identified himself with Parnok:

This period (i.e., the mid-twenties) ended up with (Mandelstam) almost confusing himself with Parnok; it almost turned him into his double. (*Vospominanija*, p. 181)

Even if there had been in Mandelstam the tiniest shred of Parnok, it vanished in early youth, when he still had no idea what "we" meant. (*Vtoraja kniga*, p. 85)

The juxtaposition of these two passages conveys an impression of self-contradiction. This impression grows somewhat weaker if it is pointed out that in the first instance Nadezhda Jakovlevna is talking about a sense of kinship with Parnok stemming from her husband's consciousness of himself as an outcast, while in the second instance the resemblance which is denied is one of character, not fate. Yet some ambivalence remains; character *is* fate, after all. Perhaps the idea of Parnok as Mandelstam's double is disturbing because it sorts so ill with the "canonical" Mandelstam, sure of his gift and of his ultimate place in Russian poetry, who appears everywhere else in her memoirs.

Nadezhda Mandelstam complains of *The Egyptian Stamp* that it is fed by "mixed sources," including impulses which should have eventuated in poems. Quite apart from the question of whether or not it touches upon a genuine failing, this comment is interesting for what it implies about the difference in the way autobiographical material is used in comparison with its use in *The Noise of Time*. If this material became prose instead of giving rise to a group of lyrics, this is another indication that Mandelstam's earlier conception of the complementarity of prose and verse had changed in some way.

The next objection offered by Mme. Mandelstam seems astonishingly irrelevant: she holds that the presence of the rudiments of a fictional plot is a weakness, inasmuch as it represents a capitulation to the then-fashionable quest for the renovation of "great literature" (*bol'šaja literatura*).[19] One can only wonder how Nadezhda Jakovlevna could see the remnants of conventional narrative fiction here as anything more than a point of departure. In this connection Segal seems closer to the mark with his idea that Mandelstam's prose—beginning with *The Egyptian Stamp*—conjures up the traces of a story line only in order to throw them off as the piece progresses.

Nadezhda Mandelstam's main criticism of *The Egyptian Stamp* is that behind it there lies an impulse to transfer the "confusion" (*sumjatica*) of the twenties back into the decade which came before. In her opinion this impulse reveals "confusion and a loss of criteria." Yet she sees a parallel displacement of the cultural atmosphere of one decade to the period which preceded it in *The Noise of Time*. If it is not objectionable there, why should it be considered a sign of weakness here?

Perhaps there is another threat here to the canonical image of the poet. Nadezhda Jakovlevna implies that poetry is aimed at an audience blessed with a higher cultural and moral development than that of the audience which reads prose fiction. Along these lines, she quotes a comment by Mandelstam that jailors need novels most of all.[20] There is an undercurrent to the effect that Mandelstam's stature and authority come from being a poet, and that to admit that prose fiction could have any but an instrumental role in his development might somehow detract from this stature. Her final stricture on the novella is that it failed even at this instrumental function: "It is indicative that, while prose always cleared the way for verse, *The Egyptian Stamp* did not perform this function."[21]

Thus all the faults to which Nadezhda Mandelstam points have to do with the outlook of the writer implicit in the text. In her opinion, this outlook seems to imply disorientation and a loss of self-confidence. It would be consistent with this reading of the novella to see in it a world more reminiscent of the Symbolist nightmare of *On the Nature of the Word*, in which "Man is no longer master in his own house," than of that ideal of Man as the measure which Mandelstam sought to serve.

On the whole, the critics have been most convincing in talking about Mandelstam's style, especially his imagery and his elliptical narrative manner. Beyond this, there are large areas of disagreement, as well as important aspects of the text that have not been commented upon. It would be hard, for example, to quarrel with Berkovskij's description of the text as a stylization in the form of a manuscript, but this provides only a starting point for the characterization of the work as a whole. Not only could more be said about its relationship to traditional narrative fiction, but the shape of its overall design could be brought out in more detail. The critical literature has relatively little to say on the question of a pattern which integrates the diverse elements of the text, except for Segal's elucidation of the semantic principles on which the work is constructed.

Given Mandelstam's orientation towards literary tradition, the topic of literary subtexts will probably prove to be inexhaustible. Perhaps it will be more productive to look at the patterns which govern the use of the more obvious references to other works, as far as this turns out to be possible, than to go through the text piling up references. It is worth pointing out in this regard that Mandelstam's articles on prose have a particularly important place among the subtexts for *The Egyptian Stamp*.

The critics seem to divide most sharply on the topics of where the boundaries lie which separate Parnok from the narrator (and Mandelstam from both) and of what the relationship is between the style of the work and the ethical assumptions that the style reflects. In practice, these turn out to be aspects of the same problem, since ethical stance is part of what is conveyed by the manner in which the implicit author is portrayed and by the attitude of this implicit author towards his protagonist.

No one seems to disagree with the assumption that there is an important ethical dimension to Mandelstam's tale but the disagreement as to its ethical content is general. Berkovskij sees an attack on the values of Tsarist culture where Brown sees a veiled disillusionment with the Revolution. Nadezhda Mandelstam sees a general—though temporary—loss of ethical criteria, while Segal treats the text as ethically exemplary in its liberation of the writer and of the writing itself. This diversity of opinion is indirect evidence of the story's density of meaning, and of its ambiguity.

What kind of a "story" is *The Egyptian Stamp*? To see the Parnok story as the basic element and the narrator's memories and reflections as somehow secondary is to make the tail wag the dog. Such an approach refers this work to the wrong conventions: those of the third-person narrative in which the narrator breaks into his story with only an occasional aside or digression. The reader should not be led astray by fragments of third-person narrative (chiefly the Parnok story) or by the echoes of such third-person tales from the Petersburg tradition as "The Nose," "The Overcoat," or *The Double*. Mandelstam's novella is actually more closely tied to the tradition of the *Ich-erzählung*, the ego-form narrative, in which the narrator's own experiences can form the chief subject of his discourse ("Diary of a Madman"; "White Nights," *Notes from Underground*).

Mandelstam innovates within this tradition. His narrator is not simply a speaker whose story happens to be recorded in some way (e.g., through the use of primary and secondary narrators or in the form of the narrator's journal or written confession); he is expressly a writer who is very consciously producing a manuscript. It is the narrator's identity as a writer which motivates the 'fiction' about Parnok. He begins by trying to write the story of Parnok in third-person form, but the condition and fate of his hero continually lead the narrator back to his own experience. He is unable to stick to his story because the material is too distressing. His sense of reality will not permit him to create a hero who grows and evolves; this same sense of reality makes it impossible for him to keep sufficient distance between himself and Parnok and to maintain a detached narrative stance.

The fact that the work takes the form of a manuscript also motivates the fragmentation of the text and the interspersion of the narrator's own experiences with those of his hero. Both these qualities of the text give it the appearance of an unpolished draft, which contains material at different stages of incorporation into the emerging design of the work. At the same time, the fragmentation of the narrative sequence and the contamination of 'fiction' and 'personal experience' also convey the implicit author's consciousness of the reality through which he is living.

Both the appearance of the text and the underlying perception of reality tied to this appearance can cause confusion during a first reading: Who is the speaker in a given passage, and about whom is he speaking? It should help to point out that Mandelstam is quite strict about not blurring pronominal references. Given the conventions of the ego-form, it therefore seems reasonable to assume that the narrator presents his own memories and perceptions in the first person, while the use of the third person indicates that the narrator is referring to Parnok or some other character. Thus the Bozio fragments, for example, have the status of material inserted into the text by the narrator/writer, and there seems no reason to view them as something thought or read by Parnok.

The above considerations help to define the work by defining the mode of narration. They also suggest suitable terms in which to discuss *The Egyptian Stamp*. For example, it seems appropriate to refer to the persona who produces the text as the 'narrator' when it is his discourse ('speech utterance') which is being emphasized, and as the 'implicit author' when either his identity as a writer or his relationship to the explicit author—Mandelstam—is in question. By the same token, 'novella,' 'story,' and 'narrative' can serve as rough designations for the text as a whole, while the second and third terms can be further qualified to refer to its components (e.g., 'the Parnok story/narrative'; 'narrative asides'; 'narrative sequence').

THE FIRE OF TIME

References to Jewish identity in *The Egyptian Stamp* are, as suggested earlier, only the most prominent of many references to different ethnic groups. Considering this stress on ethnic identity, one group is remarkable for its absence from the foreground: those of markedly Russian descent. Russian literature, needless to say, does not have to be about ethnic Russians; still, there is something peculiar about their absence from a story about the end of St. Petersburg. Except for historical and literary figures who are conjured up simply as names, no character in the tale has a Russian surname. All the named characters, plus some others who are not identified by name, have a slight air of resident aliens about them, as if the whole city had turned into a foreign quarter.

Parnok has a Jewish name, and he is framed within the consciousness of a narrator who makes his own Jewish origins clear in a series of autobio-graphical asides. Mervis is Jewish, as are the "little men" of the narrator's recollections, Nikolaj Davydovič Šapiro and Geška Rabinovič. The narra-tor's relative, Pergament, has a daughter, Aunt Vera, who is apparently a convert to Lutheranism. The motif of Lutheranism calls up the Swedish Lutherans Karl and Amalija Blomkvist and their deceased daughter El'za. Father Bruni's surname indicates his remotely Italian origins; the singer Angelina Bozio is also Italian. Kržižanovskij is a Polish name, which per-haps helps to explain why the Polish proprietress of the laundry where Parnok searches for his dress shirts takes the captain's part.

Whatever their origins, all these persons belong, in one way or another, to the culture of the former imperial capital. The Czech mirror shop, for example, where Parnok goes in search of a telephone, has been part of the city's life for over thirty years, while references to "Dutch Petersburg" and Biron carry the idea of resident foreigners back to the eighteenth century origins of the city. This cosmopolitan world has ambiguous relations with the surrounding majority culture, and this ambiguity colors the condition of the narrator and of Parnok with more than a hint of absurdity. Both are involved in maintaining a culture which is theirs and yet not theirs. It belongs to them as Peterburgers, but they stand ouside it on grounds of class and ethnicity. The atmosphere of their 'Russia' is made up of literary references (to Gogol', Tolstoj, Puškin, Dostoevskij, and Annenskij, among others) and malevolence (the lynch mob; *koncertnyj strax*, 'concert-going anxiety').

The absence of ethnic Russians is part of a more general undertow of absences and disappearances that runs through the story. Furniture, coffee beans, cocoa, coats and shirts, false teeth, and governments vanish. The powers of speech and hearing are represented by their absence. Books "melt"; emptiness (*pustota*) threatens life and art.[22] One is reminded of Man-delstam's warning (in *O prirode slova*) about the dire consequences which could come to Russia as a result of becoming mute (*onemenie*).

Taken together, these silences and disappearances signify that it is the cultural legacy of the nineteenth century which is vanishing into the "fire of time." Hence Parnok's fate involves multiple ironies. If it is assumed (mainly on extratextual grounds) that he is meant, in some sense, to be Jewish, his situation is that of a colonized member of an ethnic minority in a revolutionary society. He represents the final stage of the assimilationist trend evident in the history of the narrator's family in *The Noise of Time*; yet just at the point where ethnic identity has all but been effaced, and only his strange name remains, the sought-after cultural identity is threatened with ruin. Viewed in this light, the Parnok story acquires overtones of a grotesque comedy of manners, whose plot grows out of the utter inappropriateness of Parnok's idea of conduct as a means of coming to terms with the surrounding chaos.

Parnok's vanishing clothes are the chief emblem of the withdrawing age. Necessary to Parnok's pursuit of career and social acceptability, his morning coat (*vizitka*) and dress shirts also connect *The Egyptian Stamp* with the picture of the condition of contemporary prose that is given in "The End of the Novel." Parnok is precisely that would-be "Napoleonic" hero with the misfortune to live in an age that places a low estimate on the role of the individual, while the implicit author must cope with the "unthinkable" task of writing fiction in which the traditional, biographical "pivot" (*steržen*) is not the compositional center. His solution—in keeping with the prescription in "The Birth of Plot"—is to turn from his hopeless hero to fragments and anecdotes.

The idea of a consonance between the view of contemporary prose expressed in "The End of the Novel" (and the complementary "Birth of Plot") and the point of view embodied in *The Egyptian Stamp* is not a new one.[23] There is more to this relationship, however, than a general correspondence in points of view. "The End of the Novel," in particular, is 'quoted' whenever Parnok is juxtaposed to the heroes of the nineteenth century French novel. The leitmotif of *molodye ljudi*, 'jeunes personnes' always implies this juxtaposition. Thus when the morning coat is first mentioned, it is characterized as "the spineless girl friend of young persons" (II, 6). The next occurrence of this motif makes the link with "The End of the Novel" explicit. Thinking about getting his coat back from Mervis, Parnok is inspired by the example of the "young persons who conquered Paris" in the novels of Balzac and Stendhal (II, 8). The same passage also ties Parnok to the heroes of these novels through the motif of *tufli*. Since Parnok's *lakirovannyi tufli*, 'patent leather shoes' are presented as making him seem faintly ridiculous, the resemblance is an ironic one.

At the point of Parnok's failure to retrieve the morning coat, he is contrasted with Balzac's Lucien de Rubempré (II, 9).[24] The mock-heroic quality of this contrast is emphasized when Parnok visits the steam laundry and the narrator comments: "The times were fearful: Tailors repossessed morning coats, and laundresses made fun of young persons who had lost their tickets" (II, 15). The incongruity between the description of the times as "fearful" and the triviality of the details which justify this description says a lot about Parnok's diminished possibilities for heroism.

There is a reprise of the 'young persons' motif in Ch. VIII, when Parnok reflects on his desire to lead a normal life and get married: Then no one would dare call him "young man" (II, 37). This is probably a response to the scene in the laundry, since it is the Polish laundress who refers to him a young man (*molodoj čelovek*).

In "The End of the Novel" Mandelstam imputes a great social significance to the classical novel, which is said to have formed the values of whole generations. Parnok is represented as the dubious beneficiary of this influence. When the narrator comments: "Parnok was the victim of ready-made conceptions as to what course a love affair (*roman*) should take" (II, 13), the word *roman* suggests 'novel' as well as 'love affair,' for Parnok's ideas of conduct—now highly dysfunctional and probably inappropriate to real life at any time—come out of novels. He is a disappointed Lucien, whose Vautrin, far from providing him with a fortune, cannot even help him to reclaim a few shirts.

Because of the dislocations caused by contemporary history, disappointed Luciens are represented as now forming a whole class of people who have only a tangential connection to the surrounding reality:

> After all there are people in the world who have never come down with anything worse than influenza and are somehow attached to the present sideways, like cotillion badges. Such people never feel like adults, and at thirty they are still taking offense at someone, still calling someone to account. (II, 13)

This passage not only describes Parnok but serves as an excellent characterization of his Dostoevskian forebears, who, whatever their actual age, were also unable to find a place in society, and were thus condemned to a form of perpetual adolescence. Moreover, this description seems in some ways to fit the narrator. He attempts to distance himself from people of Parnok's caste ("I would gather them all and settle them in Sestroretsk . . ."), but fails to cover all the clues which link him to them. It appears, for example, that he belongs to Parnok's cohort by age, for his memories cover a thirty year span: "Thirty years passed like a slow fire" (II, 5). It also turns out that his preferred literary method implies a similarly tangential perspective: "Destroy your manuscript, but preserve what you have sketched in the margin . . ." (II, 41; the adverb *sboku*, translated here as "in the margin," literally means 'on or from the side' or 'sideways,' as in "people hooked on to the present age sideways.") The motif of influenza also connects the narrator to Parnok's cohort, for it serves as an analogue for "prosaic delirium," a state of inspiration to which he refers when describing his writing.

"The End of the Novel" suggests the etiology of this condition of less-than-adulthood. Mandelstam writes there of the feeling of time in the classical European novel as time "which belongs to man for acting, conquering, perishing, loving." On the one hand, such a sense of time entails a high estimate of the values and capabilities of the individual, for it implies that this gift of time is the birthright of every individual. On the other hand, it also implies a conception of a round of life in which tradition sanctions the passage through successive stages. But the world represented in *The Egyptian Stamp* is one in which this passage seems no longer negotiable. The times are out of joint and the individual has been "thrown out of his own biography." Parnok's sense of exclusion from the company of those who claim to have made the passage to adulthood and who call him "young person" is symptomatic of the chasm separating the old values from the possibility of their realization.

The narrator of the novella is preoccupied with time and its effects, even though the "time which belongs to Man" of the classical novel is conspicuously unavailable to his hero, Parnok. This preoccupation is associated with a sense of restricted space which at some points in the narrative suggests suffocation and claustrophobia. Mandelstam's abiding concern is the place of the individual consciousness within the currents of culture and history—a theme of epic sweep and scope. Yet in *The Egyptian Stamp*, as earlier in *The Noise of Time*, this epic theme is elaborated within the constricted geographical setting of Petersburg, past and present.

As if to compensate for this narrowing of spatial focus, there is great variety in the ways in which time is represented. The workings of time are evident at every level of the text. To begin with, the text is marked by time in the use of prose rhythms; as Segal points out, such features of Mandelstam's prose as the use of typographically isolated lines and the manner of its division into paragraphs and larger fragments serve the meaning of the work in the same way as rhythmicometrical divisions serve the meaning of a lyric. The use of 'biographical' links to connect images "genealogically" (as Berkovskij puts it) requires that associations be made which bridge expanses of time, as is illustrated by the implicit author's perceptions of Mervis in Ch. VII, or by the facts of literary descent that connect Parnok with Lucien de Rubempré. In the narrative sequence as a whole, time is treated as a tool of the writer, which he uses to form patterns in the manner of the Bergsonian "fan of phenomena" (*veer javlenij*) described in *On the Nature of the Word*.

In *The Egyptian Stamp*, this fan makes its connections over a progression of linear time that divides roughly into three ranges, all of which measure events in the same space. These ranges cover, respectively, Imperial Petersburg from its eighteenth century origins to its end in February 1917; Petersburg under the Provisional Government (the setting for Parnok's actions); and Petersburg-Leningrad from the Bolshevik Revolution to the time in which the narrator is setting down his thoughts (not later than 1927). Except for some references to his childhood and to his "family tree," Parnok is situated within the middle range. The narrator, on the other hand, is free to make retrospective connections among all three.

All these ways in which time shapes the text emphasize its importance as an explicit theme in the novella: a theme so pervasive that, among other readings, *The Egyptian Stamp* can be read as a meditation on time. In this respect the story forms a part of the poet's response to a text that haunts Mandelstam's writing in the twenties: the deathbed poem of the great eighteenth century poet G. R. Derzhavin. Against Derzhavin's gloomy conclusion that all human achievement is destined to be swept away by "the river of time in its coursing," Mandelstam attempts to assert the significance of the individual and the continuity of culture.

The first allusion to the theme of time is to be found in the epigraph: "I do not like rolled-up manuscripts. Some of them are heavy and greasy with time, like the archangel's trumpet." The narrator's dislike of rolled-up manuscripts anticipates his exhortation to "Destroy the manuscript" in Ch. VIII, where it is presented in the context of a prescription for his method of writing. Hence the complete significance of the epigraph is not disclosed until the end of the text. As the work progresses, it turns out that the sentiment stated in the epigraph expresses Mandelstam's distrust of prose which attempts to reproduce the continuous (hence, "greasy with time") quality of nontextual reality. In Ch. V it becomes clear that there is also a metonymic connection between "manuscripts," in this negative sense, and the "litterateurs," the representatives of embalmed, institutionalized literature, who produce pseudo-continuous prose. The epigraph thus initiates the development of an analogy whose implications are of importance to the meaning of the work:

$$\frac{\text{marginal persons}}{\text{social life}} = \frac{\text{"raznočinec-writer"}}{\text{"Literature"}} = \frac{\text{marginalia}}{\text{manuscript}}$$

In each case the relationship of the upper term to the lower is one of peripherality; in the language of the story itself they are connected "sideways."

The epigraph first presents the image of the staining of writing by time, and then begins to particularize time. The trumpet of the archangel, after all, will only sound at the Last Judgment, the end of time. This eschatological note is heard again on the first page of the narrative proper when the narrator describes the Kokorev warehouses (the repository of his family's furniture) as a "Valhalla." Prompted by the many instances of loss and disappearance which betoken the passing of the age, these forebodings are given in their most extreme form in Ch. VII, when the narrator reflects that everything is melting and growing smaller, and that the end is near ("Only a little time is left to us.") and in Ch. VIII, when the raised bridges which Parnok is approaching are made to connote the following: ". . .that all must come to an abrupt end, that emptiness and yawning gaps are fabulous goods, that there would be separation—it is inevitable—and that deceitful levers control the masses and years" (II, 36).[25] In this expanded context, the aversion voiced in the epigraph acquires a further shade of meaning: the rolled-up manuscripts are associated with the dread of the encroaching emptiness.

In the narrator's apostrophe of his family and the lost ideal of failed permanent domesticity in Ch. I, the effects of time on an individual life are presented first as a "centrifugal force" (*centrobežnaja sila vremeni*) and then as the action of a "slow conflagration" (*medlennyj požar*) with a "cold white flame." Both of these metaphors for the workings of time have parallels elsewhere in Mandelstam's writings. The motif of an external centrifugal force which dislocates attempts at preserving settled patterns of existence is another link to the speculations on the nature of prose in "The End of the Novel." The destructive action of this centrifugal force of time in the fiction contrasts with the balance of centripetal and centrifugal forces which, in Mandelstam's view, was characteristic of the old biographically-centered novel. In "The End of the Novel" these forces were abstractions, metaphors which described the attraction of ambition, summoning the provincial heroes of Balzac and Stendhal to rise and fall in Paris. In *The Egyptian Stamp*, the equilibrium of these forces has been destroyed, and the overriding centrifugal force of the times becomes almost literal, capable first of "sweeping away" (*razmetat'*) the family belongings, and then of bringing about all the numerous disappearances that follow. It would seem that Parnok, even more than the narrator, lives in an exploding universe, in which the "centrifugal" attraction of ambition is overmatched by even stronger centrifugal forces which sweep everything beyond his reach.

The idea of the fire of time is found in Mandelstam's verse and has variants in his criticism.[26] It forms a pattern of imagery that extends throughout the novella. As a description of objective time, it takes two forms, which correspond to different tempos. First there is the slow fire of time mentioned above. This image connotes those steady slow changes whose cumulative effects cannot be perceived except after a sizeable interval—in this case, a thirty-year stretch of the narrator's life. Time's ineluctable rhythms are also suggested by an image which accompanies the abduction of Parnok's coat: "The last coffee beans vanished in the crater of a coffee mill resembling a barrel-organ" (II, 6). Although it is neither silent nor slow in its action, the coffee mill is suggestive of an hourglass, hinting at the theme of the disappearances wrought by time.

In Ch. II, the slow fire of time gives way to an all-out conflagration. Describing the places where Petersburgers arrange trysts, the narrator comments that more than tradition has fixed them in his mind. Insofar as they belong to the customs of the end of the epoch, they have a special quality of finality which makes them stand out in high relief in his memory: "But just before the end, when the temperature of the age had jumped up to 37.3 and life rushed along after a false alarm like a fire engine thundering in the night along the white Nevskij Prospekt . . ." (II, 10). The fire of time takes the form here of a crisis fever, by analogy to the final fever of a terminally-ill person on the one hand, and a property fire on the other. The qualification of this fire as a false alarm seems to imply that life takes on a deceitful character at the "end of the epoch." The above-quoted passage also anticipates other directions in the development of the fire/time complex. Most importantly, it introduces the theme of feverish illness, which is explored in Chs. VII and VIII. There is, for example, a parallel between the final fever of the age and the death agony of the delirious Bozio. She too experiences hallucinations at the last moment, and there is a repetition of the motif of the fire wagon (*požarnyj oboz*), whose sounds provide the raw material which her delirium transforms into an operatic overture.

Hence the motif of fire brings together the ideas of the end of the age and of the consciousness of life as a hallucinatory, disconnected, feverish experience. There is, moreover, a link between the fire of time and literary creativity. This tie is implicit in the narrator's formula, "Fires and books— these are fine things. We shall still get to do some looking and reading" (II, 35). Here fire is construed as a type of writing, to be read and interpreted by the narrator. An earlier variation on this same thought indicates that this 'writing' is part of the Petersburg "text"; "You, wood yards—black libraries of the city—we shall yet do some reading, have a look about" (II, 35). Elsewhere the parallelism between fires and books is extended to an analogy between fever and the implicit author's state of inspiration (See below, pp. 129-32).

In Chs. VII and VIII, where the motifs of fever, fire, literature, and writing are increasingly brought together, the image of the end of the epoch is linked with another form of temporal diplacement. This new aspect is introduced by the description of Emma Bovary as "the younger sister of our proud Anna." Since *Madam Bovary* was written before *Anna Karenina*,

Emma is "younger" in the sense that she appears in a novel written when the age was younger. To describe her as the younger sister creates an impression of time running backwards. When the dying Bozio, transported back to the scene of her operatic debut by her final delirium, begins to sing in the untrained voice of a fifteen-year old adolescent, the sense of time in reverse is placed within the context of the analogy between the individual life-span and the life-span of the age. The association of reverse time with states other than normal waking consciousness is emphasized by the narrator's memory of a childhood nightmare which was accompanied by illness: ". . .everything happened backwards, as it always does in a dream" (II, 39).

The conception of time running in reverse at the end of an epoch is a familiar one in Mandelstam's writings. It appears first in "Pushkin and Skrjabin": ". . .Time can move backwards: the whole course of recent history, which with terrible force has turned away from Christianity to Buddhism and Theosophy, bears witness to this . . ." (II, 314). The return to what in Mandelstam's view are pre-Christian concepts of culture, personality, and time itself is offered here as evidence that time is coursing backwards. There is a variation on this theme in *The Noise of Time*. There the idea of the river of time running backwards from the present into the past is used in the description of the fate of the man who lives by "literary rancor": "Thus one enters the present, the modern day, as if it were a dried-up riverbed" (II, 103).

Thus it would appear that the image of time in reverse has a predominantly negative tonality. Found in contexts of nightmare, delirium, death, and cultural crisis, it seems to connote either a fear of the loss of conscious control of one's creative fantasies or an apprehension lest the cultural achievements of the past be lost.

Through the idea of repetition which is common to both, the backward flow of time is connected with that cyclic sense of time which is part of Mandelstam's conception of the poetic word. Thus the reversal of time which returns Bozio to her adolescence can also be interpreted as a cyclical return, while for Parnok, the cycle of life has been frozen at the point of a figurative adolescence.

The Egyptian Stamp also conveys the idea of cyclic movement in individual lives and in the life of culture by making use of the Persephone myth—a motif that also occurs in several of the lyrics in *Tristia*.[27] In Ch. IV, the narrator laments that Parnok might just as well have tried to call "Proserpina or Persephone, who had not yet had a telephone installed" (II, 20). Presumably, both the Roman and Greek appelllations of the goddess are given because of the sound repetitions which this makes possible:

/PROserpina, PROveden, perseFONa, teleFON; teleFON, provedEN/. This sound pattern—together with the virtual repetition of the whole phrase a few brief paragraphs later—underscores the pathos of the sentiment: the place where telephones have not yet been installed is the underworld, where Proserpina/Persephone must spend half the year. This chain of associations begins in Ch. II with Parnok's memory of an "event" (*sobytie*; in Mandelstam's lexicon, an occurrence which is significant because it is charged with *preemstvennost'*, the sign of cultural continuity) which took place in February of 1917. Watching sledloads of ice being transported, Parnok takes note of a pine branch frozen into an ice block "like a Greek maiden in an open coffin" (II, 10). This image of the Greek maiden/pine branch in the grip of winter (ice) and death (the open coffin), conveys the essence of the Proserpine myth: the cycle of death and resurrection.[28]

This incident of the pine branch is also bound up with Parnok's hopes at the moment of the great historical divide between Tsarism and Revolutionary Russia. The first mention of Parnok's desire to work for the Greek Desk of the Ministry of Foreign Affairs comes just before this passage. As the narrative proceeds, it becomes apparent that Parnok, like the Greek maiden in the ice, feels himself to be a displaced Southerner, trapped in the North. At the end of Ch. IV, for example, Parnok is characterized as "a lemon seed, tossed into a crack in the Petersburg granite" (II, 22).

The reprise of the Persephone motif arises as part of Parnok's reaction to the lynch mob. The explicit mention of Persephone refers to the summer of 1917, when the February government is vanishing. In fact, the paralysis of the government, the mobs in the streets, and the subsequent indication that the episode takes place during the White Nights all suggest that Parnok gets caught up in some mob action related to the "July Days." The contrast between the season of the year and the cultural 'season' underscores the contrasting contexts of winter and summer; social chaos, evidence of the moribund state of culture, is juxtaposed with the physical season of rebirth and flowering, when Persephone should be released from her grave.

This implicit contrast between the season of the age and the season of the year also figures in the narrator's memories of theater, ballet, and concert performances in Ch. V. The motifs of winter, the theater, an atmosphere of threat, and a sense of exclusion link these passages to Mandelstam's so-called 'theater poems.' There is also a parallel between the association of late imperial culture with winter in *The Egyptian Stamp* and the analogous pattern of imagery in *The Noise of Time*. The earlier prose piece, however, provides no parallel to the atmosphere of threat and claustrophobia in the novella. The narrator is painfully aware that "concert-going anxiety" (*kon-

certnyj strax) is one of the experiences that he shares with Parnok, and the Aleksandrinskij Theater is compared to a village bathhouse where a brutal murder has been committed. Bozio, too, dies in the winter—or even (in the poetic tradition established by Nekrasov) from the winter.

In Ch. IV, the account of the lynching episode is momentarily broken off by an apostrophe to time: "Time—timid chrysalis, flour-strewn cabbage butterfly, young Jewish girl pressed up to a watchmaker's window—you would be better off not looking!" (II, 18). Denominating different stages in the insect's life cycle, the images of chrysalis and the cabbage butterfly are also figures for cyclical time. They suggest a view of time as something fragile, like Parnok's mode of life. The idea of a threat to continuity which is immanent both in the age and in its representatives crops up again later (in Ch. VIII) in the image of the "mosquito prince," who is a projection of the situation of the narrator and of his hero.

The personification of time as a young Jewish girl partakes of the same quality of fragility, as becomes clear when she reappears in Ch. VI, with the further qualification that she is "sickly" (*bol'naja*). On this occasion, she stands for time in the aspect of memory. This casts a new associative shadow back onto the earlier passage. Time now appears as threatened in the sense that memory, which preserves the linkages among events, is itself a relatively fragile force in the face of what seems to be impending catastrophe.

ASSOCIATIVE CHAINS[29]

An exploration of the ways in which time operates in *The Egyptian Stamp* suggests that it is not only the appearance of being a manuscript which accounts for its disjunctive and asymmetrical movement; the idiosyncratic temporal sense displayed by the implicit author is also responsible. In addition to his being preoccupied with the workings of time, this implicit author can be characterized as a man whose thought processes are dominated by the operations of associative meaning. His associations are drawn from history and culture; he is most prone to draw on the historical and cultural legacy of St. Petersburg, which he views through the eyes of a long-term resident of the city who feels himself to be, nevertheless, an outsider.

The self-consciousness of this implicit author is the product of his associative mode of thinking, which first creates a dense network of interconnections in the surrounding sociocultural space and then moves from this network to the situation of the observer in relation to it. The functioning of this associative mode, which—in kind if not in quality—is a trait of both the narrator and Parnok, is illustrated most strikingly in Ch. IV. This chapter is the hinge upon which the whole work turns. Parnok's attempt to avert a lynching, which is his major and final enterprise, is its main plot element. The urgency of the situation seems to strip Parnok of his logical capabilities altogether, while the pathos of his hero's plight also seems to lead the narrator into a withdrawal from the story line into a series of 'free' associations.

This emphasis on associative processes is entirely consonant with the angle of vision shared by the narrator and Parnok. As personalities with marginal identities, they see things from the periphery, and what they tend to see are fragments. The objects observed in this disjunctive fashion readily modulate into substitute images, related to their originals by similarity, contiguity, or both. When the lynching victim, for example, is referred to at one point as a "dandruff-strewn coat hanger" (*perxotnaja vešalka*, II, 17) this image is suggested both by his immediate appearance and by his implication in the complex of contiguously-related images which includes jackets and clothes hangers or racks. This substitution illustrates the coordinate processes of metaphor and metonymy which work to assimilate events into the observer's network of private associations. At times—the "Barbizon luncheon" passage for example—the associative logic also serves to defuse emotionally distonic material by replacing the threatening image with something more benign.[30]

The oblique angle of vision, together with the fragmentation and metaphorization of what is observed, characterizes the successive approaches to the *samosud*, the lynch mob. The crowd is first glimpsed from above, from the "bird's-eye view" which, according to a hint supplied by the author, is the dominant vantage point of the work. This angle of vision is responsible for the choice of metonyms used to describe the crowd: shoulders, napes, and jutting ears. This fragmented picture dehumanizes the crowd and turns it from an assembly of individuals into a threatening mass. Even the victim is differentiated from his captors only by his role in the procession. Except for his "ill-fated collar" and the attention which is bestowed upon it, he is just another "dandruff-strewn coat hanger."

Parnok's next view of the mob has him scuttling sideways along the sidewalk ahead of it ("sidling along the sidewalk ahead of the sizeable procession of lynchers" II, 19). Emblematic of his sideways attachment to life, this posture is also expressive of his fear of the crowd, a theme that is developed later on the same page. The crowd is then viewed as part of the street scene which is broken into reflected fragments in the mirror shops.

This further disordering and decomposition of the action by the mirrors is said to render it "even more frightening and shaggy." It also provides a concrete context for the narrator's later description of life as made out of "emptiness and glass" (II, 40).

It may also be worth pointing out that when Rotmistr Kržižanovskij (the mysterious figure who comes to be in possession of Parnok's morning coat and dress shirts) appears on the corner of Voznesenskaja Street, he is at least a block away from Goroxovaja, where the mob is, for the two streets did not cross, and angled away from each other towards the Fontanka (Goroxovaja is now ul. Džeržinskogo, and Moskovskij Prospekt follows part of the course of Voznesenskaja). This topographic fact underscores how divided and strained Parnok's attention is as he tries to simultaneously keep track of the crowd, avoid its hostile attention, and find help to prevent the drowning.

While a combination like "pleči-vešalki" ("shoulder-clothes hangers") may appear to be an accidental product of the immediate situation, the selection of such associations in the novella as a whole is far from accidental. As N. Berkovskij, Clarence Brown, and Dmitrij Segal have demonstrated, *The Egyptian Stamp* gets its semantic coherence from the patterned way in which such images are chosen and combined. What follows, then, is an attempt to carry the analysis of this patterning to the syntagmatic level, where one association gives rise to another.

In Ch. IV, the first of these associative chains has to do with pain, mutilation, and dismemberment. That the episode begins with a visit to the dentist has no plot significance; there is no reason to assume that Parnok would have had better luck if he had noticed the crowd while at the laundry, the theater, or his apartment. However, the fact that he is at the dentist's office is not arbitrary in relation to the story's patterns of connotative meaning. In Ch. III, the disappearance of false teeth from dentists' offices has been presented as an ominous sign of impending civil turmoil. It is one of the indications that, despite the government's hopes, its pacific citizens will turn into the citizens comprising the mob. The narrator's almost openly sarcastic word in praise of dentists introduces another motif. Not only are dentists somehow linked with public disorder, they themselves are agents of physical violence. When the narrator affects to love the hum of the dentist's drill, the reader—unless he has perfect teeth—gets the joke.

An immediate connection is thus drawn between Parnok's own experience of physical pain and the fate awaiting the lynching victim. Another link in this chain of associations is forged when Parnok, hastening down the dentist's steps, keeps repeating the phrase, "Buttons are made from animal blood" (II, 18). The narrator comments that this sentence, which sounds like an antivivisectionist or vegetarian slogan, displaces any kind of thought. This does not mean, however, that it is devoid of significance. Parnok's phrase suggests a sympathy with animals, perceived as victims who are slaughtered by people for selfish utilitarian ends. It also carries the connotation of blood sacrifice, and is therefore tied to the description of the mob as a kind of religious ceremonial, moving along with a "prayerful rustle" (*s molitvennym šoroxom*). The subsequent comparison of the mob to "Shiites on the day of Shakhse-Vakhse" hints at the biographical source for this imagery of a dehumanized mass intent upon sacrificial bloodshed. Nadezhda Mandelstam relates how she and her husband observed this ritual procession of the Shiite sect while in the Caucasus. The participants cut at themselves with knives as a sign of their religious fervor, and the Mandelstams seem to have been shocked and upset by the bloody spectacle.[31]

Parnok's repeated phrase also suggests a sense of physical disgust at the idea of blood and offal. This reaction is triggered by the mob, with its "bloated intestines" (*kišečnye puzyri*). One nauseating thought gives rise to another as Parnok associates these stinking organs with the entrails and lungs being sold at the butchers'. The narrator makes it clear, however, that Parnok is associating two causes which give rise to the same disgust in him, and that the operative cause here is the "fearful order that bound the mob together." Thus Parnok's moral outrage at the murder which is about to take place is conditioned by the physical disgust and horror evoked in him as a result of his private associations linking killing and bloody dismembered organs. In light of the implicit tie between Parnok and the victim, both of whom are "little men," it is interesting that among the details of the victim's biography, there is mention made of his spitting (as a sign of disgust) at the Tatar butcher shops which sold bad meat; apparently, his reaction to his class of stimuli is the same as his would-be rescuer's.

The same complex of imagery figures in the description of an army of ants, "dragging the martial sections of their as yet undismembered body" (*ešče nerazrublennoe telo* II, 22). While there is no explicit connection between the description of the ants and the lynching, a parallel is suggested by a similarity in overtones (an individualized mass, moving in the manner of a military procession), and by the fact that the next detail after the mention of the ants is that "Parnok shook himself (*vstrjaxnulsja*)." This shudder suggests that it is Parnok who is making an association between the mob and the army of ants, and that this association brings a reaction which is similar to his earlier feeling of nausea.

The army of ants belongs to a pattern of associated images which is so pervasive in this chapter that it is reasonable to speak of an 'entomological' subcode. Where such images are associated in any way with the lynch mob, they have clearly repellent overtones: "And black gleaming ants like carnivorous actors of the Chinese theater in an old play with an executioner. . . ." But this is only the last and most developed entomological analogue for the crowd. There are three other direct metaphors for the mob which picture it as a swarm of insects. First, it is represented as a "strange hive" whose "queen" is the victim in its center. At another point it is described as a "cockroach-like crowd" (tarakan'ja tolpa; "beetling mob" in the Brown translation) and later as a "swarm of human locusts" that is blackening the banks of the Fontanka. What is more, it is said to have its origins "in an uncouth nursery of dandruff, *bedbugs*, and jutting ears" (II, 17). The insect motif, with similarly repellent overtones, also crops up when the lynching is represented as characteristic of the moral aspect of the city itself: "Petersburg had declared itself a Nero and was as repellent as if it were eating a soup of *crushed flies*" (II, 20). In addition to illustrating the use of the entomological subcode, this passage also anticipates the "taste of revulsion carried to the point of ecstasy" which is part of the narrator's "real truth" about Petersburg in Ch. VII.

The generally negative semantics of the entomological subcode gives it a similar function to the 'blood and guts' pattern with which it is interwoven. The use of insect imagery to help sustain negative overtones in *The Egyptian Stamp* has two kinds of referents. One source, the association of bedbugs, roaches, locusts and ants with filth, pollution of foodstuffs, feeding on the living and scavenging on the dead, is universal enough to require no special comment. But there is also an intellectual and literary tradition which comes into play here. Tolstoj wrote approvingly of swarm life in *War and Peace* while Dostoevskij, in *Notes from Underground*, expressed the fear that positivist models of social organization could, if put into practice, turn society into an antheap; both, however, illustrate a tradition of picturing the collective aspect of human life in terms of the social organization of insects. It is interesting that Mandelstam compares his ants to "carnivorous actors of the Chinese theater." Like the earlier comparison of the crowd to Shiites, this simile aligns the imagery of insect swarms with that monumental social architecture and its attendant lack of regard for the individual which Mandelstam saw as an "Asian" element in modern life, and against which he warned in "The Nineteenth Century" and "Humanism and Contemporaneity."

It would be wrong, however, to assume that insect imagery always has negative implications in Mandelstam's prose. Within the chapter that is being analyzed here, there is also a series of images linking entomological motifs with the theme of time. The characterization of time as a chrysalis and a cabbage butterfly has already been mentioned. The passage in which this apostrophe of time appears is also interesting as an example of the associative manner. A watchmaker (*časovščik*) figures in this aside, which is followed shortly by mention of Parnok's running into a watchmaker's shop in search of a phone. There is a play of entomological imagery in the description of the watchmaker's work: the watch-springs which he is inspecting through a glass are metaphorized as "gnats" (*kozjavki*), and one element in the "cocktail" of associations assembled by the distracted Parnok as he rushes out of the shop is the "babble of cicadas" (*lepet cikad*). This sound is, first of all, a metaphor for the ticking of clocks, but it is also suggestive of time in another way. Mandelstam's paronomastic dictum, "A citation is a cicada" (*Citata—cikada*) is directly applicable to this passage, which contains associations that range through centuries (Spinoza, Rembrandt, "goatish" Spanish painting). Moreover, this *lepet* is a variety of that as-yet-unarticulated babble which can be turned into literary art. Another example is the whine of the mosquito in Ch. VIII. An attribute of the summer setting, this whine develops into the pathetic speech of the "mosquito prince," of whom there is an earlier incarnation in a lyric written in 1923: "I do not know when/ This catch began;/ Isn't it to this tune the thief makes a rustling sound./ The mosquito prince whines?" In this earlier instance, as Kiril Taranovsky has pointed out, the mosquito's whine is associated with poetry,[32] but in both cases the writer projects a pattern of meaningful speech onto the insect's wordless hum.

One of the motifs which keeps recurring in connection with the use of insect metaphors for the crowd is that of blackness or darkness, which is an attribute of either the individual creatures or of their swarms. This motif is a link to another major associative pattern which can evoke either positive or negative meanings, depending on the context.

This cluster of associations has to do with dark formations on a lighter field and, more generally, with spots, stains, and blemishes. When, for example, Parnok first views the mob from the dentist's office, it is represented as a dark mass which all but obliterates the paving, whose wooden blocks are said to have "shown through" (*prosvečivalis'*) only in the open square in the center reserved for the victim and his "aides-de-camp" (II, 17). This image is repeated, in a variant form, in the observation that the "swarm of human locusts" has *blackened* (*vyčernila*) the shores of the Fontanka (II, 20).

The connection of images of spots and stains with this field becomes clearer as the chapter progresses. When the proprietor of the Czech mirror shop slams his door against Parnok in a gesture aimed at protecting his

firm, whose reputation has been "unspotted [*nezapjatnannaja*] since eighteen eighty-one" (II, 19), Parnok is implicated in this complex of motifs in a
new way. The Czech behaves as if Parnok carried the threat of spreading
blemishes of the moral variety. This detail looks forward to a passage
which is of central significance for it contains the title motif, the Egyptian
stamp.

The dynamism of the associational mode is well illustrated by the thematic modulations which lead into the mention of the stamp. First, a link
between Parnok and 'spots' is implied. Then, after his vain appeal to Kržižanovskij, he is shown running along the pavement, tapping it with "the
little sheep's hooves of his lacquered pumps" (II, 19). His fear of the crowd
is restated, and this statement is followed by a generalization which identifies Parnok as a member of a whole class of people who evoke hostility in
crowds, women and children. This passage is grammatically and themati-
cally reminiscent of the earlier generalization on that class of people who
are somehow attached to life sideways. These two generalizations complement each other, for the coefficient of Parnok's sense of himself as an outsider is his sense of an active hostility on the part of society towards him.
The lynch mob, whose immediate target is another "little man," is a realization of this social hostility in its most frightening form. In this context the
leitmotif of sheepishness used in connection with Parnok not only suggests
an attribute of his personality, but implies that he has the bearing of a
potential sacrificial victim of the crowd's displeasure.

In the following paragraph, Parnok's perception of exclusion and of
social hostility directed towards himself is implicitly traced back to his
school days. The motifs of the sheep's hooves and the patent leather pumps
are shown to have been turned against him in the form of schoolboy
insults. It also turns out that "Egyptian stamp" was another of the insulting
names applied to Parnok. When this latter motif is pondered in conjunction with the rather puzzling teasing game which was based on Parnok's
supposed talents as a "spot remover" (*pjatnovyvodčik*), a set of related ideas
takes shape whose implications extend in all directions through the Parnok
plot and the concerns of the narrator:

> His schoolmates teased him with being a "sheep," a "lacquered hoof," an
> "Egyptian Stamp," and with other offensive names. For no good reason, the
> boys spread a rumor about him to the effect that he was a "spot remover";
> that is, that he knew a special mix that would take out grease, ink, and other
> stains. Just to tease him, the boys would steal some hideous rag from their
> mothers and bring it in to class, with an innocent air suggesting to Parnok
> that he "remove the little spot." (II, 19-20).

A comparison with how bullying in school is treated in *The Noise of Time* is instructive. In the earlier piece, the narrator comments that the "flabby intellectuals" were bullied as a class by the "aristocrats." This kind of hostility is presented as a general fact of school life and its origins in class bias are made clear. In *The Egyptian Stamp* on the other hand, Parnok seems to be the sole target. The reasons for his rejection are as mysterious as the point of such epithets as "Egyptian stamp" and "spot remover." When one recalls parallel scenes in the school reminiscences of such writers as Mandelstam's friends Erenburg and Babel', one wonders if Parnok's experience is not remotely based on some childhood memory of Mandelstam's, with anti-Semitic overtones; to a child, such behavior is as incomprehensible as the hazing of Parnok "počemu-to," 'for no earthly reason'.

Omry Ronen has suggested that the insulting Egyptian stamp refers to a postage stamp issued in Egypt in 1902 and 1906.[33] To prevent this stamp from being reused, it was printed in such a way that any attempt to remove the cancellation by moistening or steaming would cause the whole printed design to dissolve. When the epithet is juxtaposed to that of the "spot remover," something of the genesis of Parnok's perspective and values is conveyed to the reader.

Viewed in this light, Parnok's outlook now appears as the result of an ambivalent process of identification with his tormentors. The mechanism is clear. He is both the cancelled stamp; i.e., a soiled object, and the spot remover. This is the result of a contiguity shift which has parallels in many societies. The Indian Untouchables, for example, are an outcast group because they work as streetcleaners, and because they are ritually impure they must work as streetcleaners. Parnok, too, seems to identify himself both with the object of the dirt-removing process and with the subject who carries this process out. In this area, the biography of the narrator can be seen to influence the categories in which his hero thinks, since fear of dirt and infection are presented as part of the atmosphere of the narrator's Jewish childhood (See below, p. 131).[34]

It is not surprising, then, that the adult Parnok is thought by the proprietor of the mirror shop to be capable of 'blemishing' his firm's record, or that the little "spot-remover" (pjatnovyvodčik) grows up with the fear that he himself will be removed:

> You will be thrown out one of these days, Parnok, thrown out shamefully, with a terrible scandal, You'll be grabbed by the arms and—pffft!—out of Symphony Hall, the Society of Defenders and Friends of the Latest Word, out of the Chamber Group for Dragonfly Music—it doesn't matter where— But you'll be thrown out, disgraced, covered with shame . . . (II, 11)

In the original, the third-plural perfective *vyvedut,* "they will throw you out," occurs three times. It is the infinitive form of this verb that is found, with the meaning 'to remove,' in the appeal to "remove this little spot" ("*vyvesti pjatniško*"); "spot remover" ("pjatnovyvodčik") is formed from the imperfective of the same verb. Therefore, if Parnok sees his outcast status as the result of some mysterious uncleanliness, he also turns this characterization around by actively accepting the responsibility of removing moral blemishes, of which the behavior of the lynch mob is an example. Thus all the associations of the mob with darkness, uncleanness, stains, and spots fall into place.

Hence the frequency with which negative images of darkness, filth, and oiliness are met in the description of the scene on the shores of the Fontanka. The impression of physical repulsion which the scene conveys qualifies Parnok's moral repulsion, and each detail has its antecedent in Parnok's childhood. The play of associations moves from rags (*vetos*) to ragdealers (*baraxol'ščiki*); from Parnok's reputation as a remover of oil and ink stains to greasy-haired students, oily, filthy waters, and 'blackened' shores (i.e., from "*černil'nye* pjatna" to "*vyčernila* berega").

Reverberations of the 'Egyptian stamp/spot remover' complex are found throughout the chapter and the text as a whole. To begin with, the list of common elements linking Parnok with the stamp can be extended. Both, for example, have the attributes of being foreign, and, in particular, Southern. There are three references to Egypt in Ch. IV: the stamp, the Egyptian Bridge, and the floor-washers whom Parnok sees "dancing with Egyptian gestures" (II, 22). In addition, there is the "dear Egypt of objects" in Ch. I, the Theban sphinxes in Ch. II, and the "mosquito/last Egyptian" in Ch. VIII.

These Egyptian motifs are, most importantly, part of the juxtaposition of North and South, and Mandelstam is interested in the similarities as well as the differences. Thus a parallel is implied between the bureaucratic order of pharaonic Egypt and the system bequeathed by Tsarist Petersburg. Both exalt the State through massive bureaucratic regimentation and monumental civic architecture, and both overwhelm the "little man." Both are vales of exile for the Jews. The idea of an alien Egyptian undercurrent in the life of modern Petersburg is suggested by the "mosquito" fragment, where the anachronistic image of the "collegiate assessor from the city of Thebes" sets off contemporary echoes from ancient Egypt. Life on the Neva estuary thus takes on overtones of life in the ancient Egyptian capital on the Nile. And when the "last Egyptian" complains, "in the north I have become nothing," his plight is suggestive of Parnok's condition, and perhaps that of the narrator too. The idea of dwindling into insignificance is presented in a parallel manner for Parnok and for the mosquito:

1) "He is a lemon seed tossed into a crack in the Petersburg granite. . . ."
   (II, 22)
2) "I am a trifle—I am nothing. I beg of the choleric granite . . ." (II, 38)

In both cases the threat of annihilation is expressed in terms of a contrast between something tiny and Southern and the massive Northern granite.

The Egyptian stamp is also part of the undertow of disappearances which run through the story. Parnok is the product of this vanishing world, and his fear of expulsion is therefore congruent with the disappearance of everything from ordinary objects like coats and coffee beans to values like honor. The equivalency between Parnok and the stamp thus has both immediate and more general implications. An analogy can be drawn between the stamp whose cancellation mark has become an attribute which cannot be destroyed without destroying the stamp itself, and Parnok, who behaves as if he felt himself to be marked in some way by his origins. This analogy implies that this stain which sets him apart from society cannot be removed without destroying his identity. The larger significance of the stamp motif has to do with Mandelstam's conception of culture and personality as something unthinkable without respect for tradition. On this level, the title motif suggests that if one tries to erase any of the marks of the past, the entire edifice of culture may be destroyed.

There is a correspondingly ambivalent attitude towards 'markedness,' in this sense, where the narrator is concerned. On the one hand, there is the profession of distaste in the epigraph for manuscripts "greasy" with time; on the other, there is the championing of marginalia, doodling, and messy rough drafts: "Scribbling is better than writing" (II, 25). This attitude can also be connected to the stamp motif. The loss of the "little grain of honor," mentioned in Ch. V, is emblematic of the loss of the individual-centered universe. The legacy of this universe can be preserved through 'disorderly' associative prose and not through "Literature." Destroy the philological core of language as a model of potential human freedom, Mandelstam warns in *On the Nature of the Word*, and the pattern of a thousand-year tradition will be obliterated.

There is also a conceptual bridge between the idea of literature as 'disorder' in this sense and the theme of drawing and painting in *The Egyptian Stamp*. The aside in Ch. IV in which the narrator describes a series of doodles gives a highly disjunctive quality to the text. The story line is broken off at a point of utter frustration for the hero (Parnok), and the interposition of a series of asides on drugstore telephones, the narrator's doodles, and French paintings before the narrator's attention comes back to his protagonist creates a rebus-like effect. The line of associations developed in relation to Parnok's efforts to prevent the lynching is not actually broken, but the continuation takes the form of a code, which is mainly based on visual imagery.

The fact that the Parnok line goes underground at the point of greatest tension and frustration is further evidence that the associative mode serves as a means of dealing with highly-charged material for the narrator as well as for Parnok. Thus the narrator produces a set of associations on the motif of pharmacy telephones as a result of Parnok's inability to telephone the police. From these reflections, he passes to the description of a series of doodles which present motifs from the proceeding narrative and which provide an iconic display of the implicit author's method of writing.

These doodled associations have the same dynamic cast as the rest of the text. The sketch of a "Greek beauty" harks back to the motif of Proserpina/Persephone in the preceding paragraphs, to the "Greek maiden in an open coffin" in Ch. II, and also to Parnok's dreams of a post in the Greek Section of the Ministry of Foreign Affairs. The fact that the girl in the sketch is "mustached" (*usataja*) situates her in the broader context of the Southern theme, since the motif of the mustache is mentioned twice in connection with the narrator's memories of his Jewish family: soot from a poorly-trimmed kerosene lamp looks to the child like "mustached butterflies" (*usatye babočki* [II, 26]), and this motif is subsequently transformed into a metonymical attribute of Jewish homes, which are said to be characterized by a "sad mustached silence" (*pečaľnaja usataja tišina* [II, 30]).

Hence the next sketch, "someone's fox-like chin," is doubly motivated. Proximity plays a part, since mustaches and chins are both facial features, but it also turns out that the chin belongs to Babeľ, many of whose stories refer to *his* Jewish background. The following metaphoric reference to Babel's glasses as "paws" is called up by the feral detail of his "fox-like" chin.

A generalization follows the first pair of drawings: "thus arabesques appear in the margins of first drafts and live an autonomous, charming, and perfidious life" (II, 21). This statement indicates that what is being described is an analogue for the writing process which is producing the novella. Mandelstam is describing a preference here for writing which still bears the traces of the work which went into it, as opposed to the smooth productions of the epigones of "Literature." The themes of writing and drawing are crossed in this passage, and, not surprisingly, there is a significant parallel between what Mandelstam looked for in writing and what he looked for in the graphic arts. In all cases, he sought an art which called attention to itself as a *human* product by involving its audience in a process of active understanding.

For example, in his notes for "Journey to Armenia" Mandelstam defines the eye (in connection with its role in painting) as a "tool for thinking" (*orudie myšlenija*), and the context suggests that it serves both artist and audience in this way (III, 169). In the "Conversation About Dante," he draws an analogy between poetic speech and an ornamental rug, and identifies the dynamic element of poetry with the constituent "ornaments" rather than with the overall design: "What is good about the ornament is that it preserves the traces of its origins like a *performed* piece of nature" (II, 365; Mandelstam's emphasis). The overall design of the poem or rug is equated with that which can be 'paraphrased'; i.e., extracted from the poem and expressed in some other medium. Design (*uzor*), in this sense of a static, subordinate element, is a term which, by extension might be applied to the plot of a work like *The Egyptian Stamp*. The divisions of the text, phonological figures, subcodes and other clusters of imagery are 'ornaments' brought together in an associative network which "preserves the traces of their origins."

The narrator's sketches involve the pen and eye in precisely things "to think with." In addition to the motifs already mentioned, his doodles include "little men shaped like violins" (*skripičnye čelovečki*; and how much better to be a violin-shaped *čeloveček* than one who is about to be drowned by a mob!) and the French horns of the Mariinskij Theater, images that evoke concert-going Petersburg and look ahead to the presentation of the theme of music in a visual subcode in Ch. V. "Artur Jakovlevič Hoffman" is Parnok's contact at the Greek Section, but his surname also recalls one of the virtuoso performers in "The Concerts of *Hoffman* and Kubelik," an association which interlinks it with the musical motifs.

The last line in this passage is the most allusive: "I pustoe mesto dlja ostal'nyx" ("And an empty place for the rest"). Its referents would seem to be Kržižanovskij, the mob, the vanishing government and the police. Since these figures are all bound up with the atmosphere of crisis and disorder, to represent them by an empty space is an act of displacement and therefore goes along with the use of associative logic as a defensive reaction. As is the case with the passage as a whole, the phrase also has to do with the implicit author's method of writing. "I am not afraid of incongruities and breaks," he proclaims in another fragment that is connected to this one both through its typographical arrangement (a series of one-sentence paragraphs) and its intent, which is to describe the text. This second significance of the "blank space" is not unrelated to its first meaning. As the text progresses, the writer comes to treat the tide of absences as not just the cause of the "end of the novel" but as a resource for a new prose. The atmosphere of threat produces a fear which in Ch. VIII is treated as an impulse to creativity: "Terror takes me by the hand and leads me" (II, 41). As the wording suggests, this fear is related to Dante's *paura* as Virgil lead him by the hand through the Inferno. It is also akin to the intuitive animal alertness which Mandelstam identified as a trait of the "outlaw" writer as early as his essay on Villon. *Pustota*, "emptiness," is therefore a strongly bivalent concept in *Egipetskaja marka*. It points both to the fear of catastrophe and to the literary means for its prevention and "subordination to a central sun," as Mandelstam put it in "The Badger's Burrow."

The fragment that follows the narrator's description of his drawings uses French painting of the Barbizon School as its raw material. The text follows an ascendent line from the narrator's black-and-white sketches, to his memory of looking at landscapes through colored glasses from a broken coronation lantern,[35] to the vivid colors of the Barbizon painters. The contrast between the landscapes produced in this way and the art of the French painters is presented as a manifestation of the North/South opposition, which here is given as a contrast between the vivid pallette of the Barbizon painters and the "Gloomily Flemish" Hermitage. French art is presented as the feast of an alien culture to which the narrator has no invitation. His childhood attempts to produce a world of color and sunlight result only in sickening combinations of hues.

An act of imaginative reconstruction makes it possible for him to participate vicariously in this sunlit world. The whole "Barbizon lunch" fragment develops through associations connected with "the sun of Barbizon," "plein-air painting," and "coloring that is like spinach with croutons" (II, 21). Images of sunlight and vegetation predominate, and the scene begins with a description of a mother tossing a salad. This sunny scene is not, however, there for its own sake so much as for the sake of contrast with the lynching. A close reading suggests that Mandelstam chose the details of the Barbizon passage with a view to creating a maximal semantic opposition between its motifs and those of the Parnok narrative. Thus the former presents a family grouping and crowds of peaceful bourgeois engaged in their Sunday pursuits, where the latter presents a lynch mob. This opposition extends to details of dress and appearance and also to the connotations of the terms used to refer to the characters. On the one hand, there are "guests in wide trousers and leonine velvet waistcoats"; on the other, thick-necked citizens who exude foulness, and who wear second-hand jackets with wadded shoulders. The image, in the Barbizon section, of women shaking ants from their rounded shoulders is the antithesis of both the dandruff-strewn shoulders of the mob and of the negative entomological images connected with it. The Barbizon scene has a rural and idyllic setting, whereas the lynching has an urban, naturalistic one (e.g., "mother-of-pearl filth," dandruff, greasy hair, rag dealers). And the vegetable motifs in the Barbizon passage are not only there to introduce bright springlike colors which are absent from the Northern granite; they also create a positive 'vegetarian' semantic field, opposed to the negative 'carnivorous' semantics of the lynching episode: "lettuce" vs. "soup made from crushed flies." The overall effect is one of contrast between French bourgeois civilization at its zenith and Russian culture at a moment of crisis.

The Barbizon passage is also the first development of an associative device which is applied again in Ch. V: the assimilation of the other arts to the art of writing. When the narrator is describing his own sketches, he is talking about an activity that is clearly a part of the process of composing his text. In the Barbizon scene, the connection with the writing process is less evident, but it is still there, in the form of a search for verbal equivalents for the colors and themes of French painting. In the fragment of Ch. V that represents musical compositions as a form of writing, the narrator first transposes the theme of music from an aural to a visual code by talking about the symphonic score rather than the musical performance. He then gives a series of visually-oriented metaphors which are based on the appearance of scores by Mozart, Beethoven, Chopin, Schubert, Schumann, Handel, and Bach. However, as these metaphors develop into miniature scenes, a further shift takes place. The vehicle takes over from the tenor, and the real subject becomes, not the appearance of the scores, but the historical and idiosyncratic personal associations conjured up by the music.

A page of sheet music is a revolution in an old German town.

Children with large heads.[36] Starlings. A prince's carriage is being unhitched. Chessplayers run out of the coffeehouses, gesticulating with their queens and pawns. (II, 24)

Induced by the look of Beethoven's scores, this sequence of associations reflects Mandelstam's belief that the essence of a historical period could be concentrated in a work of art. These lines concern music which is presented initially as a form of writing—writing which fits in with the rest of *The Egyptian Stamp* by presenting variations on material that also crops up elsewhere in the text. The most important connection has to do with the treatment of Beethoven's music as a product of the Age of Revolution.

Hence there is a parallel with the revolutionary period of 1917. This parallel is supported by an image of urban disorder ("Rasprjagajut karetu," "The carriage is being unhitched") which, moreover, anticipates an attribute of the writer's creative fear in Ch. VIII: "Strax *rasprjagaet lošadej* kogda nužno exat'," "Fear unharnesses the horses when you need to go" (II, 41). In Ch. VI, Parnok as a child is described as a "six-year old padded Beethoven," because his earmuffs make him deaf. Parnok shares with the narrator a love of music, and the association of an image of music with an image of silence forms a minor pattern of repetitions in the story. There is a clear pathway of associations leading from the description of a group of deaf-mutes whose signed speech is visual rather than aural, through the visual approach to music (sheet music), to the narrator's reminiscence of his own music lessons (a memory which is linked to another variety of sign language, that of a semaphore tower) to his memories of the family piano, first seen vanishing along with the rest of the family belongings in Ch. I, to his fear of merging with Parnok.

Ch. IV is particularly dense with references to Petersburg locations, especially streets. The pattern of events and associations seems to spring from the very topography of the city. The street map becomes a cognitive grid for the narrator and his hero, a ready-at-hand framework through which to run the threads of association. The lynch mob, for example, is classified by the narrator as part of the flora and fauna of Petersburg, having its origins somewhere between Haymarket Square (*Sennaja*) and Flour Lane (*Mučnoj pereulok*). Their jackets come from the Apraksin Arcade (*Apraksinskij dvor*; hence "apraksinskie pidžaki"). These locations are all within the vicinity of Goroxovaja street, where Parnok first sees the mob from the dentist's office. Moreover, there is a phonological and semantic connection between the "dandruff-strewn jackets" (*osypannye perxot'ju pidžaki*) of the mob which comes from the area of *Mučnoj* and the narrator's apostrophe of time as a "flour-strewn cabbage butterfly" (*obsypannaja mukoj kapustnica*). The first image seem to give rise to the second, with the result that the flour with which time is dusted has the appearance of being somehow connected with the mob, which gives it distinctly negative psychological overtones.

An angrily dismissive comment also reinforces the idea of a close link between the capital and its people: "What of it! The Egyptian Bridge has never so much as had a whiff of Egypt, and not one respectable person has ever been face-to-face with Kalinkin" (II, 20). Here the narrator seems to transfer his outrage from the mob back to the city which gave rise to the mob. The implication is that there is something mendacious even in the place-names of this city which has "declared itself a Nero." The speaker's desire to 'discredit' the two bridges stems from the fact that both crossed the Fontanka, scene of the drowning.

Ch. IV ends with two variants on the idea of Parnok as overwhelmed by large impersonal forces: the Petersburg granite and the loom of approaching night. In view of the way images linked with Petersburg and with darkness are used in this chapter, its conclusion is suggestive of Parnok being annihilated by those forces, immanent in the city and in the times, against which he has been struggling.

READING, WRITING, DELIRIUM

Literature has already been alluded to as an important source of associative links in *The Egyptian Stamp*. The novella's debt to Gogol' and its orientation towards Flaubert and Balzac have been mentioned as particular instances of its relationship to literary tradition. As is the case with *The Noise of Time*, the angle of vision of the narrator has a lot to do with the manner in which literary subtexts are used. In order to understand the narrator's perspective on the literature of the past, it is necessary to bring out his relationship to Parnok in more detail.

The opportunist Kržižanovskij implies an equivalency between Parnok and the victim of the mob by significantly confusing the two: ". . . Don't worry about him: Word of honor, he's having a tooth filled. I'll tell you something else: Today on the Fontanka, it's not clear which, either he stole a watch, or his was stolen. Attaboy! A filthy story!" (II, 29). The narrator, for his part, fears that he is too similar to Parnok: "I, too, am sustained only by Petersburg—concert-going, yellow, glowering, ruffled-up and wintry" (II, 25). Despite the fact that Parnok seems deracinated and the narrator makes frequent references to his Jewish background, they even seem to share a relative, Aunt Ioganna. True, as the narrator's aunt, she is a member of a Jewish wedding party, while as Parnok's relative she is a dwarf, described in terms which bring the eighteenth century to mind. These motifs include the Empress Anna Leopoldovna, Biron, and the mention that she is a dwarf (*karlica*), of whom the eighteenth century rulers were fond.[37]

All this suggests the areas of resemblance between Parnok and the narrator. Both belong to the class of little men and to the literary tradition encompassed by the "Petersburg text." The narrator takes pains to stress that Parnok is not an isolated instance, but a member of a whole class of people who are described in successive asides as "attached to the present sideways," as inspiring the hostility of crowds, "living under the star of scandal" (II, 27-28), and as the descendants of Captain Goljadkin (II, 37). A generic thread extends from the *raznočincy* with whom the narrator of *The Noise of Time* comes to identify his fate to the "little men" and "young persons" of *The Egyptian Stamp*. Just below the surface of the novella there is a similar ambivalence towards the legacy of the nineteenth century. Instances of this ambivalence include the idea of Parnok as a victim of outworn literary conceptions, and as an almost literal victim of the barber-executioner as he readies himself to go out to a concert. The undertone of dread that accompanies Parnok's cultural pursuits, is his strongest connection to the narrator, who uses the epithet *strašnyj* ("fearful" or "terrifying") twice in one paragraph in reference to his own theater-going experiences (II, 25).

The text conveys this same dualistic response to literature. The lynch mob, for example, speaks in a collective voice to juxtapose their victim with Anatole France: "It is not Anatole France whom we are burying in a cata-falque adorned with ostrich feathers . . . instead, we are taking a certain little man to be drowned in the Fontanka, off the live-well barge" (II, 18). The folkloric device of a negative comparison—highly anomalous in this context—serves to frame an implicit contrast between the "little man" and the French writer. The reference to France's state funeral, moreover, is an anachronism, since he died in 1924. As an allusion to an event which occurs beyond the temporal frame of the Parnok episodes, this reference is illustrative of Mandelstam's tendency to associate events according to their "inner connections" (*vnutrennie svjazi*) rather than their temporal sequence.[38]

In this instance, the "internal connection" has to do with Mandelstam's association of himself with the little man and outsider-writer, facing the hostility of society and of the literary Establishment, whose honors are reserved for the likes of Anatole France.[39] A similar constellation of motifs appears in "Fourth Prose": "For some little Frenchman, it's '*cher maître*'— dear teacher, but with me, it's 'Hey Mandelstam, go scratch the dogs!' To each his own" (II, 191).

From the opposition between the little man and the literary Establishment it is a small step to the substitution of the type of writer who corresponds to the little man, the *raznočinec*. The contempt felt by the *raznočinec*-writer for the litterateur surfaces in a fragment from the fifth chapter that also contains the strongest echoes of Dostoevskij. Here is its opening paragraph:

> Scandal is the name of the devil discovered by Russian prose, or by Russian life itself, in the forties or thereabouts. It is not catastrophe but its ape, a base transformation, when a dog's head grows on a man's shoulders. Scandal lives

by a greasy out-of-date passport granted by literature. It is literature's off-spring, its favorite child. A little grain has been lost: a homeopathic dragee, a miniscule dose of a cold white substance . . . In those far-off times when they had recourse to the cuckoo-duel, consisting of two opponents in a dark room shooting with pistols at china cupboards, inkwells, and family portraits, this grain was called "honor" (II, 27).

The narrator goes on to abuse the litterateurs, whose faces, as they pose for a group photograph, express "one urgent and profound question: what is the current price of a pound of elephant meat?"

The opening paragraph restates several motifs from the first page of the story. Insofar as the argument can be paraphrased, it can be said to establish an opposition between scandal and literature on the one hand, and catastrophe and life on the other. If scandal did reflect some genuine feature of Russian life when it appeared as a literary theme in the 1840's, it has now long since become a cliched convention, in life as in literature. The implication is that scandal is a diminution of tragedy, and its rule is a sign of the loss of the heroic; Parnok is a figure in a "filthy story," not a tragedy. The "greasy out-of-date passport" granted by literature to the demon of scandal is a variant of the same idea as the rolled-up manuscripts, smeared with time, which are presented as an object of aversion in the epigraph. As such, it also belongs to the same field of meaning as the manuscripts which the implicit author advises his readers to destroy in Ch. VIII. But the demon of scandal also has antecedents in *The Brothers Karamazov* and *The Possessed*. Ivan Karamazov, too, feels diminished by the banality of his devil. However, the line "It is not catastrophe but its ape" alludes first, to the scene in *The Possessed* where Stavrogin, mocking Petr Verxovenskij, tells him "I am laughing at my ape"; more generally, to Stavrogin's failure to achieve anything more tragic than the series of scandals organized in large part by Petr.

In a virtual refrain of Parnok's dream with which the story began, the demon of scandal is pictured as the beneficiary of the loss of the convention of honor. In the enlarged context, the significance of this dream of the "American duel-cuckoo-game" becomes more apparent, as does its relevance to Ch. I: ironically, Parnok is dreaming about the conventions of heroism while Mervis is making off with his coat.

In view of Mandelstam's many clashes with literary officialdom and with literary "names," one wonders if the contention that scandal is under the protection of literature does not also reflect on the habits of the Soviet literary Establishment. The conception of scandal as a "base transformation" (*podloe prevraščenie*) of catastrophe is very much in keeping with the quality of Mandelstam's indignation over the "Ulenspiegel affair" as it is expressed in "Fourth Prose": "To Perish at Gornfel'd's hands is as stupid as getting killed by a bicycle or pecked to death by a parrot" (II, 185). Here too there is a note of disgust over the ascendency of mere scandal and over the lack of respect for the dignity of the individual that it entails.

To the extent that there is a convergence between Parnok and the narrator, there is also an overlapping of identity between the outsider whose status in "adult" society is uncertain and the champion of outlaw prose. The many references to Dostoevskij's works in the story are mainly in the services of this alliance. It is Dostoevskij as the poet of adolescent rage, of the resentment of the outsider who, no matter what his calendar age, is treated as a minor, who is referred to in *The Egyptian Stamp*. Thus in that same fragment from Ch. 5, the narrator equates the litterateurs with the audience that shouts down poor Ippolit in *The Idiot*: "That evening, at a dacha in Pavlovsk, these gentlemen literateurs called the poor youth Ippolit on the carpet. That is why he was unable to get through his oilcloth-covered notebook. Here's another Rousseau for you!" (II, 27).[40]

If Dostoevskij is used as an authority on the outsider, Pushkin is treated from the point of view of an outsider. References to Pushkin in the novella do not fit in very well with the idea of Mandelstam's reverential attitude towards him; it can hardly be said that Pushkin is referred to only in exalted contexts in the story.[41]

When Mervis (in Ch. I) breaks off his discussion with Parnok, leaving the latter to contemplate the "rather strange iconostasis" that partitions the tailor's room, there is a suggestion of a parallel with the scene in which the narrator of "The Stationmaster" describes another example of folk iconography, the series of scenes depicting the story of the Prodigal Son, which decorate the Stationmaster's quarters.

In the pictures which decorate Mervis' partition, the iconography is entirely secular, and Pushkin himself appears in one of the icons. This picture is described in a way that implies a contradiction between its surface meaning and its latent meaning:

> There, his face contorted, dressed in a fur coat, was Pushkin, whom some gentlemen resembling torchbearers were lifting out of a carriage as narrow as a sentrybox and, ignoring a startled coachman in a Metropolitan's cap, were preparing to toss into a doorway. Farther off some Dutchmen on stilts were depicted, running with a crane's gait all over their little country. (II, 9)

What can be the meaning of this strange scene, in which the national poet is given such a distorted appearance and seems to be suffering such undignified treatment? What looks like the aftermath of a drunken carousal can, in fact, be nothing other than the depiction of the mortally wounded poet being carried home after his duel with D'Anthes in January 1837. Whether the ambiguous quality of this picture is the result of its innate crudity, or whether the confused perception of what it represents comes from Parnok, the scene is an allusive one. The motif of the duel, for example, connects the image of Pushkin to the thematics of the "cuckoo duel" and the lost grain of honor. Hence the apparent debasement of the image of Pushkin, the highest figure in Mandelstam's literary Pantheon, forms a counterpart to Parnok's diminished possibilities for individual heroism. Moreover, the equation (through proximity) of Pushkin with the balloonist Santos Dumont—who, significantly enough, has been thrown out of his balloon—and with a scene of "Dutchmen on stilts, who were running with a crane's gait all over their little country" comments on Parnok's status, for it parodies his yearnings for culture, adventure and travel.

Taken as a group, the scenes on Mervis's "iconostasis" serve as an ironic comment on the story, just as "The Prodigal Son" does in "The Stationmaster." At the same time, they also suggest the growing remoteness of Pushkin's legacy; if popular culture has turned him into an icon rather than a living presence, he has become as exotic as the explorer or the Dutchmen on stilts.

At a later point in the narrative, when Parnok is reflecting on his failures, his thoughts seem to take the form of an angry rejoinder to Pushkin's "Vospominanie":

1. Kogda dlja smertnogo umolknet šumnyj den'
    I na nemye stogny grada poluprozračnaja
    Naljažet ten' i son, dnevnyx trudov nagrada .   .   .
2. Prokljatyj *son*! Prokljatye *stogny* bessty žego *goroda* (II, 26)

1. When, for mortals, the noisy day falls silent,
    And on the city's mute squares there settles
    A half-transparent shadow and sleep,
    The reward for daily labors
2. Accursed *sleep*! Accursed *squares* of a shameless city!

(Because of its rarity, *stogna*, "square or wide street," is an especially strong signal of an implicit response to Pushkin here.)

The lyric plot of Pushkin's poem represents a measure impossible of attainment for Parnok. His "daily labors" have been entirely futile, and the city appears to him as a delirious, deceitful dream. Despite the pangs of conscience experienced by the lyric hero of "Vospominanie," the poem ends on an affirmative note: "But I do not erase the sad lines." Parnok's memories lead to no such resolution:

> He recalled his inglorious victories, his disgraceful rendezvous: the standing
> in the streets, the telephone receivers in beerhalls, as frightening as crayfish
> claws . . . the numbers for unnecessary, burnt-out telephones. (II, 26)

It is hardly surprising that Parnok should be thinking about telephones
after his attempt to avert the drowning. The implication here seems to be
that they have not served him much better in his erotic adventures. The
dominant impression produced by this passage is one of seemingly ineradi-
cable shame, which goes along with Parnok's fears of social disgrace (". . .
but you'll be thrown out, disgraced, covered with shame . . .").

The text to which the greatest number (4) of explicit references are made
is *Anna Karenina*. Tolstoj's novel is mentioned in "The End of the Novel"
as one of those texts that are said to have had a tremendous formative
influence on nineteenth century society. It is not surprising, then, that *Anna
Karenina* is referred to in contexts having to do with the confusion or inter-
action of life and art. The question of relations between these two realms is
implicit in the first mention, when a member of the audience at the Mariinskij Theater wonders where Anna's seat was located. This confusion
sounds in a more pathetic key in an aside in Ch. VII, which has been
quoted earlier in a different connection:

> Books melt like chunks of ice brought into a room. Everything grows
> smaller. Everything seems to me a book. Where is the difference between a
> book and a thing? I do not know life: they switched it on me as long ago as
> the time when I recognized the crunch of arsenic between the teeth of the
> amorous French brunette, the younger sister of our proud Anna. (II, 34).

The idea of a surrogate life, a life that is counterfeit, alien to one's true
nature, or poisoned by an unhappy passion, is a recurrent theme in Mandelstam's prose and verse in the twenties. For him, even great literature, if it is
infected by "hidden Buddhism," can be an agent for this substitution. Perhaps this belief of Mandelstam's helps to explain the "sistership" of Anna
Karenina and Emma Bovary. In "The Nineteenth Century" the poet pro-
poses Tolstoj as a counter to the French analytic novel: "Tolstoj's novels
are pure epic and a completely sound European form of art (II, 282)." In
mentioning Emma and Anna in the same breath, perhaps what Mandelstam is doing is alluding to a style of reading, one which is particularly
invited by *Bovary* but which can take any novel as its object in the substitution of art for life.

The narrator traces his disorientation to a childhood cause: his early
immersion in books and innocence of life. "Immersion" is, if anything, too
mild a term. The first reading of *Madame Bovary* is presented as an experience of either metempsychosis or anamnesis, depending upon whether

one interprets the Russian *uznat'* as "to discover" or "to recognize." Either way, there is an intense and total identification with Emma and, by implication, with Anna. The narrator's professed ignorance of life, pictured here as a realm of vague and inconstant forms, contrasts with the tactile precision of that "crunch of arsenic"; yet to have one's greatest intensity of experience in this beautiful "molecular" world, characterized in "The Nineteenth Century" as a world of stasis, separation from life, and sterility, is to undergo a kind of death. Thus if the narrator's words allude to the vanishing of that nineteenth-century culture which formed his consciousness, they also suggest something malign in the influence of this receding world.

That Anna is now mentioned in connection with suicide is also illustrative of the manner in which associative chains are forged. The motif of death also figures in the third and fourth mentions of Anna's name. Both these references come in Ch. VIII. The third is part of a programmatic statement on the nature of the new "railroad prose":

> The railroad has changed the whole course, the whole structure, and the whole tempo of our prose. It has given prose over into the power of the senseless muttering of the little French *mužik* from *Anna Karenina*. Railroad prose, like the lady's handbag of this little peasant from the hour of death, is filled with coupler's tools: delirious particles and prepositions like hardware fittings, which belong in a display of legal evidence. It is done without any concern for beauty and roundedness. (II, 41)

Noteworthy for the ways in which the source text is transformed, this passage refers to several scenes from the novel, moves about nouns and epithets from their places in Tolstoj, and creates new meanings out of these shifts.

The "*little mužik*" (peasant) is drawn from Anna's recurrent nightmare, which is said to go back to the period of her first meeting with Vronskij: "A little old man with a disheveled beard did something hunched over the iron, accompanying his actions with senseless French words . . ."[42] This little old man seems to be based on the watchman who is crushed by the train on which Anna arrives in Moscow, an accident she takes as an evil omen (*durnoe predznamenovanie*). A "hideous peasant" who walks past her train window also reminds her of the figures from her nightmares, and she recalls the watchman when she makes her own decision to throw herself under the train. The nightmare figure appears again as the last image in her consciousness (hence "predsmertnyj," 'from the hour of death,' in Mandelstam) before she dies.

Mandelstam shifts the attribute of 'Frenchness' from the peasant's language to his nationality. The oxymoron which results, "French *mužik*" is, on the surface, as "senseless" as the figure's words. The woman's purse or handbag (*Damskaja sumočka*) of Mandelstam's "little peasant" is also partly the product of a contiguity shift. In the novel, it is Anna, and not the nightmare figure, who is carrying a handbag. Tolstoj mentions this red bag (*krasnyj mešoček*) twice, as an object which Anna must get rid of in order to be able to jump under the train at the right point: "She wanted to fall under the first car, the middle of which was drawing level with her. But the red bag, which she began removing from her arm, held her back . . ."; ". . . she flung the red bag away . . ."[43] In *The Egyptian Stamp* this bag, which attaches Anna to life against her will, is transferred to the little peasant.

The motif of the bag also has an antecedent in Mandelstam's story. His peasant is described as having a *sumočka*, not a *mešoček*. The two terms are synonymous, but the *sumočka* is associated with Parnok, for it is a detail from his dream which begins Ch. I: "That night he dreamed of a China-man, festooned with ladies' handbags (*damskie sumočki*) as if with a neck-lace of partridges . . ." The Chinaman is a semantic equivalent to the French *mužik*. Since Parnok does not understand Chinese, the Chinese fig-ure stands for "senseless" speech. This babble has broader implications in the story than in the novel. It is implicit in Parnok's dream, but it belongs to the wider field of meaning of that *lepet* out of which modern life is said to be made. The motif of the lady's handbag is therefore not a piece of surrealism but a characteristically Mandelstamian riddle, whose meaning is to be unraveled by placing it within a broadened thematic context as it is repeated later in the text. It is a metaphor for the principles of semantic coherence of the new prose. These principles turn out to be the semantics of delirium: "delirious particles" and "prepositions like hardware fittings," the coupling devices appropriate to composition that is based on the path-ways of associative meaning.

A similar cluster of images occurs in the narrator's description of his "prosaic delirium" (*prozaičeskij bred*):

> Then, I confess, I cannot stand to be quarantined, and I march boldly, after breaking the thermometers, through an infectious labyrinth, festooned with subordinate clauses as if with jolly chance purchases . . . into the open sack there fly crisp brown žavaronki [little rolls named after the lark, or žavaronok], as naive as the plastic art of the first centuries of Christianity . . . (II, 40)

The narrator takes the place here of the Chinaman/little peasant, hung about, not with the bag, but with its contents. The sack which catches the swallow-buns brings to mind the Chinese's necklace of partridges, inas-much as both images seem to connote successfully captured meanings. It is also worthy of note that *žavaronok* 'lark' is a metaphor for *fabula*, 'story,' in "The Birth of Plot," and that both birds and baked bread are associated with poetry in Mandelstam's verse.[44]

The last reference to *Anna Karenina* is found on the last page of the story. Kržižanovskij, travelling on the Moscow express, samples "railroad coffee, prepared according to a recipe unchanged since Anna Karenina's day, made of chicory with a slight admixture of cemetery earth or some other vileness of the sort." (II, 42) Thus the discussion of railroad prose modulates into the description of an actual train trip.

The "railroad prose" passage associates writing with delirium, train travel, and death. In linking the style of his novella with that of *Anna Karenina*, Mandelstam is alluding to Anna's stream-of-consciousness monologue, which runs through Chs. xxviii to xxxi of Part 7, as well as to her nightmare. Set mainly in her carriage and in and around the train, this monologue incorporates memories, Anna's reflections on her fate, and her reactions to shop signs and passers-by. Its movement from one motif to another shows no regard for logical sequence. As an example of a literary rendering of a delirious chain of associations it does have something of the quality of *The Egyptian Stamp*—with the difference that its 'delirious' style is clearly subordinated to the requirements of the plot. But when the narrator/implicit author of *The Egyptian Stamp* speaks of how the railroad has given Russian prose into the power of that unintelligible peasant from *Anna Karenina*, he is alluding to a shift in sensibillity evident in his text not Tolstoj's. Naming *Anna Karenina* as the fountainhead of what he takes to be the most vital tendency in the prose of his own day, Mandelstam's narrator is thus inventing a tradition for himself, just as he invents a literary ancestry for Parnok. This he accomplishes by reinterpreting a secondary current in Tolstoj's prose in order to appropriate it as the dominant of his own.

The narrator's "prosaic delirium" is but one of many items from the category of "illness." Among the diseases and disorders mentioned are scarlet fever, measles, colds, influenza, diptheria, chickenpox, trachoma, sclerosis, and tuberculosis. Many of these illnesses have in common the fact that they are either typically thought of as childhood diseases or they produce fever and delirium, or both. The theme of illness is connected in the story with childhood, with Petersburg, and with literary inspiration. It is revealing that in Ch. VIII, Parnok and the implicit author are linked through the motif of childhood illnesses. Parnok has a perception of Petersburg as a feverish mirage he identifies with a childhood illness, while the narrator recalls a nightmare (the episode of the City of Malinov) which accompanied an attack of illness in his childhood. This nightmare is semantically connected with the passage on pharmacy telephones in Ch. IV (through the 'raspberry' motif[45]) and with his memory of his family's hypochondriacal response to soot and drafts in Ch. V. Since delirium is both a traditional analogy for poetic inspiration and a state of consciousness in which syllogistic thought is replaced by free association, childhood fevers can be seen as one experiential source of the manner of thinking shared by the narrator and his hero.

The narrator's account of his journey to "Malinov" is revealed as a dream experience: "Everything happened backwards, as it always does in a dream." The "Malinov" fragment thus links two states of consciousness—fever and sleep—which exemplify the processes of non-syllogistic thought. Apart from references to feverish dreams, the motif of sleep also appears in Parnok's dream in Ch. I and then in his repudiation of Petersburg as an "accursed dream" in Ch. V. The exhortation in Ch. VIII to "Destroy the manuscript" makes the analogy between the associative writing process and sleep explicit: "Destroy your manuscript, but preserve what you have sketched in the margin out of boredom or lack of skill and as in a dream."

The description of Petersburg as either the source of this delirium or as the fever itself serves to carry the illness theme outwards from Parnok and the narrator into the macrocosm of culture and history. Where Parnok thinks of the city as the illness itself, the narrator repeatedly refers to illness as a property of the city. This pattern of associations begins with his reference to the "diptherial reaches" (*difteritnye prostranstva*) surrounding his family's apartment in Ch. V (II, 26). In Ch. VIII, the pattern is picked up again. First there is a simile which compares Petersburg's subsurface layers (*podspudnye plasty*) with a source of diptherial infection: "One need only remove the film from the Petersburg air and then its subsurface layer will be revealed. . . . But the pen that removes this film is like a doctor's teaspoon, infected by a spot of diptheria. It is better not to touch it" (II, 37-38). Later the "delirium of Petersburg influenza" (*peterburgskij influencnyj bred*) is mentioned in an aside as one of the materials from which the lives of the city's residents is made (II, 40). These passages reinforce and localize the connection between the fever of the dying age and the fire of time which was made in Ch. II. The Petersburg influenza delirium appears to be a manifestation of the fire of time, and the overtones of feverish delirium in the creative state which the narrator calls "prosaic delirium" signal his engagement in the life of his times.

In the simile quoted above, the pen, by virtue of its association with the doctor's teaspoon, is both a healing and an infected object. Like the spot-remover theme, the illness theme has a dual significance. In the course of the narrative, both these themes tend to undergo a change in value from negative to positive. The two themes are linked through their joint implication in the semantic field of 'impurity.' Thus the coherence of *The Egyptian Stamp* is illustrated by the fact that the lynch mob, with its moral and physical uncleanness, is characterized as a source of infection (*zaraza*) produced by the city. In Ch. V, the link between 'illness' and 'uncleanness' is traced to the fear of dirt and infection which appears to have been an important element in the outlook of the narrator's family:

> In our house what was feared most of all was "soot," that is, the lampblack from the kerosene lamps. The shout "soot! soot!" sounded like "fire!" "we're burning!" Into the room where the lamp was acting up they would run. Wringing their hands, they would stand there and sniff the air, which seethed with mustached, living, fluttering tea-leaves.
>
> The guilty lamp was punished by having its wick lowered.
>
> Then the little ventilation windows would be quickly flung open, and through them would shoot in frosty air like champagne. Like an ether-bearing chill or a sublimate of pneumonia, the cold air would hastily penetrate the whole room, with its mustached butterflies of "soot," which had settled on the pique blankets and pillowcases.
>
> "You can't go in there!" mother and grandmother would whisper. "The ventilation window!" (II, 25-26)

The picture emerges of a household in which nothing is to be feared more than dirt and fresh air. The reader is struck by the disproportionate intensity with which the narrator's mother and grandmother are said to have responded to the periodic appearance of soot from the lamps. The scene conveys an impression of the home as a precarious island in a universe of dirt and infection that is continually threatening to overwhelm it. The hint of overprotectiveness (You can't go in there . . .") is illuminating, for it suggests the direction in which his upbringing has influenced the character of the narrator. When he discourses on his ignorance of real life, it would appear that the manner in which his family insulated him from the world of dirt, fresh air, and raw, unboiled water has as much to do with this ignorance as do his early reading or those revolutionary changes which seem to signal the end of culture to him.

When it is placed in the broader context of the work as a whole, the motif of conflagration ("fire, we're burning") takes on a doubly ironic quality. On the one hand, the analogy between a wick which needs trimming and an outbreak of fire is ironically incommensurate; the narrator seems to be making fun of his maternal relatives' hyperbolic reaction. On the other hand, the narrator is recalling this family trait from a distance sufficient to enable him to see the dissolution of his family as a gradual effect of the metaphorical fire of time. From this vantage point, the soot episodes appear as a sign of the workings of this unnoticed conflagration, and the reaction to these soots, with its parallel to responses to fire, looks like unconscious prophecy.

In opposition to the exaggerated and overprotective reaction of the mother and grandmother, there are glimpses of the child's attraction to the world outside. His gravitation to this world is clearly implied by their injunction to stay away from the ventilation window (*fortočka*), through which the "frosty air like champagne" rushes in. This simile connotes something stimulating and intoxicating; along the same lines, the "forbidden chill" is perceived by the narrator as a "miraculous guest from diptherial space." Hence the narrator's identification of his manner of writing with delirium can be read as a development of this childhood attraction to what is forbidden and infectious. The end point of this development is the last apotheosis of illness as the writer's "dear prosaic delirium."

THE IMPLICIT AUTHOR

The implicit author of *The Egyptian Stamp* endows his hero with his own manner of thought, but on a more restricted scale. The kinship with Parnok which so distresses the narrator is based on an apprehension of shared social status. The writer is linked with Parnok through his sense of displacement and his concern for the loss of the conventions of personal honor and dignity. He is, however, blessed with two strengths which Parnok does not have. While Parnok attempts to escape from his sense of victimization and failure by seeking comfort in memories of childhood, the narrator objectifies both his own condition and Parnok's by placing their experiences within the broader perspective of the Petersburg cultural tradition. What is more, the narrator can turn his reflections on his existence into prose—an avenue of achievement that is not open to Parnok.

Parnok is the chief actor in the narrator's fiction, but the narrator's presence is not limited to this alter ego and to the persona of the implicit author—at least not just in the role of 'writer.' He also invests himself in other roles, each of which implies a different perspective on the text. One of the most curious guises of the implicit author grows out of a tacit identification of the narrator's perspective with the angle of vision of a bird. The importance of this alternative perspective is suggested by the fact that one of Mandelstam's few recorded comments on his novella characterizes it as a "bird's-eye view" of events.[46]

This idea is echoed within the text, in Ch. VII: "A bird's eye, filled with blood, also sees the world in its own fashion" (II, 34). The meaning of this thought is in large part a function of the context in which it appears. It is preceded by the narrator's cryptic declaration of the "real truth": "Cod-liver oil is a mixture of fires, yellow winter mornings, and whale oil: the taste of torn-eyes, swollen to bursting, the taste of revulsion brought to the point of ecstasy." This truth is only superficially about the taste of cod-liver oil. It is actually a truth about Petersburg, and about the narrator's attitude towards the city. One part of this attitude can be surmised from the fact that the image that gives rise to this declaration is a simile for Mervis which compares the tailor to a thief in a marketplace, "ready to shout a final irrefutably convincing word" (II, 33). It can hardly be a coincidence that the narrator also represents himself as hurrying to tell the real truth. His haste, like that of the thief in the marketplace, springs from the conviction that time is running out for him—an idea which is given its most forceful expression in the passage on "melting books" that follows the comment on the bird's eye.

Each constituent of the definition of the taste of cod-liver oil is drawn from the complex of imagery that signifies Petersburg. The connotations of cod-liver oil are made explicit in "Leningrad," a December, 1930, lyric in which several of the associative patterns of *The Egyptian Stamp* reappear. One of the consequences of the speaker's return to Petersburg-Leningrad is given in the second stanza: "You've come back: then hurry and swallow/The cod-liver oil of the Leningrad streetlights by the river!" In both the story and the lyric, this truth leaves a repellent taste. "Fires, yellow winter mornings, and whale oil," the elements that produce this taste, also have their counterparts elsewhere. As mentioned earlier, conflagrations (*požary*), connote the fire of time and the fever that is one of its manifestations as well as actual fires, such as the one which coincided with the death agony of Bozio, or the bonfires that were lit on the winter streets near the theaters. The use of yellow as an emblematic color for Petersburg is well attested in the poetic tradition.[47] Mandelstam makes use of it in *The Noise of Time* as well as in such lyrics as "Leningrad" and the much earlier "Petersburg stanzas." The motif of whale oil (together with an etymological and phonological play on the root R/V) is also found in the 1935 lyric, "Net, ne migren', no podaj karandašik mentolovyj" ("No, it isn't migraine, but give me the stick of menthol"). In her commentary on this lyric, Mme. Mandelstam states that the image of "rotten whale oil" (*tuxlaja vorvan'*) connotes the smell of decay. This, together with the etymological connection with the idea of something which is torn out, is congruent with another associative pattern in *The Egyptian Stamp*: the complex of imagery having to do with bloody, dismembered flesh and organs. This particular pattern becomes more marked in the rest of the predicate, which presents the "taste of torn-out eyes . . . the taste of revulsion brought to the point of ecstasy" as an equivalent for cod-liver oil.

This last idea is more ramified. It is an instance of a moral habit that is also illustrated by the treatment of the theme of uncleanness and the theme of illness: the transformation of a negatively-charged concept into something positive; from "revulsion" to "ecstasy." In this trait, the narrator shows himself to be a true descendant of the Underground Man, who knew that for the isolated consciousness, the pain of existence could become a source of aesthetic pleasure.

The comment on the bird's eye is a modulation of this highly-charged material. It is connected with the image of the torn-out eyes in the preceding paragraph, but it establishes a literal and psychological distance between the narrator and his "truth." The bird's eye sees things from a height, in less detail, and perhaps without comprehension of their human significance. Hence the narrator, in making this statement, is momentarily drawing back from the perception of the reality of Petersburg, and is also implying an affinity between the rapid, darting movement of the bird's eye and the pattern of selection of details in his prose.

The bird's-eye view is also met with in other parts of the story. The swallows of the Hermitage, for example, chirp about the Barbizon sun—presumably the town lies in the path of their annual migration—while the swallows in the Park of Mon Repos converse with the ravens about the etiquette of Lutheran funeral announcements. Another example of the association of the image of the writer with bird imagery is not so much metaphoric as it is metonymic: since the writer's pen (*pero*) is etymologically connected with the bird's feather, the motif of the pen represents the writer's activity in language drawn from the 'bird' complex. What is salient in the handling of this motif is that the pen tends to be presented as an autonomous subject with a will of its own, and not as an object manipulated by the writer. The passage on drawing in Ch. IV, for example, begins "My pen sketches" ("Pero risujet") rather than "I sketch with my pen" ('perom risuju'). In Ch. V, the writer's agitation at his awareness of his similarity to Parnok is indicated by a loss of control over his pen: "My pen is being refractory: It has split apart and has spattered everything with its black blood . . ." (II, 25). The pen-actor reappears as the agent which exposes Petersburg's subsurface layers in Ch. VIII: "But the pen that removes this film . . ." The image of 'the pen which writes by itself' is in harmony with the representation of the writing process as a variety of delirium. In both cases there is a loss or repudiation of a certain controlling logic; it is not possible to write in a conventionally logical manner with such a pen. The pen is thus an instrument of the associative mode. As is the case with the bird-complex as a whole, it implies a disjunctive way of looking at things and is an extension of the implicit author's vision.

The narrator also presents himself metaphorically in the role of a tailor. This hypostasis motivates two classes of imagery: sartorial metonymy and textural imagery. The story is replete with mentions of clothing, accessories, and associated ideas. Echoes of clothing motifs contribute to the coherence of the text. Thus Parnok's missing coat and shirts are brought to mind in Ch. V, when the deafmutes who are observed in their passage across Palace Square seem to be weaving a shirt. The lynch mob is contrasted to the guests at the Barbizon lunch through differences in apparel. In the portrait of Father Bruni, it is his clerical cassock (*rjaska*) which is emphasized. At one point it gives him the appearance of a clothesrack or hanger (*vešalka*)—a motif which reappears in the description of the crowd in the following chapter. The appealing quality of the portrait of the guests at the Barbizon lunch is retroactively undercut when it turns out that the pompous litterateurs in Ch. V wear the same wide trousers (*širokie pantalony*)—apparently the costume of men of assured social status. Ch. III takes place in a laundry, a setting which is implicated in the theme of cleanliness and uncleanness. And the motif of the ladies' handbag, presented as a riddle in the first chapter which is answered in the last, helps to frame the entire story.

A single such reference can embody the essential features of a moment in history. This is true of Parnok's morning coat, one of the emblems of his rootedness in an outmoded literary past. It is also true of the senatorial uniform ordered from Mervis by a "Lawyer Gruzenberg" in January 1917 and mentioned by the tailor when he is trying to turn the conversation away from Parnok's repossessed coat (II, 8). The owner of this coat must be O. O. Gruzenberg, who served in the last two Dumas, was the only Jewish lawyer in the Bejlis case, and defended Trotsky in 1906.[48] As a well-known fighter for Jewish rights who became, for a brief moment at the end of the imperial period, a Russian senator, Gruzenberg represents one solution to the problem of bicultural identity that is a tacit theme in Mandelstam's story. There is a nice irony in the fact that his name is brought up in connection with the official uniform which marks the high point in his official career just when Parnok is attempting to retrieve the coat which he needs to make a career.

This emphasis on details of dress is a traditional ingredient of the Petersburg tale, with antecedents in Gogol's synecdochic catalog of strollers represented by their attire in "Nevskij Prospekt," Akakij Akakievič's overcoat, and the imposing uniform worn by the unfortunate Kovalev's nose. The use of sartorial metonymy in this tradition signifies a value system in which social status and rank are rigidly stratified along bureaucratic lines and clothes really do make the man. As a throwback to this world, Parnok's manner of dress is out of keeping with his low status and with the times.

The numerous references to details of dress can also be said to express the sensibility of a tailor or a worker in one of the textile trades. This sensibility also informs the complex of textural images. Allusions to cloth and textiles, to the process of weaving or sewing them, and to their tactile qualities form a semantically stable group in Mandelstam's writing from his first published lyrics to the last Voronež notebook.[49] The basic import of this complex of imagery is the assertion of an analogy between the process of writing or composing and the process of weaving yarn into cloth or of making clothing from fabric. In *The Egyptian Stamp* this analogy is made explicit at two points. The first is found in Ch. V in one of the digressions on the method by which the text is being produced:

> I am not afraid of incongruities and breaks
> I cut the paper with a pair of long scissors.
> I glue on ribbons of paper as a fringe.
> A manuscript is always a storm, frayed and shredded.
> It is the draft of a sonata.
> Scribbling is better than writing.
> I'm not afraid of seams and the yellowness of the glue.
> I do a tailor's work. I spend time doing nothing.
> I sketch Marat in his stocking cap.
> Martins and Swifts. (II, 25)

In addition to identifying the writer's activity with the tailor's (*Portnajzu*), the implicit author describes how he actually 'tailors' the manuscript, cutting it, gluing on fringes, not hiding the seams or the glue lines. As he describes this activity, he represents it iconically. In the manner of the digression on drawing in the preceding chapter, the writer's thoughts are not presented in an integrated paragraph, but rather in the form of discrete blocks of material. The arrangement of these blocks produces an impression of "incongruities and breaks" which is counteracted by the associative threads with which the parts are sewn together.

In the final apostrophe of railroad prose in Ch. VIII, Mandelstam attributes textural properties to prose itself:

Yes, there, where the beefy levers of steam locomotives drip with hot oil, there it breathes, *all stretched out at full length; giving false measure*, the shameless creature, *winding on its life-devouring measuring rod* all the sixty-nine versts of the Nikolaev line, with carafes of misted-over vodka. (II, 41)

This sentence begins with prose as the concrete subject and the railroad as a metaphor for the dynamism of prose. In midsentence, however, this metaphor becomes the tenor of a new vehicle, one which serves as a figure for the operations both of prose and the railroad. The new metaphor converts the dynamism of prose and the speed and distance of the train journey into textural processes. The sequence of operations which is described is one which applies to fabric, which can be spread out, given in false measure, and then rolled up.

From the general analogy between writing and the processes of weaving and sewing there follows the possibility of extracting a wide range of connotative meanings from the visual or tactile properties of different kinds of yarn or fabric. In *The Egyptian Stamp* certain fabrics with this power of allusion are the subjects of limited repetitions. These fabrics are canvas (*xolst*) and vaguer *sukno*; 'cloth,' 'broadlcloth,' 'linen.' References to canvas are concentrated in Ch. I. In Parnok's dream, the opponents fire at the "family portraits," i.e., 'canvases.' A map of the hemispheres made of canvas (or coarse linen) paper, *xolščevaja bumaga*, is said to have signified the consoling idea of stability in Parnok's early childhood, and Lucien de Rubempré is described at the beginning of his career as wearing "rough linen" (or "homespun") underclothes (*gruboe xolščevoe beľe*). The different contexts in which the motif of *xolst* appears have in common their membership in the semantic field of 'beginnings': family and childhood for Parnok, the clothing of his native Angoulême for Lucien.

The other link among these images is that they are correlates for rather abstract situations, which is a characteristic of many of the textural images in the story. In this case, the situations are, respectively, the lost grain of honor, the dream of domestic permanence, and the hope of achieving a career. The other repeated cloth motif, *sukno*, is found only twice, but in contexts where both the abstract significance and the emotional implications of the image are stressed. *Sukno* appears in nearly identical descriptions of the sky in the first and last chapters. In Ch. I, Bozio's hopes are deceived by the "low sky like a [cloth-] draped" ceiling of the eighteen fifties, while the trip to Malinov takes place under a "low police-linen sky" (*nizkoe sukonno-policejskoe nebo*). In the passages on fear in the same chapter, one of its attributes is that it sends "dreams with unnecessarily low ceilings" (*sny s bespričinno-nizkimi potolkami*). There is a similarly claustrophobic overtone in Ch. V, when the narrator speaks of the dread aroused in him by the low-ceilinged vestibule of the Aleksandrinskij Theater. Hence *Sukno* is connected, via some private chain of associations, with the condition of claustrophobia. This condition can be referred to the anthropocentric planetary model favored by Mandelstam. On the surface, feelings of claustrophobia would appear to be a strange response to a situation in which objects and values seem to be receding and vanishing. A fear of empty space might be logically expected here, not a fear of enclosed space. Yet Parnok's exploding universe and the narrator's contracting one are expressions of the same phenomenon. This claustrophobia is cultural in origin, and is consonant with Mandelstam's image of post-Revolutionary Petersburg as a coffin.[50] Parnok's fate reflects the decline of the role of the individual hero. The narrator, in creating a world in which individual opportunity is beyond reach, is thrown back upon his own isolated consciousness, and this retreat gives rise to a sense of claustrophobic constraint.

Another limited repetition involves a cloth object rather than a type of fabric. This object is a shaggy towel (*moxnatoe polotence*) worn by Parnok at the barber's in Ch. II: "Under the shaggy towel his rabbit blood instantly warmed up" (II, 13). The towel crops up again among motifs associated with Parnok's early childhood in Ch. VI: "The first loss of contact with people and with himself and, who knows, the first presclerotic hum in the blood, still for the time being rubbed warm by the shaggy towel of life's seventh year, coalesced in the earmuffs. And the six-year-old quilted Beethoven in leggings, armed with his deafness, was pushed out onto the stairs" (II, 32). It is interesting that in both cases the towel is mentioned in association with musical motifs. Parnok's presence at the barber's is part of his concert-going ritual, while the temporary deafness of the child makes it possible to describe him as a "six year-old Beethoven" (See above, p. 120). Moreover, the towel in both instances is represented as a stimulus to life and is mentioned in connection with warmed blood. Yet a life of ambiguous promise is to be inferred, for there are overtones of resistance to this stimulus: the child must be shoved out of doors, and Parnok's attendance at concerts is presented in terms which are more suggestive of sacrifice than of pleasure. The second passage also serves to foreshadow Parnok's fate: a loss of contact with people and with oneself. The child's deafness therefore anticipates the whole trend of silences and other absences which will be the dominant feature of his adult world.

Other textural images (muslin, gauze, *polotno*; 'linen,' madepollam) are either simple descriptive details of the scene in which they appear or are part of the pattern of textural images which signify abstract situations, but only appear once. If textural imagery in general is so widespread in Mandelstam's writing, it is because such images fit in well with a poetics which treats the word as material that can be worked into a design built on associative meanings without loss of concrete, denotative meaning.

THE DESIGN OF *THE EGYPTIAN STAMP*

It is easier to talk about the semantic structure of a fragment of the novella or to trace a recurring motif through its successive embodiments than it is to discover an overall design that governs the arrangement of all fragments which make up the text. Shaping forces such as the persona of the implicit author, the requirements imposed upon the text by its ostensible identity as a manuscript, and the dominance of associative meaning have, for the most part, been examined in relation to individual sections of the text. What manner of description of the text as an entity grows out of the analysis of these informing ideas?

To a limited extent, *The Egyptian Stamp*, can be characterized through the very act of recognizing its opacity to critical description. Indeed, given the importance of the concept of emptiness in the story, there is a certain appropriateness to this fact. On the one hand, the text is continually spiralling back upon itself. It becomes almost inevitable that a passage that is commented upon in one connection will have to be taken up a second time in order to discuss some other theme. On the other hand, Mandelstam's literary prose is remarkable in its resistance to being uprooted, for purposes of critical discussion, from the broad cultural-historical context in which it exists.

Another approach to the overall design of the novella is to look at how its large-scale divisions—its eight chapters—organize the text. The abstract function of this division into parts has been described by Segal. Just as in the case of such smaller units as sentences and paragraphs, Mandelstam's chapter divisions serve to increase the semantic density within the section of text which is marked off in this manner. The lack of logical transitions across these boundaries signifies the discontinuous quality which Mandelstam thought essential to the new prose.

In attempting to account for how the chapters operate as elements of a unified design, it is illuminating to contrast the tale's use of chapters with the use of stanzas in Mandelstam's poetry of the twenties. In his study of the "Slate Pencil Ode" ("*Grifel'naja oda*"), for example, Omry Ronen has discovered a series of striking correspondences between the semantic structure of the poem and its stanzaic structure. No such wide-ranging parallelisms and symmetrical oppositions can be found in the story, a fact which says something about the contrasting uses of prose and poetry in Mandelstam's work. His earlier views on the complementarity of prose and verse seem to have little application here but his conception of prose as the arena of "contradiction, disorder, polyphony" ("raznoboj, razlad, mnogogolosie") fits in very well with the character of railroad prose. If there is an overall design in the progression from chapter to chapter, it is closer in character to the design of a drama than that of a poem.

As far as the Parnok plot is concerned, it is dramatically appropriate that the action should begin with the theft of the morning coat in Ch. I and the dress shirts in Ch. III; that they should turn up in Kržižanovskij's possession in Chs. VII and VIII; and that the story should conclude with Kržižanovskij finding his place in the sun; that is, with the furthest development of the theft in Ch. I (Nadezhda Mandelstam mentions a report that the Hotel Select was commandeered right after the Revolution for workers at the Ljubjanka Prison. Hence this detail is a rather strong hint as to where Kržižanovskij's career ambitions were taking him [*Vtoraja kniga*, p. 590].).

It has been mentioned in another connection that the culmination of Parnok's story comes in Ch. IV, with his failure to save the lynching victim and the disclosure of the meaning of the stamp motif. And here a narrative symmetry does come into play: the culmination of the narrator's growing self-awareness at a high point—the paean to railroad prose—in Ch. VIII. The narrator's self-consciousness begins to coalesce in Ch. V, right after Parnok's major failure, in the course of an attempt to differentiate himself from Parnok. Another symmetry between Chs. IV and VIII underscores this contrast. The disclosure of the meaning of the Egyptian stamp motif points to the unity of Parnok's fate from childhood onwards and accounts for his character in chiefly biographical terms. The narrator's comment in Ch. VIII that life is a tale without a plot and without a hero accounts for the selection of an anti-hero like Parnok and confirms his status as a representative figure. In this way it provides an insight into the fictional strategy of the narrator as writer—an insight that parallels the insight into Parnok's behavior provided by the stamp motif.

In roughly the second half of the text, the writer becomes the main subject of his own prose. Two shifts in emphasis accompany the displacement of Parnok by the implicit author. First, literature and the arts become explicit themes. This process begins with the fragments on drawing and painting in Ch. IV, continues in the next chapter in the discussion of literature, litterateurs, and the ballet, and, in subsequent chapters, takes the form of open references to literary subtexts such as *Anna Karenina* and *The*

Double. These literary motifs signal an increasingly bookish sensibility. Parnok's reflections on his lineage and his perception of Petersburg (in Ch. VII) as a text at various stages of production illustrate this cast of mind. It is even more marked in the narrator, for whom, in Ch. VII, life is completely subsumed by literature ("Everything seems like a book to me").

Second, as the narrator emerges into the foreground, he provides the reader with an increasing quantity of biographical information about himself. In the first four chapters, biographical episodes (and this does not exhaust all biographical references) are limited to the narrator's toast to his family in Ch. I and his memory of Nikolaj Davydovič in Ch. II. Both these fragments embellish the theme of a stable world which existed in the past and which now has been lost. The first passage, with its talk of failed domestic immortality and its imagery of furniture going off into exile, treats this theme openly. The lost world is an implicit theme in the second passage. The narrator's fondness for Nikolaj Davydovič is said to stem from the fact of the latter's dependence upon the narrator's father. This dependence is taken by the child as a proof of the existence of a fixed social hierarchy in which he occupies a secure position. The "Nikolaj Davydovič" fragment is placed just after a passage whose theme is Parnok's fears of social exclusion and disgrace. The contrastive intent of this arrangement is obvious: a secure social status is precisely what Parnok lacks; his life is a mere congeries of circumstances, determined by a "wild parabola" (II, 11).

The second half of the story contains four biographical fragments: the reminiscence about kerosene soots in Ch. V, the digressions on Geška Rabinovič and Aunt Vera in VI, and the Malinov episode in VIII. As a group, they seem to be selected less as illustrations of the world that has been lost than as clues to the narrator's intellectual formation and social origins.

It would be an oversimplification to read the second half of *The Egyptian Stamp* as the record of an uninterrupted spiritual ascent for the narrator. Nor is Parnok utterly crushed; in Ch. VIII he still hopes to awaken from his Petersburg illness, to make a career, marry, and rid himself of the tag of "young person." As for the narrator, there is nothing upbeat about his declaration in Ch. VII that everything on his cultural horizon is melting and growing smaller.

It is from this impending catastrophe that the narrator escapes into "prosaic delirium"—hardly an unqualified victory. Mandelstam's novella embodies a contradiction which is present in much of the best Soviet prose of the twenties, as well as in such later works as *The Master and Margarita* and *Doctor Zhivago*. The narrator's dilemma is one which he shares with

Babel's Ljutov, Oleša's Kavalerov, and the heroes of Bulgakov's and Pasternak's novels: the triumph of verbal imagination is contrasted with failure in the realm of social action and achievement. In *The Egyptian Stamp* this realm can hardly even be said to exist. Mandelstam's tale presents a moment during which an old value system is in a state of dissolution and no new culture has established itself in the place of the old. Thus its universe is a grotesque one, in which a continual tension exists between the implicit author's delight in his powers of literary invention and his eschatological forebodings.

While this tension in no way detracts from the work's aesthetic power, it does suggest that there is some justice in Nadezhda Mandelstam's contention that the story grew out of her husband's spiritual crisis without doing anything to resolve it.

According to the ideal of language for which Mandelstam used the metaphor of Hellenism, the literary word ought to model and protect a belief in the dignity of the individual. But the language of *The Egyptian Stamp* serves less to "humanize the surrounding world"—a purpose ascribed to Hellenism in *On the Nature of the Word*—than to portray a nightmare reality. The story's moral sympathies are clear enough, but it is a deeply pessimistic work, ambivalent about the legacy of the past and apprehensive of the future. It is therefore not surprising that in Mandelstam's later prose he abandoned the device of a fictitious hero altogether; how could Parnok become the spokesman for an affirmative vision? While "Fourth Prose" and "Journey to Armenia" have close stylistic affinities with Mandelstam's novella, they do away with the divorce between narrator and actor. When the narrator of these later works speaks of the beauty and terror of existence, he does so without showing any overt symptoms of a divided consciousness.

CHAPTER FOUR

"FOURTH PROSE" AND "JOURNEY TO ARMENIA"

"Fourth Prose"[1] exhibits that tension between surface meaning and deeper significance which is a hallmark of Mandelstam's writing. What appears to be topical satire in the form of a diatribe against the Soviet literary bureaucracy turns out to be something closer to a vision of Hell. Particular instances of injustice are absorbed into the picture of an existence that has become a phantasmagoria.

The central concerns of "Fourth Prose" are moral ones. Jane Gary Harris has aptly characterized the text as a set of variations on the theme, "Thou Shalt Not Kill."[2] In the course of his invective, Mandelstam equates officially sponsored coercion with the violence of a lynch mob, and appeals to the judgment of history against both. His clash with the Soviet literary establishment is presented as a descent into a modern Inferno; like Dante, Mandelstam appears to use his writing as a means to obtain a literary revenge against his enemies.

Considered in this light, Mandelstam's *cri de coeur* shows a certain kinship with Bulgakov's *Master and Margarita*. Both works are directed against the same literary establishment, and Mandelstam's writers, editors, and critics show a family resemblance to their counterparts in "Griboedov House." Picturing the literary world as the domain of the devil, both writers express the belief that injustice is never final. In the fantasy that "manuscripts don't burn," one senses the same impulse as in the declaration by the implicit author of "Fourth Prose" that "the legal proceedings are not over, and—I make bold to assure you—will never be over" (II, 186).

At the core of the text lie two confrontations with officially-sanctioned injustice: Mandelstam's intercession on behalf of five elderly bank workers, condemned to death on some vague charge in the spring of 1928; and his own involvement in the so-called "Ulenspiegel Affair," a protracted ordeal that lasted from summer 1928 into the early part of 1930. These two episodes were linked not only by temporal proximity but by the poet's appealing, in both cases, to Nikolaj Ivanovič Buxarin. It was Buxarin who was able to get the death penalty set aside in the earlier case, and then to put a stop to the policy of using the Ulenspiegel business as an instrument for the semiofficial persecution of Mandelstam.[3]

In "Fourth Prose" it is clearly the Ulenspiegel case that is the precipitat-
ing event, the affair of the clerks serving chiefly as evidence that the lynch-
mob morality displayed in the juridical and journalistic attack on Mandelstam was a manifestation of the spirit of the times. When the publisher of
Mandelstam's revision of two earlier Russian translations of Charles de
Coster's *La Légende de Thyl Ulenspiegel et de Lamme Goedzak* issued the
book with Mandelstam listed as the sole translator, a scandal ensued. The
poet was the first to notify the critic and translator A. G. Gorn'feld, whose
translation of *Ulenspiegel* had been the chief resource of the new version, of
the oversight. Despite the fact that Mandelstam stated that he held himself
morally responsible, Gorn'feld, in a letter to the editor of the *Red Evening
Newspaper* (*Krasnaja večernjaja gazeta*), accused the poet of plagiarism. The
dispute was finally adjudicated by the Federation of Soviet Writers' Organizations (referred to in the text under its acronym FOSP).

The Federation's decision essentially repeated Mandelstam's own declaration of moral responsibility. Mandelstam, however, was outraged at this
finding. The dispute with Gorn'feld had served as the pretext for an organized campaign to blacklist the poet; yet even apart from the hardships he
experienced as a consequence of financial deprivation and slander, there
would, in his view, have been a world of difference between a judgment
dictated by his own conscience and a decision handed down by "Literature," that is, the literary establishment, its allies, and its bosses. As he put
it in a letter to the members of FOSP:

> Now I look back with bitterness on the whole of my life's path. A testimo-
> nial fit for a dog has been my reward. What an example of respect for labor
> and for the worker's personality you provide for our country, writers. The
> trouble is not that you have broken my life in two, barbarously destroyed my
> work, and poisoned my air and my bread; but that you have managed to get
> away with not even noticing any of this.

Another letter addressed to the same readership makes it clear that the
poet understood the plagiarism case as "Literature's" way of avenging itself
upon him for his campaign to end the exploitation of translators. FOSP, he
charged, had "responded with the staging of a scandalous criminal trial to
the first attempt in the USSR by a writer to intercede in publishing mat-
ters." For years Mandelstam had been fighting on two fronts against the
"howling chronic disgrace" that summed up the translator's conditions of
work. Publicly, in a series of articles, he called for higher standards of
translation and a more selective approach in the choice of foreign texts.
Privately, in his correspondence with the publishing houses, he railed
against pressuring translators to work at record speed for low rates of pay;

pay which might in any case "be held back right up to the point where a number of translators had been forced to sell everything they owned down to the last chair."

The arbitration proceedings served as the last straw. According to Nadezhda Mandelstam, the Ulenspiegel affair put an end to her husband's attempts to reach an accommodation with the Soviet order: ". . . the 'sick son of the age' suddenly understood that he was the healthy one."[4] In comparison with *The Egyptian Stamp*, "Fourth Prose" conveys a strikingly different picture of the relationship between the writer-outsider and the representatives of literary society. Instead of the ambiguous affirmation of "prosaic delirium," there is a ringing self-affirmation on the part of the authorial persona, a clear appeal to "Truth with a capital letter" and to the judgment of posterity. Nadezhda Mandelstam describes the liberation brought about by the writing of "Fourth Prose" in these terms:

> In "Fourth Prose" O. M. described our country as "bloody," pronounced his curse upon official literature, tore the literary overcoat off his shoulders, and again extended his hand to a *raznočinec*: Akakij Akakievič, the most senior Komsomol.[5]

In this reading, "Fourth Prose" serves as both an extended curse and a declaration of personal allegiances.

As for the manner in which its themes are presented, an obvious point to be made is that the process of fragmentation has accelerated. In a text approximately half the length of *The Egyptian Stamp*, there are twice as many chapters: sixteen, as compared to eight. In the novella, the fragmenting of the text was a conscious device, motivated by the "manuscript" quality of the work. An outline of the thematic connections that link the fragments of "Fourth Prose" suggest a somewhat different connection between matter and manner.

The chapters of this diatribe accentuate stages in the narrator's developing self-awareness. As Segal has pointed out, a movement towards increased consciousness of self can be found in each of the three literary "proses" written in the manner that first appears in *The Egyptian Stamp*.[6] In "Fourth Prose" the process of self-definition begins obliquely, through references to the case of the bank officials. Mandelstam does not mention his own intercession on their behalf, nor does he draw any explicit parallels with his own ordeal. In Ch. 1, there is an implicit tie between the lynch-mob mentality and the loss of the "bourgeois" values of "fastidiousness" (*brezglivost'*) and "decency"—a correlation that is also implicit in the novella, with its motif of the lost pill of honor. In Ch. 2, the riddle of the "genre painting," a scene of bullying and class oppression fostered by Communist Party cadres, serves as an allegorical expansion of the same theme.

Ch. 3 begins with a reference to the "lame girl" (*devuška xromonožka*), without mentioning that she is the editor of *Moscow Komsomol* (*Moskovskij Komsomolec*) or that Mandelstam worked there for a time. Ch. 3 chiefly consists of a series of illustrations of the motif of officially sponsored violence, which has been introduced in the first two chapters. This context implies a kinship between the lame girl and the "agitmamas" who egg on the little bully in Ch. 2. By the same token, Ch. 3 conduces to an implicit identification by the narrator (who begins to describe his own experiences only in Ch. 4) with the little boy who is victimized in Ch. 2. Touching upon various instances of violence and coercion, Ch. 3 finally settles into a characterization of the demonic atmosphere of a Moscow newspaper office; thus from Ch. 2 to Ch. 4 there is a progression from impressions of the moral state of society at large, to the spirit of contemporary journalism, and finally to the author's personal experiences in journalistic circles.

In Ch. 4, the narrator begins to elaborate upon the representation of himself as an outlaw. Like Parnok, who is despised by doormen and women, Mandelstam states that he was hated by the servants at *Cekubu*.[7] Unlike Parnok, however, he is proud of his outlaw status. There is a natural progression from his account of how he was compelled to steal soap from the respected scholars residing at the *Cekubu* house to his outburst in Ch. 5 against "writers who write things to order" ("pisateli, kotorye pišut zaranee razrešennye vešči").

In Ch. 6, the narrator's revulsion against the literary establishment represented by *Moscow Komsomol*, *Cekubu*, and Herzen House serves as a background against which to define his own literary manner: "I have no manuscripts, no notebooks, no archives. I have no 'handwriting' because I never 'write.' In Russia I alone work from the voice, while all around the shaggymaned scum writes. What the hell kind of writer am I? Be off, you fools" (II, 182). This opposition between "working from the voice" and "writing," by means of which the speaker distinguishes himself from the writers' pack, has a programmatic relevance to the text as a whole. The rapid transitions and brief fragments suggest a transcript of oral speech. The choppiness of the text also creates a tempo that is appropriate to a state of anger and of impatience beyond all bounds.

The progression from the angry outburst, "Be off, you fools!" to the discussion of the qualities of the Gillette razor blade carries a note of challenge. The Gillette is first mentioned as a tool with which the author's stolen pencils—another badge of his outlaw status—can be sharpened. When the speaker goes on to state that the Gillette blade has always seemed to him to be one of "the noblest products of the steel industry" he is continuing his implicit praise of the bourgeois world (the home of the values of fastidiousness and decency) and offering an indirect insult to Soviet culture. The Gillette blade is also mentioned in one of the Voronež lyrics, No. 334, which begins: "With the thin blade of a Gillette/ The bristles of hibernation are easily removed" ("Plastinkoj tonenkoj žilleta/ Legko ščetinu spjački snjat'"). The blade thus seems to carry associations of being an object that is foreign, well-made, has the ability to make things sharp (in the literal sense of "sharpening pencils" in the prose and in the figurative sense of "quickening" or "contributing to a state of alertness" in the lyric), and which, to quote the prose again, "bends but does not break"; i.e., it belongs to the semantic group of objects that are at once both fragile and strong—a combination that Mandelstam elsewhere ("The Concerts of Hofmann and Kubelik") associates with artistic culture and with those who, like Parnok, are its legatees.

Ch. 7 introduces the leitmotif of Chinese identity: "I am a Chinese, no one understands me." As is the case with Parnok's dream in the beginning of *The Egyptian Stamp*, "Chineseness" is linked with the idea of incomprehension. In Ch. 7, the author continues to define himself in relation to a hostile environment. In Ch. 8, he again takes up the theme of his revulsion against "Literature." A verse of the poet Esenin is offered as a potent spell against the baneful influence of hackwork, and this detail echoes an allusion to Zoščenko in the previous chapter in a similarly positive context. Ch. 8 also concludes the treatment of the theme of philology, which begins with the contrasting of attitudes toward the literary word in Ch. 5.

The lament, in Ch. 8, for "Mother Philology" sets the stage for the first open and specific attack on Gorn'feld, who is identified in Ch. 9 as a member of the class of killers and would-be killers of Russian poets. Chapters 9 through 11 are linked by the motif of 'petitions for redress.' In Ch. 9 Mandelstam attacks Gorn'feld's letters to the *Red Evening Newspaper* as an appeal to an alien authority, while in Ch. 10, the poet alludes to his own application for help, addressed to Buxarin, who at that time was in charge of *Pravda*. The theme of petition continues in Ch. 11, which takes the form of an appeal to Herzen, whom the speaker holds accountable for what is going on at "his" house. Calling upon the judgment of posterity, Ch. 11 also evokes the second meaning of "pravda," "Truth with a capital letter," and introduces the terminology of legal proceedings: "judicial proceedings," "litigate," "enter in the official record," "trial." (*sudoproizvodstvo, sudit'sja, zanesti v protokol, process*).

Ch. 12 takes up the theme of judgment. The FOSP decision in Mandelstam's case is transformed into a sacrificial ritual of "literary circumcision," which is carried out by the tribe of writers. This ritual motif is intensified in Ch. 13, when the author refers to it as an attempt to castrate him. The sense of strangeness and fear produced by this confrontation is underscored by a reference to the opening lines of the *Inferno*. Mandelstam seems to imply a kinship between Dante's situation and his own; like Esenin and Zoščenko, Dante also belongs to the line of "real" writers, and to evoke his shade in connection with an attempted castration is to evoke a genuine literary tradition in the face of suffering imposed by a false one.

Ch. 14 contains Mandelstam's rejection of the "literary overcoat,"[8] which in this context takes on the quality of a badge of initiation, marking one's passage through the ritual described in Chs. 12 and 13. Hence the penalty suffered by Mandelstam for foregoing literary circumcision/castration is a refusal to acknowledge his adulthood: ". . . others get more respectable every day, while with me it's just the opposite—time runs backwards." This passage, from Ch. 15, recalls the theme of perpetual enforced adolescence from *The Egyptian Stamp*.

In the final chapter, the writer offers a definition of labor that will encompass his own work and associates himself with an archetype from Russian Jewish jokes, with the implication that he and Gorn'feld have acted out such a joke. There is a pathos in this identification that enhances the note of personal unhappiness (as opposed to anger or indignation) that crops up in the last two chapters when the author complains of his poverty and of the disrespect shown him.

Against a background of brutal acts committed in the name of humanity, the author asserts his private values. Mandelstam unmasks the dominant morality, which attempts to justify itself on grounds of historical inevitability, as nothing better than lynch law. The implicit argument of "Fourth Prose" is that there is a causal relationship between these scenes of coercion and murder and the attitudes promulgated in literature and the press. The bully in Ch. 2 is egged on by Komsomols, and the paper that Mandelstam describes is *Komsomol Pravda*. When writers help to disseminate the political morality of the day, and that morality is equivalent to lynch law, then words can kill. The idea of literature and the press as a lethal force is introduced in the third chapter, when a Moscow editor is portrayed as a "frightening and illiterate horse-doctor[9] of happenings, deaths, and events, who is pleased as can be when the black horse's blood of the epoch spurts like a fountain" (II, 181). "Happenings, deaths, and events," ("proisšestvie, smerti, i sobytija") the ordinary subject matter of a newspaper, take on a malign quality here, as though Tolstoj's Polikuška were ministering to a beast from "The Horseshoe Finder" or "The Age."

The image of this editor is drawn from a passage that portrays literary Moscow as a landscape filled with demons:

> Here there is a perpetual accounting-office night, illuminated by the yellow flame of a second-class waiting room in a railroad station. Here, as in Push-kin's tale, a Jew is married to a frog; that is, a perpetual wedding is taking place, uniting a goat-footed fop, ejaculating theatrical roe, with a fellow evil spirit out of the same bathhouse: a Moscow editor-coffinmaker, who makes brocaded coffins on Monday, Tuesday, Wednesday, and Thursday. He rustles a paper shroud. He opens the veins of the months of the Christian year that preserve their pastoral-Greek names: January, February, and March . . .

This phantasmagoria takes place in the endless night of a Hell whose traditional fires have been replaced by the yellow glow of those waiting-room lamps. Combining in themselves the attributes of grotesques out of nightmare and the literary fairytale, the demons who occupy this office complex on Tverskaja are portrayed as the agents of a funereal under-world. In the image of the editor-coffinmaker, rustling his paper shroud, there may also be an allusion to Pushkin's short story "The Coffinmaker" ("Grobovščik"), which also describes a nightmare gathering of spirits. Both 'funereal' and 'veterinary' images serve to fill in a picture of the Moscow press as an institution whose ostensible purpose is to serve the public, but whose actual intent is murderous.

The image of the "goat-footed fop, ejaculating theatrical roe" (*ikra*, 'fish eggs,' 'caviar') includes a recurrent motif ('goatishness') that helps to extend the demonic and infernal overtones throughout the text. This pat-tern of imagery, which depends upon the traditional folkloric depiction of Satan with cloven hooves or, more specifically, with goat feet, apears first in Ch. 2, where the privileged little bully is wearing kid boots (*kozlinnye sapožki*). Since the leading connotation of this image is 'privilege,' the demonic overtones appear only in retrospect, in the light of the whole set of images connected with goats. The lame girl from *Komsomol Pravda* is also obliquely associated with this pattern of imagery: "One of her legs is shorter than the other, and the clumsy prosthetic shoe calls to mind a wooden hoof" (II, 180). The motif of the hoof recurs a few lines later in a simile that seems to imply something demonic in the Komsomol outlook: "Our conception of schooling has the same relationship to scholarship as a hoof does to a foot, but that doesn't bother us." This is followed by an address to the whole staff of the paper that generalizes the epithet "cloven-hoofed" (*parnokopytnyj*): "I have come to you, my cloven-hoofed friends . . ."

In Ch. 11, the speaker prophesies that a crowd of students and police-men, "led by a goat-choirmaster" (*kozel-regent*) will carry the remains of his case out of District Court in a "police coffin." Suggestive of some medieval parodic rite (perhaps preserved in some student custom?), the image of the "goat-choirmaster" forges an associative link between the motif of 'goatishness' and the Ulenspiegel affair. This link is echoed in Ch. 13, where it is mentioned that the "tribal elders," that is, the officials of the writers' organizations, have a smell compounded of "onions, novels, and goat meat (*kozljatina*)". This telltale stench is hardly surprising in a clan which the speaker considers to have "sold their souls to the poxy devil for three generations in advance," and who are referred to in another context as "rogataja nečisť," 'horned evil spirits' or 'horned riffraff.' In Ch. 15 Man-delstam represents his agreement with GIZ, the State Publishing House, as a pact with the devil: "...I signed a grandiose, unperformable contract with Beelzebub or GIZ ..." (II, 190). The suggestion that the author's dealings with official literature constitute an agreement with the powers of evil makes it possible to see "Fourth Prose" as an act of conjuration, whose goal is to release the poet from the consequences of this unholy pact.

As is the case with the narrator of *The Egyptian Stamp* and with Parnok, the implicit author of "Fourth Prose" is involved in a dialectical process of identification, in the psychoanalytic sense. The negative component of this process is most evident in the writer's rejection of the "literary overcoat." The motif of the overcoat (*šuba*) is, characteristically, introduced obliquely in Chs. 4 and 7

1.   When I moved to a different apartment, my fur coat lay across the cab, as is customary with people who are leaving the hospital after a prolonged stay or who have just been released from prison (II, 182).

2.   Sluts and slobs![10] Let's go to Azerbaidjan! I would have taken courage with me in a yellow straw basket packed with a whole pile of clean-smelling linen, and my fur coat would have hung from a golden nail. And I would have come out at the Erivan railroad station with a winter fur coat in one hand and an oldster's walking stick—my Jewish staff—in the other (II, 184).

In these two passages references to the overcoats serve as metonymic attributes of the implicit author. In the first, the *šuba* develops the negative characterization of *Cekubu* by implying that leaving the quarters managed by that organization is like leaving a hospital or a prison. In the second pasage, the overcoat is mentioned in connection with the author's wish to journey away from Moscow, to Alma-Ata, Azerbaidjan, or Armenia; what is interesting here is the conjunction of the overcoat with the writer's "Jewish staff," a combination that is emblematic of his two cultures. Both allusions to the overcoat indicate that it continues, as in *The Noise of Time*, to be a motif with both positive and negative overtones. Thus it would appear that when the narrator declares, "I tear the literary overcoat off my shoulders and trample it underfoot" (II, 189), he is casting off something more than an externally-imposed sign of status. This declaration acquires an added shade of meaning when it is compared with the conclusion of "In a Fur Coat Above One's Station," where Mandelstam warns that nineteenth-century Russian culture is concluded and unrepeatable. The "furry hide" (*pušnaja škura* [II, 108]) of the metaphorical "beast" of the last century's literature has been transformed, in the hands of Soviet writers, into an oppressive burden: a "literary pelt" (*literaturnaja pušnina*), that almost suffocates the narrator of "Fourth Prose" before he frees himself of it.

The author's affirmation of his Jewishness clearly has a part in his rejection of membership in the tribe of writers: "I insist that the writing confraternity, as it has taken shape in Europe and especially in Russia, is incompatible with the honorable title of Hebrew, of which I am proud" (II, 187). As is the case with allusions to Dante, Zoščenko, and Esenin, this evocation of "the honorable title of Hebrew" represents an appeal to a genuine authority against the claims of a spurious one. If the treatment of Jewishness in "Fourth Prose" is contrasted with the earlier handling of the same theme in Mandelstam's prose, the difference that emerges is that now the Jewish theme is not simply a matter of origins and milieu. No longer a condition that threatens or complicates the writer's identity, Jewishness now operates as a positive force, providing a moral perspective that enables Mandelstam to judge his judges.

In the discussion of *The Egyptian Stamp*, it was argued that the stamp motif serves as an index of Parnok's character, extending the reader's sense of Parnok by hinting at how he has in part identified himself with his enemies and, in part, has inverted their representation of him. An analogous process is at work in "Fourth Prose." In a striking passage in Ch. 12, the author takes negative images that might be applied to one outcast group, the Jews, and reassigns them to writers, who are metaphorically pictured as a tribe of Gypsies—another traditional group of outcasts.

Mandelstam's writer-Gypsies are practitioners of the (Jewish) ritual of circumcision (*obrezanie*). When the poet metaphorizes his treatment at the hands of FOSP as an attempted castration, he is extending the symbolic implications of this rite to the limit. By the same token, the writers' clan is presented as being avaricious, prone to thievery, and lacking in genuine loyalties. Finally—and most primitively—they are said to have "a repellent odor to their skins" (II, 188). In all these respects, writers-as-Gypsies become, in effect, Mandelstam's Jews.

This deflection of antisemitic and other xenophobic stereotypes is accompanied by allusions to what may be called "high" and "low" Jewish traditions: the writer associates himself both with the patrician lineage of "shepherds, patriarchs, and kings" and with one of the lowly figures from the large class of jokes that begin with the phrase "Xodjat dva evreja," "Two Jews are walking along." The formal situation that Mandelstam ascribes to these anecdotes offers a parallel to his own position during the course of the Ulenspiegel scandal: ". . . and one asks and asks, while the other keeps on evading a straight answer, and there is no way for them to disengage" (II, 192). In Ch. 15, Mandelstam himself resorts to this strategem in response to the threats and solicitations of the arbitrators of his dispute:

> What sort of character is this Mandelstam, who for such-and-such a period of years is supposed to have done such-and-such—*and keeps on dodging his way out of it, the scoundrel? . . . Will he dodge his responsibilities for much longer?* . . . I am guilty, there can be no two ways about it. I can't wangle my way out of my culpability. I live under unrepayable obligations. *Dodging responsibility is my salvation. Must I go on dodging much longer?* (II, 189-90)

In the two passages just cited, the verbs *krutit'* and *izvoračivat'sja* (translated as, respectively, "evade" and "dodge") suggest a range of defensive maneuvers that enable the narrator to preserve some measure of freedom. These maneuvers, moreover, are transformed from being the subject of an accusation against the writer to being an activity he claims as a necessary condition of his existence. Hence Mandelstam implies a kinship with the humble figure from the joke cycle, who is always able to slip free from an annoying or threatening situation.

"Fourth Prose" ends with a proverb: "And on the city crest in Armavira is written: 'A dog howls, the wind carries the sound'" (II, 192). Thus the last word in this diatribe is directed against the members of FOSP, earlier likened to a pack of hounds through the description of them as "shaggy-maned scum." (Although it is used figuratively, either in the sense of "the genuine article" or "having some negative quality in the highest degree," the epithet *gustopsovaja* is applied to purebred dogs when it is used in its literal meaning of "shaggy-maned.") In Russian, the Armavira motto reads: "Sobaka laet, veter nosit"; Mandelstam was to return to this well-known saying in one of the Voronež lyrics, No. 354, encoding it into the third stanza:

> Neščasten tot, kogo, kak ten' ego,
> *Pugaet laj i veter kosit,*
> I beden tot, kto, sam poluživoj,
> U teni milostyni prosit.   (I, 240)

Unhappy the man, whom, like his own shade,
The barking frightens, and the wind slashes;
And pitiable is he, himself but half-alive,
Who of a shade begs charity.

By this time (January 1937), Mandelstam knew that many of his enemies would share his fate.

JOURNEY TO ARMENIA

Because much of the work is not explicitly connected with the subject announced by Mandelstam's title, a reader of the "'Journey' to Armenia" is apt to be struck by the question of the work's relationship to its presumed genre, travel writing. Several circumstances make genre an issue here. First of all, Mandelstam was, as we might say, "on assignment." Like other Soviet writers of the period, he was supposed to celebrate the achievements of Soviet Power. Yet, as Henry Gifford puts it, what Mandelstam ended up celebrating were "all those qualities that resisted the Bolshevist innovators and revealed the unbroken ties of this people with the Christian and classical culture of the Mediterranean."[11] What the poet does, in effect, is to struggle against his celebratory task, redefining it in such a way as to praise what he deems genuinely praiseworthy. On this level, the seeming disjunction between the work's title and the body of the text marks an attempt to replace an illegitimate authority, i.e., a Stalinist appropriation of a literary tradition, with a legitimate one.

To do this Mandelstam must recover the tradition. Discussing the "Journey" in the context of Russian and Soviet-Russian travel writing, Carol Avins points out that the Russian traveler is always using his experience of travel as a way of rethinking the meaning of home.[12] But for Mandelstam, the notion of home cannot be localized in the Soviet Russia of the Cultural Revolution; certainly it is not to be identified with the gloomy Zamoskva-reče quarter in Moscow, where Mandelstam is glad to be only a temporary resident and where what Stalin called the *velikij perelom*, "the great transition," literally "the great break," is ominously figured in the felling of a mighty linden by a tenants' committee. Indeed, as Avins points out, while it is an expectation of the genre that the journey will end with the traveler's return home, Mandelstam's journey implies a loss of home, mitigated by a temporary reprieve, the "one more day" granted to King Arshak in his dungeon in the final chapter. The writer must therefore make his real home in writing, and he must make his writing at home in the history of literature. This circumstance, too, motivates the stretching of generic limits in "Journey to Armenia": the actual journey becomes an analogue and jumping-off point for a whole series of attempts at cognition of the world, and these attempts, which lead from the physiology of organic growth to what Mandelstam calls the physiology of response to a painting and ultimately to the "physiology of reading," seek to make the world cohere by linking organic processes and textuality.

The habit of introducing reflections on other writings into the literature of travel also contributes to the hybridization of the genre and is a token of the modernist cast of Mandelstam's prose. The "Journey" shows affinities with Gide's *Voyage to the Congo.* Writing a few years before Mandelstam, Gide offers an account of his travels which is not only an expose of colonialist abuses but a voyage through a series of texts, e.g., La Fontaine, Goethe, Bossuet, Scott, and especially Conrad. The French author's appeal to literary tradition as a way of crystallizing his own perceptions of an alien place parallels Mandelstam's invocation of the writings of Dante and Goethe as he strives to make the Soviet Armenia of 1930 a ground for Mandelstamian ethics and poetics.[13]

A second quality of the "Journey" is its markedly polemical and didactic cast. In this respect, the Armenian material has a heuristic function in the poet's staking out of his aesthetic and ethical position. His reaction to a swarm of fireflies performing a dance of death in the section headed "Suxum" typifies the continual alternation between the rhetoric of perception and the rhetoric of argument and persuasion:

> Once I saw a Dance of Death, the Wedding Dance of tiny phosphorescent insects. It seemed at first as if dots of light from tiny wandering cigarettes were flashing, but their flourishes were too daring, free, and bold.
>
> The devil only knows what they were up to!
>
> Coming closer: Electrified, frenzied ephemera were blinking and twitching, tracing and devouring the black bestseller [*černoe čtivo*] of the present moment.
>
> Our solid, heavy bodies will evanesce in the same way, and our actions will turn into the same wild tumult of senseless signals, if we do not leave behind us substantial proofs of being.
>
> It is frightening to live in a world that consists only of exclamations and interjections! (II, 158)

To a certain extent, this polemical quality is generated by the device of presenting parts of the text as an imaginary dialogue between the poet and his biologist friend B. S. Kuzin, whom Mandelstam first met in Armenia: "With these belated reflections, B. S., I hope to make it up to you, if only in part, for having interfered with your chess game in Erevan." However, the device of the absent interlocutor suggests that the first audience for the writer's arguments and interpretations is Mandelstam himself. In other words, the "Journey to Armenia" has a noticeable undercurrent of auto-communication.[14] In his ongoing process of authorial self-creation, Mandel-stam in 1930, having exorcised the demons of the Writers' Union in "Fourth Prose" and having affirmed his own integrity as a writer and a Jew, needed to elaborate a voice and a vision that would be potent against the destructive force of the Cultural Revolution, now in full flood.[14] The appeal to a quasi-scientific vocabulary that draws upon contemporary trends in biology and physiology is part of this enterprise. Although this rhetorical move reaches its fruition in the thirties (e.g., the injunction in the *Conversation About Dante* "Poetry, be envious of crystallography!"), it has its origins in the somewhat more playful use of geological and botanical subcodes in *The Noise of Time*. When Mandelstam assimilates the world-view of Tjutčev to that of Kautsky in "The Erfurt Program," he is hinting at a mode of "scientific" knowledge that includes both aesthetic perception and "scientific socialism." In the "Journey" he is using the language of the life sciences to explode Stalinism's claims to authoritativeness as a scientific approach to reality.

In 1930 such a position could hardly be taken openly in a piece which, unlike "Fourth Prose," was written for publication. In the "Journey" for the first time, at least in the literary prose, the semantic poetics takes on an explicitly hermetic cast, figured in a tripartite formula Mandelstam ascribes to the closing of Armenian folktales: "Three apples fell from heaven: the first apple is for the one who told the tale, the second for the one who listened to it, and the third for the one who understood it." In context this formula hints at two audiences, only one of which receives the text's full esoteric meaning. Here Mandelstam's discourse seems to ally itself with the Russian tradition of "Aesopian language," meant to convey one kind of meaning to the profane and another to the initiated. However a passage from one of Mandelstam's letters suggests that the language of the "Jour-ney" is meant to have a performative edge, to actually elicit the illumination of the model reader:

> My little book states that the eye is a device for thinking, that light is a force, and that ornament is thought. It is converned with friendship, science, and intellectual passion, and not with "things."
> One should always be making journeys, not just to Armenia and Tadjiki-stan. The greatest satisfaction for an artist is to set into motion those who think and feel differently than he himself. (III, 169)

This series of propositions corresponds to three major themes of Mandel-stam's text: vision, the poet's friendship with Kuzin and his circle, and the theme of journeying, literally and figuratively. In speaking of ornament as thought and placing "vešči," 'things,' in quotation marks, Mandelstam is also taking a stand in favor of ornamental prose in the face of calls for an unadorned and concrete style—"vešči" in this acceptation being a late Formalist catchword.

Every page of the "Journey" reveals a concern with vision, with its re-awakening, and with the regeneration of the senses and the spirit. The eye is a "device for thinking," not simply because visual representations can be the basis for mental ones, but because the vision about which Mandelstam is writing is a contemplative process that involves the mind in what the eye sees. In "The French," a chapter whose immediate subject is the paintings of the Impressionists and Neo-Impressionists, Mandelstam breaks down the process of viewing a painting into three stages. The first stage is a brief glance, serving as a trial immersion to acquaint the eye with a new visual medium (*sreda*). The second viewing aims at detaching the painting from the surrounding reality, with which, "like any object," it is connected. This stage seems to be analogous to the reader's suppression of consciousness of a poem's concrete addressee, a procedure the young Mandelstam had advocated in "On the Addressee" as a means of enhancing the poem's properties as an aesthetic communication. Finally, in the third stage, a direct confrontation with the idea of the painting ("očnaja stavka s zamy-slom") takes place. Albeit in a less formalized manner, these stages of contemplation operate throughout the "Journey" to turn the visual (*zritel'noe*) into a property of the imagination (*umozritel'noe*).

Sila, "force," in the expression "light is a force" belongs to a semantic group that is important for the "Journey." Forming part of the Neo-Lamarckian subcode, this group also includes such terms as *tjaga, pritjaže-nie, silovoe pole, silovoe natjaženie,* and *temperaturnye volny*: "pull," "gravi-tation," "field of force," "tension field," and "temperature waves." Lamarck seems to have provided Mandelstam with a new metaphor for his concern with the prospects for human freedom. As Mandelstam portrays him (in "Around the Naturalists" and the lyric "Lamarck"), Lamarck is not so much an experimental scientist as a moralist, a "fighter for the honor of Nature." What attracted the poet in Lamarckian biology was the dignity and auton-omy that it confers upon nature: "Hence for its environment the organism is a matter of probability, desirability, and expectation. For the organism the environment is a force that invites; not so much an envelope as a chal-lenge; (II, 164). Light, taken in this context, is a force that functions as just such a creative "challenge" (*vyzov*) to the "organism"-observer.

Mandelstam's Lamarck takes on the characteristics of an ideal reader of nature, an observer whose approach to his subject matter resembles the manner in which the "poetically literate reader" in Mandelstam's criticism responds to the discontinuities of the literary text. As indicated by the second and third passages quoted below, this resemblance is even stronger in the draft version of "Journey to Armenia," where both Lamarckian biology and the prose narrative are said to be centrally concerned with the intervals in the respective series, i.e., evolution and extratextual reality (*dejstvitel'nost'*), upon which they reflect:

1.   Lamarck is sensitive to the gaps between classes. He hears the pauses and syncopations in the evolutionary series. (II, 164)

2.   Lamarck is sensitive to the *gaps* between classes. (These are the intervals in the evolutionary series. The voids gape.) He hears the syncopations and pauses in the evolutionary series. (III, 161; Mandelstam's emphasis.)

3.   Reality has an uninterrupted character

      The prose that corresponds to it . . . always forms a discontinuous series . . . Hence the prose narrative is not other than a discontinuous sign of the continuous . . . (it is concerned only with the intervals) . . . (III, 166-67)

These passages offer an implicit critique of that "naive realism" which would finally congeal as Socialist realism. The literary text and the 'text' observed by the naturalist become analogues of each other; the "gaping voids," "syncopations," and "pauses" in the evolutionary series are paralleled by the intervals and disjunctions of the literary text. The intervals confronted by the naturalist and the ideal reader generate tension fields to which each must adapt; each, in his own way, faces the challenge of "restoring the missing signs," as Mandelstam put it in "Vypad."

The idea that "ornament is thought" anticipates the reflections in the "Conversation About Dante" on ornament as a product that "preserves the traces of its own origins." It is to be understood within the context of the neo-Lamarckian current in the "Journey" as well. In the course of his imaginary dialogue with Kuzin (in "Zamoskvoreče") Mandelstam contemptuously dismisses the writer M. E. Kozakov to the seventh circle of Dante's Inferno because Kozakov has offered a public recantation for the fault of having been an "Ornamentalist" (II, 154). The reference to Kozakov is interposed in the midst of Mandelstam's reflections on the process of growth in nasturtium petals. These reflections include the following definition of growth:

A plant is a sound, elicited by the wand of a theremin, cooing in a sphere that is oversaturated with wave processes. It is the emissary of a living storm, permanently raging in the universe, equally akin to stone and to lightning. A plant in the world—is an event, an occurrence, an arrow, and not boring, bearded "development." (II, 154)

Here teleology and freedom are brought into harmony; growth is understood not as something that is compelled but as something that is "elicited" (*izlečennyj*).

Hence to be an "Ornamentalist" is to align oneself with the principle of growth (*rost*), according to which all organisms are viewed as capable of free responses to their environment. It is this conception of growth, resembling a cybernetic feedback process, that Mandelstam opposes to the idea of "development" (*razvitie*) or "progress," according to which change in the human and natural realms are *determined* by the environment. The Ornamentalist writer, then, selects and combines his raw materials (to continue the textile analogy from the "Conversation About Dante") in such a way that the reader will, in Mandelstam's phrase, be "set into motion," establishing his or her own connections among the elements of the text. "Ornament" in this sense becomes both the product of thought and a stimulus to it.

When the poet in his letter speaks of "friendship, science, and intellectual passion," he is referring, in the first instance, to his friendship with Kuzin, who started Mandelstam reading the naturalists (Lamarck, Linnaeus, Buffon, Pallas, Darwin) and who seems to have rekindled the poet's interest in German literature.[15] The chapter title "Around the Naturalists" therefore refers both to the classics about whom the poet is writing and to the circle of scientists with whom he became acquainted through Kuzin. The influence of Kuzin can also be seen in the references to Goethe that appear in both the draft and published versions of "Journey to Armenia." It is illustrative of Mandelstam's tendency to find a common motivation in the intellectual and artistic productions of an epoch that the main references to Goethe's works (*Wilhelm Meister* in the final version and *Italienische Reise* in the draft variant) should associate the German author with the theme of the traveler-naturalist.

Mandelstam's works and letters, as well as his wife's reminiscences, make it clear that "friendship, science, and intellectual passion" were qualities that the poet sorely missed in Moscow. "Journey to Armenia" suggests that one of the restorative functions that the trip South fulfilled was to provide the poet with evidence that, at least on the peripheries of the Soviet state, human decency was still an abundant quality. The episode of the chemist Gambarian's heart attack and its aftermath is a vivid example. Here is how Mandelstam describes the reaction of onlookers to the rescue of the stricken man: "It was the most splendid applause I had ever heard in my life: a man was being saluted for still being alive" (II, 141-42).

The injunction "One should always be making journeys" hints that Mandelstam's travels in Armenia and Georgia are not the only journeys with which his work is concerned. In this context, the idea of travel takes on the quality of metaphor for any sustained and independent act of thought, vision, and imagination. "Journey to Armenia" is as much concerned with Mandelstam's vicarious participation in Kuzin's travels as it is with his own. While he addresses Kuzin as if he expected to join him in Armenia, Mandelstam was apparently convinced that he would never be permitted to return there.[16] Thus one form of 'journey' is the fantasy of returning to the South.

In "The French" Mandelstam speaks of the "traveller-eye" (*putešestvennik-glaz*), which delivers to the consciousness the "diplomatic credentials" (*posol'skie gramoty*) it has carried back from its successful "entry" (*vxožde-nie*) into a painting. *Glaz* here is a synecdoche which stands for the complex "eye-mind-object of vision and intelligence." Looking at the works of French painters is treated as a form of travel that is analogous to a Southern journey—an analogy that enables Mandelstam to pass smoothly from his meditations on the Black Sea to his impressions of the painters. That the works of the Impressionists and their successors were evocative of Southern associations in Mandelstam can be judged from his response to Paul Signac's *From Eugene Delacroix to Neo-Impressionism*: "Signac sounded the call to arms for the final, mature gathering of Impressionists. Into clear camps he called Zouaves, burnooses, and the red skirts of Algerian women . . . It seemed to me as if I had exchanged my hoof-shaped and dusty city shoes for light Muslim slippers" (II, 145).

Like the ancient geographers he calls the best writers of the classical world, Mandelstam's natural scientists are indefatigable travelers; like the painters, they are also artists who can set their readers off on journeys of the intellect and the imagination. In the same vein, Kuzin, their spiritual heir, is depicted as a Gumilevian New Adam, at home anywhere, familiar with distant places, and capable of doing his research "on the run" (*na xodu*).

All of Mandelstam's 'travels' have the same object. They are all pilgrimages in search of healing for the soul and renewal for the senses. Thus, for example, contemplation of the Black Sea is metaphorized as bathing the eye in an eye-cup "so that every mote and tear comes out of it" (II, 159). In the draft version, healing is also said to be a goal of art: "By nature the artist is a doctor, a healer. But if he heals no one, to whom and for what is he needed?" (III, 159). Signac's theory of painting ("the law of optical fusion," *zakon optičeskoj smesi*) is said to have the power of "invigorating and strengthening the nerves" ("bodrjaščaja i ukrepljaščaja nervy") (II, 145)—an effect which is reminiscent of the lesson drawn from the example set by the Armenians: ". . . Look lively, don't fear your time, don't be devious" (". . . ty *bodrstvueš*, ne bojsja svoego vremeni, ne lukav" [II, 143]).

Reading the great naturalists is said to have a similarly restorative influence: "Reading the systematizing naturalists (Linneaus, Buffon, Pallas) has a splendid influence on the condition of the senses, steadies the glance, and imparts a mineral, quartz calm to the soul" (II, 162). This blend of physiological and geological motifs suggests that Mandelstam conceives this process of healing and renewal as a Lamarckian adaptation to the texts in question.

The section headed "Sevan," which begins the "journey," implies that it is not only reading that can stimulate this adaptive and regenerative process. As a result of the atmosphere of expectation (*ožidanie*) which is said to be characteristic of life on any island, "the helix of the ear becomes very attenuated and acquires a new coil" (II, 140). Later the accommodation of the eye to the "climate" of a painting is presented in a similar manner. The eye is described as a "noble but stubborn animal" whose adjustment to the "material environment" of a painting is much more a matter of "internal secretion" i.e., of physiological adaptation, than of "apperception," which Mandelstam glosses as "external perception" (*vnešnoe vosprijatie* [II, 161]).

The representation of healing and renewal as a neo-Lamarckian process culminates in the last two chapters, which treat Mandelstam's travels in the vicinity of Ararat, his ascent of Mt. Alagez, and his attempts to learn the Armenian language. Both the language and the mountains exert a similar "attraction" (*tjaga, pritjaženie*) upon him:

1.   The Armenian language is wearproof, a pair of boots made of stone. Well, of course: thick-walled words, layers of air in the semivowels. But does all its charm consist in this? No! What is the source of its attraction? How can it be explained? Made sense of? (II, 170)

2.   I have developed in myself a sixth sense—an "Ararat" sense: a feeling of the gravitational pull exerted by a mountain. (II, 170)

For Mandelstam, the same forces "permanently raging in the universe" result in the metaphoric word-stone and the massive stoniness of a mountain; that the mountain in this instance is named Ararat is suggestive of another tie between word and mountain: both the geography and culture of Armenia are valued by Mandelstam for their links to Biblical history. Mandelstam's "sixth sense," moreover, is both the sensation caused by the pull of the mountain, and the aesthetic sixth sense of Gumilev's lyric—the 'attraction' exerted by a poem. A passage in which the contours of Alagez evoke yet another kind of *tjaga*, the "imperative verbal gravitation" of the Latin gerundive, "that which ought to be," provides another instance where language and geology meet. Since Mandelstam's example of the gerundive is rendered as "dolženstvujuščaja byt' xvalimoj," 'that which ought to be praised' it is apparent just where language and mountains converge: the mountain inspires a moral purposiveness. It is the emblem of those Armenian influences which reawaken the senses and inspire moral firmness, imparting what Mandelstam called in his drafts "zvukoodetost', kamennokrovnost' i tverdokamennost'" (III, 168). Translated by Jane Gary Harris as "total immersion in sound, steadfastness, and vigor," this string of neologisms has the literal meanings of 'sound-clothedness,' 'stone-bloodedness,' and 'firm-stoniness.'

The significance of the Armenian journey is summed up in the adaptation of the Armenian historical legend of Arshak and Shapuh that is inserted just before the end of the text. The first eight verses catalog the deprivation of the senses suffered by the imprisoned King Arshak. The next several verses describe King Shapuh's campaign against the Kushani people, and the conduct by which the eunuch Darmastat distinguishes himself during the fighting. The fifteenth verse takes up the theme of Arshak's evil fortune: "Yesterday he was king, today he has fallen into a crack; he is doubled over in the womb like a baby. He warms himself with lice and takes pleasure in scratching" (II, 176). The contrast between past and present parallels a line of No. 218, written during Mandelstam's stay in Tbilisi: "Persons were we; now we're mere personnel" ("Byli my ljudi, a stali ljud'e"). The king's tribulations also bring those of Parnok, "thrown into a crevice in the granite of Petersburg," to mind. Thus it is tempting to see what Nadezhda Mandelstam calls a "hidden self-disclosure" ("skrytoe avtopriznanie") in the representation of Arshak.

In the seventeenth and final verse, Darmastat asks a reward for his valor: "I would like Arshak to spend one more day[17] full of sounds, tastes, and smells . . . ." This wish is very close to a thought in Mandelstam's drafts, where he gives as the goal of his visit a search for the sensuous: "In May of 1930 I made my way with a straw basket to Yerevan/to a foreign country, in order to feel with my eyes its cities and graves, to take in the sounds of its speech, and to breathe for a time its highly difficult and noble historical atmosphere/" (III, 149). Sensuous pleasure, in this statement, becomes a component of the most rarefied spiritual experiences; for Mandelstam, Armenia's sounds, tastes, and smells afforded a physical and moral palliative to the effects of the oppressive atmosphere of Moscow. A palliative and not an antidote: If there is an idyllic quality to "Journey to Armenia," its pleasures, as in any idyll, pertain to a foreign place and an alien condition, marked by its remoteness from the situation of the poet and his readers, whether Alexandrian or Muscovite. Shaped by the terrors it seeks to escape, it is not only concerned with "that which ought to be" but with a reality which ought not to be. Hence it is, as Sidney Monas puts it, also "a vision of the end."[18]

The work's generic affinities, as well as its rhetorical qualities, can be elucidated by juxtaposing Mandelstam's "Journey" with another, called to mind by the very title of Mandelstam's text: Pushkin's *Journey to Erzerum*. Superficial similarities abound: both poets were looking for a respite from governmental interference in their creative and personal lives; in traveling south, both were returning to regions associated in their writings with freedom, with the legacy of the classical world, and with the Biblical world; Mandelstam's travels took him to places mentioned in Pushkin's account: the Caucasus, Georgia (both spent time in Tbilisi), and Armenia (both travelled in the vicinity of Ararat).

However, it is easier to make a case for possible allusions to *Journey to Erzerum* in Mandelstam's Armenian lyrics than in "Journey to Armenia." Thus in No. X of the Armenian cycle, Mandelstam mentions the *Kurdiny*, a mountain tribe that has ". . . reconciled God and the devil/ Rendering to each their half." In their religious views, these tribesmen remind the reader of Pushkin's *jazydy* (mentioned in the third chapter of "Journey to Erzerum"), who worship God but do not curse the devil. Although the goal of Pushkin's journey is mentioned twice in Mandelstam's lyrics, it appears there under the modern spelling of "Erzerum," and not in the obsolete form used by Pushkin, "Arzrum."

Despite the weakness of such echoes, there is still reason to see an implicit dialogue with Pushkin in "Journey to Armenia" and to seek additional meanings in Mandelstam's work by juxtaposing it with Pushkin's . Indeed, the very scarcity of Pushkinian echoes in a work whose setting includes regions associated with Pushkin and whose author so revered Pushkin seems significant. It invites conjecture as to why this should be the case.

Differences in the conception of literary prose and—more narrowly—in the literary-polemical content implicit in the two texts may well account for the lack of overt references to the earlier "Journey" in the later one. Thus where Pushkin's work seems to be directed against the "poetic" ornamental prose of such writers as Chateaubriand and Marlinskij, Mandelstam's explicitly "ornamental" prose takes aim at literary parallels to what he calls "the harmless plague of naive realism" in the graphic arts. In this connection, Mandelstam's claim that "ornament is thought" can be read (with the emphasis on the copula) as a response to Pushkin's position on the primacy of thought in prose and to the exclusion of ornamental devices which, in Pushkin's view, this primacy entailed. The spareness of Pushkin's prose gives rise to a distinctive prose rhythm. As A. Z. Ležnev has pointed out, the basic rhythmic unit is the brief, unadorned subject-predicate phrase, groups of which follow one another in rapid succession. Sequences of such short phrases alternate with relatively more complex sentence structures, which, in turn, are succeeded by a balanced cadence, which resolves the whole development.[19] Examples of such rhythmico-semantic blocks tend to be found in their purest form in sections of *Journey to Erzerum* that treat the activity of travel:

> The moon was shining; everything was quiet; only the hoofbeats of my horse resounded in the nocturnal silence. I rode for a long time, not meeting with any signs of habitation. Finally I saw a solitary hut. I started knocking on the door. The owner came out. I asked for some water, first in Russian and then in Tatar. He didn't understand me. What wonderful unconcern! Thirty versts from Tiflis and on the road to Persia and Turkey, he knew not a single word in Russian or in Tatar.[20]

The opening sentence-paragraph of "Journey to Armenia" provides an obvious contrast to the syntax, rhythm, and semantics of Pushkin's prose:

> On the island of Sevan, which is distinguished by two most worthy architectural monuments of the seventh century, as well as by the dugouts of lice-ridden hermits who had recently died off, thickly overgrown with nettles and thistles and no more frightening than the cellars of abandoned dachas, I spent a month, enjoying the stillness of lake water at an altitude of four thousand feet and getting accustomed to contemplating some twenty to thirty tombs, scattered in the manner of flowerbeds amidst monastery dormitories that had been rejuvenated by renovation. (II, 137)

These two passages illustrate two different principles of syntagmatic progression: where Pushkin's prose presents a montage of ideas, arranged in grammatically discrete subject-predicate clauses, Mandelstam's prose is characterized by the elaboration and modulation of ideas within a single sentence.[21] Thus, for example, in the passage quoted above, the basic 'material,' "I spent a month on the island of Sevan," is elaborated through an accretion of epithets and subordinate clauses. The convoluted syntax surrounds and contains the grammatical subject "I" and offers an iconic parallel to the thematic significance of the sentence: Sevan as a geographical and cultural space which contains artifacts of great historical diversity (e.g., architectural monuments of the seventh century, dugouts of recently-deceased hermits), all in different stages of decay and renewal, and all as densely interconnected and commingled as the elements of the sentence itself. At the same time, Mandelstam's beginning thematizes the author's situation. His persona is caught in a force field of heterogeneous styles, ranging from the diction of guidebooks (e.g., "Sevan . . . is distinguished by two most worthy architectural monuments of the seventh century"), to something suggestive of the language of Soviet-style militant atheism ("the dugouts of lice-ridden hermits who had recently died off"), to the language of autobiographical reminiscence ("no more frightening than the cellars of abandoned dachas"). As these examples suggest, the clashing diction also emphasizes the writer's suspension between past and present, foreign and native, pleasure and fear.

While this passage is of more than average complexity, it is not unrepresentative, for it only exaggerates the ornamental style of the text as a whole. Because it opens the work, it can be said to announce that style and to indicate the texture of what is to follow. In this respect, while "Journey to Armenia" belongs to the same line as *The Egyptian Stamp*, there seems to be a shift in the choice of leading devices from the fragment to the ornament. Where the implicit author of the earlier work declares "I am not afraid of incoherence and gaps," his counterpart in "Journey to Armenia" seeks to demonstrate the contention (not found in the text itself) that "ornament is thought."

CONCLUSION

Influenced by the semantic principles of his verse, Mandelstam's literary prose at its best has a richness of meaning that is equal to anything in the Russian tradition. Yet it must be remembered that, for all its fascination, Mandelstam's prose was a minor activity in comparison with his verse. Nadezhda Mandelstam's comments on the creative history of her husband's works, as well as D. M. Segal's insights into the texts themselves, suggest that Mandelstam used prose as a writer's workshop in which he could reassess his values and experiment with his language. In trying to establish a perspective on Mandelstam's literary prose, it must be borne in mind that these four brief pieces, occupying a total of only 158 pages in the *Collected Works*, were written over a period of only eight years in a literary career that spanned roughly thirty.

Yet these eight years were a period of major turmoil in the poet's life. They coincided with the spiritual crisis of the mid-twenties and with the prolonged poetic silence, lasting until the fall of 1930, which was associated with it. 1928 saw the publication of three books by Mandelstam (*On Poetry, The Egyptian Stamp*, and *Verses*), yet it was also the year in which the Ulenspiegel affair began. Although Nadezhda Mandelstam mentions the years 1922-26 as the worst period in her husband's life, it seems clear that the poet's personal crisis was not resolved until the winter of 1929-30 (the period during which "Fourth Prose" was written). The "Journey to Armenia" may be taken as evidence that the months of travel that followed strengthened Mandelstam's inner equilibrium, to that extent that such a thing was possible under the conditions in which the poet lived his last decade.

In Mandelstam's postrevolutionary verse and prose the border between literature and extratextual reality is an open one. His prose reflects the evolution of his attempt to come to grips with his increasingly isolated literary and personal position. Thus Mandelstam's literary prose contains evidence of 'growth' in the sense in which this term is used in "Journey to Armenia." This process of change underlies the variations in what Mandelstam would call the "stylistic conception" (*stilističeskaja mysl'*) embodied in each piece. The evolving image of the implicit author is also a sign of this growth.

As mentioned earlier, there is an obvious change in the style of Mandelstam's prose from *The Noise of Time* to *The Egyptian Stamp*. The question arises as to why, apart from a brief outline for a story to be called "The Bassoonist," there was no real continuation of *The Egyptian Stamp*, which remained his only venture in the realm of narrative fiction. The probable answer is that after 1928, fiction in the manner of Mandelstam's tale would have been unpublishable; "Fourth Prose" was written 'for the drawer,' while "Journey to Armenia" contains a nod in the direction of the journalistic sketch (*očerk*). Yet in "Journey to Armenia" Mandelstam also seems to take a stand with the out-of-favor Ornamentalists. As the most self-consciously ornamental of the four literary "proses," "Journey" perhaps hints at what Mandelstam's program would have been had he continued his experiment with literary prose.

In Mandelstam's prose, changes in the author's attitude towards his own creativity are signalled by shifts in the intentions (the "stylistic impulses" referred to above) achieved in successive texts, and also by changes in the leading motifs that serve as emblems for the authorial persona. In *The Noise of Time* the dominant intention realized by the text is the distancing (*otstranenie*) of the past, which is linked to the attempt to resolve the tension between Jewish and Russian elements in the narrator's cultural legacy. Consonant with this focus on the past, the narrator's memory is his chief emblem. The theme of biculturalism is also important in *The Egyptian Stamp* but there it is subordinated to "prosaic delirium." In keeping with both the quality of this threat and the manner in which it is met, the metonymic attributes that are emblematic of the implicit author of the tale are his insubordinate pen and the disjointed manuscript which it produces.

The idea of "prosaic delirium" is closely bound up with the conception of the world of natural and cultural objects as so many texts. Although the affirmation of a continuity between writing and the world is a trait that runs throughout Mandelstam's *oeuvre*, his prose—after *The Egyptian Stamp*—reveals a decided shift in the connotative value of this relationship. In *The Noise of Time* and, still more obviously, in *The Egyptian Stamp*, the conversion of other forms of experience into texts has overtones that seem to be symptomatic of illness, of a diminished self-control and a weakened capacity for experiencing life. When the narrator of Mandelstam's novella admits to a confusion between books and things, the pathos of his declaration is expressive of a conflict he has inherited from both the *raznočincy* and his Jewish forebears, the "people of the Book." The manner in which extratextual experience is assimilated here to reading suggests a split between thought and action that is irreconcilable.

In "Fourth Prose" writing is represented as the characteristic activity of the despised and alien tribe of litterateurs. Accordingly, the voice replaces the pen and the text in the metonymic representation of the implicit author, while the theme of extratextual experience as 'writing' is absent. The organizing intention achieved by the work is the narrator's affirmation of his private values and his rejection of the values and concerns of "Literature." Both the Jewish and the *raznočinec* traditions reinforce each other in a positive manner in the conception of the implicit author as a literary "outlaw." When the theme of nature as a text returns in "Journey to Armenia," it is devoid of negative connotations, and the metaphoric equivalency of the two realms is expressive of a sense of harmony and unity between humanity and nature.

Implicit in the analogy between writing and tailoring in *The Egyptian Stamp*, the theme of the narrator's assessment of his own activity as labor (*trud*) becomes explicit in "Fourth Prose." Declaring that he would forbid litterateurs to have children, the author characterizes real work, in effect, as that which constitutes a tradition: "How can they have children—children, after all, must continue for us, must finish saying the main thing for us . . ." (II, 182). Subsequently he formulates a definition of genuine work that embraces his own activities as well as the work of those who are more narrowly defined as "workers" (*trudjaščiesja*): "Real work is Brussels lace;

the main thing in it is what supports the pattern: air, perforations, truancies" (II, 191). Characterizing labor as the interpolation of pattern upon emptiness, Mandelstam implicitly rejects the position that labor is genuine only insofar as it resembles industrial labor, whose output can be planned and measured. On the contrary, all varieties of work are viewed as genuine to the extent that they resemble his own art, with its characteristic tension between pattern and emptiness.

In "Journey to Armenia," Mandelstam returns to the theme of work in relation to posterity, for example, in his reflections on the fate of human activity prompted by the fireflies' dance. He seems to put behind himself the question of the values of his own work as "substantial proofs of being" when he affirms that "Every kind of labor is deserving of respect" (II, 148)

This statement suggests what is at stake in the "Journey." Mandelstam's account of his travels is his most joyous prose work and—in its concern with "that which ought to be praised"—his most openly didactic. In keeping with its emphasis on the importance of vision for teaching that "life is a precious and inalienable gift" (II, 167), the motif of the eye is its leading emblem for the implicit author.

"Journey to Armenia" conveys intimations of a harmony hitherto unattained in Mandelstam's prose. In many respects, however, this harmonious outlook suggests a return to the vision embodied in his works from before the years of artistic crisis. While there is growth in the image of the implicit author in Mandelstam's literary prose, the mutable elements of his vision fit into a a larger framework which is remarkably stable and self-consistent. One is struck by the extent to which Mandelstam returns in the 1931 "Journey" to the imagery and concerns of his 1922 essay *On the Nature of the Word*. The 'neo-Lamarckian' aesthetics of the "Journey," for example, are simply a variation of the "organic poetics" of the earlier piece, in which Mandelstam treats Acmeism as an attempt to give poetics a biological basis. The reconciliation of man and nature, as well as the sacralization of everyday life which is part of this reconciliation, is a theme found in both texts. When the author of the "Journey" expresses a longing to return to Armenia, "where human skulls are equally splendid in the coffin and at work" (II, 147), his thought conveys the same humane ideal as the anti-Symbolist polemics of his early criticism.

Mandelstam's concern for the fate of philology is at once the most important constant of his literary prose and its most important link to his earlier verse and criticism. In *The Noise of Time*, respect for the poetic word as the bearer of tradition and model of potential freedom is associated with the figure of V. V. Gippius. The threat of a catastrophic break in the continuity of culture is much stronger in *The Egyptian Stamp*, where the agent of philology's survival is "prosaic delirium"—an idea that is not free of a pathological residue, despite attempts to find antecedents for it in the prose of Tolstoj and Dostoevskij. The new stress on the oral, rather than the written word in "Fourth Prose" seems to be motivated in part by the disrepute into which the written word, in Mandelstam's view, has fallen; "Literature" appears to have hopelessly compromised the position of "Mother Philology" in Soviet Russia.

The condition of the philological spirit seems much improved in "Journey to Armenia." In Mandelstam's account of his journey, the renewal of the senses is complemented by a revival of the awareness of language as the embodiment of tradition and avatar of human freedom. It is Mandelstam's exposure to classical and modern Armenian which is represented as the main stimulus to this revival. By using terms like "wearproof," "stone boots," and "thick-walled words" as metaphoric correlates for Armenian, Mandelstam endows it with the same materiality and durability which he had ascribed to the Russian language in *On the Nature of the Word* and his other critical pieces.

In the course of this study, Mandelstam's literary prose has, at times, been viewed as the locus of an attempt to transfer the dominant of prose from its traditional centers in plot or character to a new center in language. In the last analysis, however, language is not the hero of Mandelstam's experiment. On this point, as on many others, the prose tends to corroborate the evidence yielded by Mandelstam's criticism and verse. His deepest concerns as a writer are not linguistic but moral. He cherished the ideal of language which he portrayed with the aid of the metaphor of "Hellenism" because he hoped that language, understood in this way, could keep alive the tradition that humanity is called to be master in its own house.

NOTES

INTRODUCTION

1. Nadezhda Mandelstam, *Vospominanija* (N. Y.: Chekhov Press, 1971). See especially the chapter entitled "Pereocenka cennostej," pp. 177-87.

2. All references to Mandelstam's works are based on *Osip Mandelstam: Sobranie sočinenij*, ed. G. P. Struve and B. A. Filipoff, 2d ed., 3 vols. (N. Y.: Inter-Language Literary Associates, 1971); vol. 4 (Paris: YMCA Press, 1981). Except for notes on publication history, all references will be included in the text.

3. Nadezhda Mandelstam, *Vospominanija*, pp. 177-78.

4. Letter to the Federation of Soviet Writers, first published in *Vestnik russkogo xristianskogo dviženija*, No. 120, pp. 246-47; rpt. in *Sobranie sočinenij*, IV, 127.

5. In "Puškin i Skrijabin," originally a paper presented to the Religious and Philosophical Society in 1913.

6. Dmitrij M. Segal, "The Connection Between Semantics and the Formal Structure of a Text," *Mythology*, ed. Pierre Maranda (Middlesex, England: Penguin, 1972), pp. 215-49.

7. In the discussion of literary prose, I am drawing upon Roman Jakobson's model of language functions and the communications network, as presented in his "Concluding Statement: Linguistics and Poetics," *Style in Language*, ed. Thomas A. Sebeok (N. Y.: M.I.T. Press and John Wiley & Sons, 1960), pp. 350-57.

8. O. Mandelstam, "Egipetskaja marka," *Zvezda*, Leningrad, May 1928, pp. 51-76; rpt. in book form by the Leningrad publishing house "Priboj," 1928; rpt. in *Sobranie sočinenij*, 11, 5-42.

9. O. Mandelstam, *Šum vremeni* (Leningrad: "Vremja," 1925); rpt. in *Egipetskaja marka* (Leningrad: "Priboj," 1928) and in *Sobranie sočinenij*, II 45-108.

10. O. Mandelstam, "Četvertaja proza," *Sobranie sočinenij*, II, 177-92.

11. O. Mandelstam, "Putešestvie v Armeniju," *Zvezda*, No. 5 (1933), pp. 103-125; rpt. in *Sobranie sočinenij*, II, 137-76.

CHAPTER I

1. Other major poets of Jewish or partly Jewish descent are Boris Pasternak and Vladislav Xodasevič. Also prominent among the "newcomers" are women poets (Zinaida Gippius, Anna Akhmatova, Marina Cvetaeva) and poets from the peasantry (Sergej Esenin, Nikolaj Kljuev).

2. Clarence Brown, *Mandelstam* (Cambridge, England: Cambridge University Press, 1973), p. 9.

3. In her reminiscences of Mandelstam, Anna Akhmatova confirms the fact reported by Georgij Ivanov in *Peterburgskie zimy* (Paris: Rodnik, 1928; p. 117-18) that Mandelstam visited Warsaw during the war years. She adds that the ghetto made a strong impression on him. (Anna Akhmatova, *Sočinenija*, vol. 2 [Munich: Inter-Language Literary Associates, 1968], p. 170).

4. One source of ambiguity here is an eschatological undercurrent that seizes upon the bleak conditions in postrevolutionary Petersburg, e.g., the absence of food, shelter and clothing, and tries to make a positive virtue of them: 'Having lost everything, we have attained inner freedom.' But there are also the two contrasting ways in which the relationship between culture and faith can be construed: 'genuine culture requires adherence to Christianity' vs. 'the situation of the cultured person is analogous to that of the Christian.' However, the metaphorical equation of culture with church, cultured individual with monk, undercuts the first reading. The whole passage can therefore be read as growing out of the kernel, 'culture has become the

new faith.' Mandelstam's paradox brings to mind the complementary claim voiced a few years later by Marina Cvetaeva: "In this our most Christian of worlds, all the poets are Yids! (Cvetaeva uses the pejorative *židy* in place of the neutral *evrei*, "Jews," to emphasize the common status of poets and Jews as pariahs.)

5. Lidija Ginzburg, "Poetika Osipa Mandeľstama," *Izvestija Akademii nauk SSSR, Serija literatury i jazyka*, vol. 31, part 4 (1972), p. 309.

6. Nadezhda Mandelstam, *Vospominanija*, p. 281.

7. Omry Ronen, "Mandelshtam, Osip Emilyevich," in *Encyclopeia Judaica Yearbook*, 1973, p. 295.

8. The motif of the homeland that will not recognize the poet-son appears to be a commonplace of the Russian-Jewish verse of Mandelstam's mother's generation. Cf. the opening of a lyric by M. Abramovič, quoted in V. Lvov-Rogačevskij, *Russko-evrejskaja literatura* (Moscow, 1922), p. 104 (emphasis in the original):

> *Isxoda net.* Sražen, porugan
> Moj padšij bog-otec-narod;
> Otčiznu-mať zovu ispugan,
> No syna mať ne priznaet.

> *There is no Exodus!* Crushed and profaned
> Is my fallen god, father, people;
> In fright I call to the Homeland-Mother*
> But the mother will not acknowledge her son.
> *literally "Fatherland-Mother"!

9. Nadezhda Mandelstam, *Vtoraja kniga* (Paris: YMCA Press, 1972), p. 56.

10. Clarence Brown, *The Prose of Osip Mandelstam*, pp. 55-56. A. K. Zholkovsky, "Invarianty i struktura teksta, II. Mandelstam: 'Ja pju za voennye astry'," *Slavica Hierosolymitana*, 4 (Jerusalem: The Magnes Press, 1979), p. 161.

11. There is something of a precedent for the use of a lullaby for ironic purposes in Nekrasov's "Kolybeľnaja pesnja" (1845), itself a parody of Lermontov's "Kazačja kolybeľnaja pesnja" (1840).

12. Sergej Bobrov, *Pečať i revoljucija*, 4 (Moscow, 1923), p. 261.

13. Cf. Ju. I. Levin, D. M. Segal, R. D. Timenčik, V. N. Toporov, and T. V. Civjan, "Russkaja semantičeskaja poètika, kak potenciaľnaja kuľturnaja paradigma," *Russian Literature*, No. 7/8 (1974), p. 50:

> [Contemporary history] produces a vector opposed to the poet's conscious intention. Hence the tragic and dynamic tension between the creative process and what is actually created. At a certain stage of culture, this tension is actualized in the reader's perception, where a set of values takes shape that corresponds to the task which the poet sets himself in history.

14. According to Steven Boyde, *Osip Mandeľštam and His Age*, Harvard Slavic Monographs, No. 1 (Cambridge: Harvard University Press, 1975), p. 47, "Sumerki svobody" was originally subtitled a hymn. The triad "sun, judge, people" may represent a transformation of the traditional coronation hymn triad "sun, judge, king." Cf. V. V. Ivanov, "K tipologii drevnebližnevostočnyx gimnov solncu," in *Sbornik statej po vtoričnym modelirujuščim sistemam*, ed. Ju. M. Lotman (Tartu, 1973), p. 46.

15. If there are references to Agamemnon here, the leader's fatal burden may correspond to Agamemnon's putting on the "yoke of necessity."

16. Kiril Taranovsky, *Essays on Mandeľštam*, Harvard Slavic Studies, No. 6 (Cambridge: Harvard University Press, 1976), p. 61.

17. Ibid., p. 60.

18. Ibid., p. 34.

19. In his study of Mandelstam's lexicon ("O častotnom slovare poèta," *Russian Literature*, 2 1972, pp. 5-36), Ju. I. Levin points to a general shift in the poet's diction from the elevated, abstract, and spiritual to the democratic, concrete, and physical. Dmitrij Segal attributes an instrumental role in this shift to the literary prose. See Segal, "Voprosy poètičeskoj organizacii semantiki v proze Mandel'štama," p. 327.

20. Nadezhda Mandelstam, *Vospominanija*, p. 185.

21. Jane Gary Harris, "An Inquiry into the Use of Autobiography as a Stylistic Determinant of the Modernist Aspect of Osip Mandel'štam's Literary Prose," in *American Contributions to the Eighth International Congress of Slavists*, Vol. 2, Literature, ed. Victor Terras (Columbus: Slavica 1978), p. 240.

22. I have taken the term "structure of thought and feeling" from Raymond Williams, *The Country and the City* (New York: Oxford University Press, 1973). However, Williams uses it to emphasize those qualities of a text that reflect the social relations of the place and time in which it is produced, rather than shifts in the outlook of an individual writer.

23. The poet declares his allegiance to the *raznochintsy* in No. 144, "I Janvarja 1924 g.," where he refers to them as "the Fourth Estate."

24. In "Mandel'štam, poèticien formaliste?" (*Revue des Études Slaves*, Vol. 50, fasc. 1 Paris: 1977), Agnes Sola explores Mandelstam's relationship to formalism, tracing his attempt to develop his own theory of poetic language to its culmination in the polemical sections of the "Conversation About Dante."

25. The full title is "Literaturnaja Moskva. Roždenie fabuly," *Rossija*, No. 2, 1922, 26-27; rpt. in *Sobranie sočinenij*, II, 332-38.

26. *O poèzii*; rpt. in *Sobranie sočinenij*, II, 266-69.

27. Mandelstam may have been familiar with Dmitrij Merežkovskij's translation of *Daphnis and Chloe* (*Dafnis i Xloja. Drevne-grečeskaja povest' Longusa o ljubvi pastuška i pastuški na Ostrove Lezbose* St. Pbg.: M. V. Pirožkov, 1904). In his introductory essay, Merežkovskij describes *Daphnis and Chloe* as the first step toward the 19th century "psychological-romantic novel." With respect to the notion that the novel has its origins in a shift of focus to the fate of individuals, Mandelstam may be following A. N. Veselovskij, whose "Grečeskij roman" (rpt. in *Izbrannye stat'i*, Leningrad: "Xudožestvennaja literatura," 1939) traces such a development away from an original focus on the mythical and religious event.

28. The phrase is from O. Mandelstam, "Poèt o sebe," *Čitatel' i pisatel'*, No. 45 (1928), p. 3; rpt. in *Sobranie sočinenij*, II, 217.

29. Georg Lukács, "The Ideology of Modernism," *Realism in Our Time*, trans. John and Necke Mander (N. Y.: Harper and Row, 1971), pp. 17-46.

30. O. Mandelstam, "Devjatnadcatyj vek," *Gostinica dlja Putešestvujuščix v Prekrasnom*, No. 1 (1922), pp. 8-11; rpt. in *O poèzii* and in *Sobranie sočinenij*, II, 276-83. Jane Gary Harris, in *Mandelstam: The Complete Critical Prose and Letters* (Ann Arbor: Ardis, 1979), p. 624n, mentions Herzen's essay "Buddhism in Science" as an influence on Mandelstam's pejorative use of "Buddhism." Nadezhda Mandelstam (*Vospominanija*, p. 266) traces her husband's usage back to Vladimir Solov'ev. Cf. Solov'ev's "Buddistskoe nastroenie v poèzii" ("The Buddhist Tendency in Poetry") in V. S. Solov'ev, *Sobranie sočinenij*, vol. 7 (St. Pbg.: "Prosveščenie," 1907), pp. 81-89.

31. Translation quoted from Francis Steegmuller, *Flaubert and Madame Bovary*, 2nd rev. ed. (Boston: Houghton-Mifflin, 1966), p. 247.

32. O. Mandelstam, "Andrej Belyj. Zapiski čudaka. Tom II," *Krasnaja nov'*, No. 5 (1923) pp. 399-400; rpt. in *Sobranie sočinenij*, II, 421-24.

33. A partial inventory of terms designating this conflict in Mandelstam's writing would include not only "Buddhist" vs. "European" tendencies and genuine writing vs. "Literature," but also the "friends of the word" vs. its enemies; the philological vs. the antiphilological spirit; "vulgate" vs. "Latin" tendencies in the Russian language; the notions of growth (*rost*),

event (*sobytie*), abrupt displacement (*sdvig*) and being (*bytie*) vs. "progress" in a shallow, positivistic sense, the inertia of daily life (*byt*), and non-being (*nebytie*); and of "monumental" cultures that build *with* Man vs. humane cultures that build *for* Man.

34. O. Mandelstam, *O prirode slova* (Kharkov: 1922); rpt. in *O poèzii* and in *Sobranie sočinenij*, II, 241-59.

35. Clarence Brown, *Mandelstam* (Cambridge, England: Cambridge University Press, 1973), pp. 154-55.

36. Mandelstam uses "Hellenistic" as an epithet for the whole world of Greek antiquity rather than as a historical label for what Mikhail Rostovtseff, defining Hellenism for the 1904 edition of the Brokgauz-Efron Encyclopedia (vol. 80, pp. 651-55), called "the cultural and political formations that developed from the fusion of Greek and oriental elements" in the empire of Alexander the Great and its successor states.

37. Nadezhda Mandelstam, *Vtoraja kniga* (Paris: YMCA Press, 1972), pp. 562-63.

CHAPTER II

1. Nadezhda Mandelstam, *Vospominanija*, p. 260.

2. On the publication history of *Šum vremeni*, see Clarence Brown, *Mandelstam*, p. 101; N. Ja. Mandelstam, *Vospominanija*, pp. 118, 260; *Vtoraja kniga*, pp. 211, 221, 380-81, 482.

3. N. Ja. Mandelstam, *Vospominanija*, p. 178.

4. Andrej Belyj, *Kotik Letaev* (Petrograd: "Èpoxa," 1922).

5. Ibid., p. 142.

6. Cf. *Egipetskaja marka*, p. 11: "S detstva on prikrepljalsja dušoj ko vsemu nenužnomu, prevraščaja v sobytija tramvajnyj lepet žizni . . ."; lyric No. 283 ("Skaži mne, čertežnik pustyni"): "On opyt iz lepeta lepit"; "Razgovor o Dante": "Ešče čto menja porazilo,—èto infantiľnosť itaľjanskoj fonetiki, ee prekrasnaja detskosť, blizosť k mladenčeskomu lepetu, kakoj-to izvečnyj dadaizm."

7. N. Ja. Mandelstam, *Vtoraja kniga*, p. 130.

8. Gregor Aronson, "Jews in Russian Literary and Political Life," *Russian Jewry* 1860-1917, ed. Jacob Frumkin, Gregor Aronson, Alexis Goldenweiser, tr. Mirra Ginzburg (N.Y.: T. Yoseloff, 1966), pp. 253-254.

9. The Mandelstam family embodies several of the stereotypes of assimilationist fiction described by V. L'vov-Rogačevskij in *Russko-Evrejskaja literatura* (Moscow, 1922). The narrator's paternal grandparents are unenlightened "temnye ljudi," his father is a "Berliner," and his mother speaks the correct but lifeless Russian of the first assimilated generation. This last stereotype is also made use of by Babel, who describes the heroine of "Gjui de Mopassan" in these terms: "Benderskaja pisala utomiteľno praviľno, bezžiznenno i razvjazno—tak, kak pisali ranše evrei na russkom jazyke."

10. Demetrius J. Koubourlis, ed., *A Concordance to the Poems of Osip Mandelstam* (Ithaca: Cornell University Press, 1974).

11. N. Ja. Mandelstam, *Vospominanija*, p. 182.

12. Steven Broyde, *Osip Mandeľstam and His Age*, Harvard Slavic Monographs, No. 1 (Cambridge: Harvard University Press, 1975).

13. Kiril Taranovsky, *Essays on Mandeľstam*, pp. 44-45.

14. This motif is repeated twice on p. 97: "'Vojna i mir' prodolžalas' . . . 'Vojna i mir' prodolžaetsja."

15. See the discussion of Mandelstam's use of the metaphor of a planetary system on pages 39-40 of this study.

16. N. Berkovskij, "O Proze Mandeľštama," *Tekuščaja literatura* (Moscow: "Federacija," 1930), p. 160.

17. The treatment of the theme of music in *Šum vremeni* is paralleled by lyric No. 125, "Koncert na Vokzale" (1921), which also draws upon memories of the Pavlovsk concerts.

18. Other examples of this reductionist binary logic include: "U francuženok cenilos' iskusstvo mnogo i bystro govorit', u švejcarok—znanie pesenok . . ." (II, 54); "U menja vpečatlenie, čto mužčiny byli isključiteľno pogloščeny delom Drejfusa, denno i noščno, a ženščiny, to est' damy s bufami, nanimali i rasščityvali prislug . . ." (II, 47).

19. D. M. Segal, "Voprosy poètičeskoj organizacii semantiki v proze Mandeľštama," 'Problems in the Poetic Organization of Semantics in Mandelstam's Prose,' in Thomas Eekman and Dean Worth, eds., *Russian Poetics: Proceedings of the International Colloquium at UCLA, September 22-26, 1975* (Columbus: Slavica, 1983), pp. 342-44.

20. Lev Semenovič Vygotskij, *Myšlenie i reč* (Moscow: soc.-èkonomičeskoe izdateľstvo, 1934), rpt. 1956 (Moscow: Izd. akad. pedagogičeskix nauk). Vygotskij discusses "non-spontaneous concepts" (*nespontannye ponjatija*) in Ch. 6, "Issledovanie razvitija naučnyx ponjatij v detskom vozraste."

The epigraph to Ch. 7, "Mysľ i slovo" is taken—without attribution—from Mandelstam's "Ja slovo pozabyl" (No. 113).

21. Other examples include "intelligent," "učaščajasja molodež," "sgorel," and "èto" (II, 59-61).

22. This question transposes a quotation from the introduction to *Mednyj vsadnik*: "Ljublju voinstvennuju živosť/ Potešnyx Marsovyx polej/ Pexotnyx ratej i konej/ Odnoobraznuju krasivosť."

23. N. Ja. Mandelstam, *Vospominanija*, p. 185. The phrase is probably from "Utro Akmeizma": "Soznanie svoej pravoty nam dorože vsego v poèzii . . ." (II, 321).

CHAPTER III

1. For the publication history of *The Egyptian Stamp* see note 8 to the Introduction to this study.

2. Although he does not explain his use of these terms, Clarence Brown's references to *The Egyptian Stamp* as a 'novella' or a 'tale' seem to me to be justifiable on several grounds (see *The Prose of Osip Mandelstam*, pp. 32-33). 'Novella' suggests a form intermediate in scope and complexity between a short story and a novel, and in this acceptation it translates the Russian term *povesť*. But *povesť* also has the older meaning of 'tale'; hence it carries the suggestion of the place of Mandelstam's fiction in the tradition of the "Petersburg tale." It can be inferred from Mandelstam's own testimony that he considered his work to be a *povesť* in one or both of these senses. In a letter to the editorial assistant Korobova concerning the publication of *The Egyptian Stamp* in book form, Mandelstam concludes with the statement, "Vtoraja povesť v Zvezde *budet*" (II, 494; Mandelstam's emphasis). This second tale or novella must be either "Smerť Bozio," announced in *Zvezda* in 1929 and 1930, or the rejected story "Fagot" (see II, 497). The obvious implication is that *The Egyptian Stamp* is also a *povesť*, the first by Mandelstam to apppear in *Zvezda*. Finally, Cf. *The Egyptian Stamp* p. 40: "Strašno podumať, čto naša žizn'—èto povesť bez fabuly i geroja . . .", a statement which seems to apply to the text as well.

3. To the studies discussed here must now be added Daphne M. West's *Mandelstam: The Egyptian Stamp* (Birmingham, U. K.: Birmingham Slavonic Monographs, No. 10, 1980). In addition to providing a helpful analysis of the tale's structure, West discovers many echoes from Mandelstam's endeavors in the twenties. Her discussion of the links between the novella and the children's verse written by Mandelstam between 1924 and 1926 is very illuminating, as is her handling of allusions to Mandelstam's translations of Barbier.

4. N. Berkovskij, "O proze Mandeľštama," p. 161.

5. Ibid., p. 176 ff.

6. Ibid., p. 179.

7. Clarence Brown, *The Prose of Osip Mandelstam*.

8. Ibid., p. 55.

9. Brown, op. cit., p. 39.

10. V. Aleksandrova, in her article "Evrei v sovetskoj literature," (*Kniga o russkom evrejstve*, ed. Ja. G. Frumkin et al, Vol. 2 N. Y.: [Sojuz russkix evreev, 1968], p. 279 ff.) mentions the following examples of Jewish tailors from the literature of the twenties: Red-headed Motele, the hero of Iosif Utkin's "Povest' o ryžem Motele, gospodine inspektore, ravvine Isaje, i komissare Blox"; Lazik Rojtšvanc, hero of Il'ja Erenburg's *Burnaja žizn' Lazika Rojtšvanca*; and Eli Rubanovskij, the central character in Mixail Kozakov's "Čelovek, padajuščij nic."

11. Nadezhda Mandelstam, *Vtoraja kniga*, p. 359.

12. Although Professor Brown does not mention the reflection of Yiddish and Russian Jewish writing and dramatic literature in the figure of Mervis, he does point out the "thoroughly Semitic" atmosphere of *The Egyptian Stamp*.

13. See note 19 to Ch. II.

14. Dmitrij Segal, "Voprosy poètičeskoj organizacii . . . ," p. 328.

15. "American duel": the Russian is "amerikanskaja duèl'-kukuška," a composite image that needs glossing. According to Kiril Taranovsky, in an "American duel"—a piece of Russian folklore to which the American counterpart would, I suppose, be "Russian roulette"—the duelists are supposed to have their encounter inside a darkened room. *Kukuška*, according to the same authority, refers to a deadly game of hide-and-seek played—also in a darkened room—by prerevolutionary Russian army officers; the game consisted in one participant calling out "Cuckoo!" and then rapidly dodging out of the way, as the other fired a pistol in the direction of the call. Because the novella later connects the image of the duel with the theme of honor, there may also be an echo here of Pushkin's "Vystrel," whose protagonist also fires into "family canvases."

16. Segal, pp. 335-36.

17. Ibid., p. 348.

18. Ibid., p. 346.

19. Nadezhda Mandelstam, *Vtoraja kniga*, p. 212.

20. Cf. "Četvertaja proza": "Tjuremščiki ljubjat čitat' romany i bol'še, čem kto-libo, nuždajutsja v literature" (II, 188).

21. *Vtoraja kniga*, pp. 212-213.

22. The terms *pustota/pustoj* appear three times. The narrator's description of a page of his sketches ends with the line, "I pustoe mesto dlja ostal'nyx" (II, 21); in Ch. VIII, raised bridges connote "that everything must come to an abrupt end, that emptiness and yawning gaps are fabulous goods . . . ("čto vse dolžno oborvat'sja, čto *pustota i zijanie*—velikolepnyj tovar . . .")" (II, 36); the same chapter contains a description of life as "made from emptiness and glass ("iz *pustoty* i stekla")" (II, 40). In 1926, Mandelstam wrote an article on his friend, the actor Jaxontov, in which he included the following remark, not only making a similar association between emptiness and Petersburg, but offering an instructive clue to the prehistory of *Egipetskaja marka*: "Osnovnaja tema 'Peterburga' (a solo theater piece by Jaxontov which consisted of a montage of Petersburg tales)—èto strax 'malen'kix ljudej' pered velikim i vraždebnym gorodom. V dviženijax aktera vse vremja čuvstvujetsja strax prostranstva, stremlenie zasloniť sja ot nabegajuščej pustoty" (III, 113).

23. Segal refers to "Konec romana" in "Voprosy poètičeskoj organizacii . . . ," as does Boris Filipoff in his introduction to Mandelstam's prose in *Sobranie sočinenij*, II.

24. Lucien Chardon de Rubempré, who appears in Balzac's *Illusions perdues* and *Splendeurs et misères des courtisanes*, belongs to the type of hero with whose creation Mandelstam credits Balzac in "Konec romana": "Tipičeskaja biografija zaxvatčika i udačnika Bonaparta raspylilas' u Bal'zaka v desjatki tak nazyvaemyx 'romanov udači' (*roman de réussite*), gde osnovnaja sila ne ljubov', a kar'era, to esť stremlenie probiť sja iz nizšix i srednix social'nyx sloev v verxnie" (II, 267-268).

25. This passage, in particular the phrase "čto vse dolžno oborvaťsja," recalls the theme and language of "1 Janvarja 1924," st. 2, lines 13-15: "Ja znaju, s každym dnem slabeet žizni vydox,/Ešče nemnogo—*oborvut*/Prostuju pesenku o glinjanyx obidax."

26. Cf. lyric fragment No. 245: "Zamolči! Ni o čem, nikogda, nikomu—/Tam v požarišče vremja poet. . . . One could also connect "the fire of time" with the "philological" and "antiphilological flames" of *O prirode slova*.

27. See Donald C. Gillis, "The Persephone Myth in Mandelstam's *Tristia*," *California Slavic Studies*, IX, ed. N. V. Riasanovskij, Gleb Stuve, and Thomas Eekman (Berkeley: U. of Cal. Press, 1976), pp. 139-159.

28. The pine branch (*xvojnaja vetka*) is also associated with death, inasmuch as funeral wreaths are made from evergreen boughs in Russia.

29. Parts of this section have appeared in *Russian Literature*, No. 5/3 (1977), pp. 257-76.

30. Cf. Nils Åke Nilsson's discussion of a similar phenomenon in Oleša, in his "Through the Wrong End of the Binoculars: An Introduction to Jurij Oleša," *Major Soviet Writers: Essays in Criticism*, ed. Edward J. Brown (N. Y.: Oxford Univ. Press, 1973), pp. 254-279.

31. *Vtoraja kniga*, p. 78.

32. Kiril Taranovsky, *Essays on Mandel'stam*, p. 31.

33. Omry Ronen, "Leksičeskij povtor, podtekst i smysl' v poètike Osipa Mandel'štama," p. 378.

34. In Mandelstam's writing, the language-metaphor that equates moral and physical blemishes is not restricted to fiction. Cf. his Letter to Soviet Writers, published as no. 5 in the selection that first appeared in *Vestnik russkogo xristianskogo dviženija*: "Neuželi vy mogli podumat' čto ja budu dal'še razgulivat' s ètim pjatnom v vašej srede . . . ?"

35. *Vtoraja kniga*, p. 530.

36. The motif of *bol'šegolovye deti*, 'children with large heads,' links this passage to the lyric "Jazyk bulyžnika mne golubja ponjatnej," in which the Jacobins of the French Revolution are metaphorically described as "large-headed lions": "A podrastut oni (l'vjata)—to razve goda dva/ Deržalas' na plečax bol'šaja golova./ Bol'šegolovye—tam ruki podnimali/ I kljatvoj na peske kak jablokom igrali" (I, 109-10).

37. Anna Leopoldovna, mother of Ioann VI, ruled from 9 November to the night of 24 November 1741, when she was ousted by Elizaveta Petrovna, who was supported by members of the Preobraženskij Regiment. Anna Leopoldovna's brief reign followed Biron's regency. Parnok's history is faulty: Anna Leopoldovna was not invested with the title of Empress (*Imperatrica*). Her title was *pravitel'nica*, 'ruler.' Nadezhda Mandelstam suggests that the "Biron" passage reflects the family history that her husband first heard from his father, and later (after *The Egyptian Stamp* had been written) heard in a more circumstantial version from a distant relative whom the Mandelstams met quite by chance. Biron is supposed to have been responsible for bringing the first Mandelstam, a jeweler and watchmaker from Courland, into Russia (*Vtoraja kniga*, pp. 576-77). The editors of Mandelstam's *Collected Works* have uncovered a 1926 article by Valentin Parnax (upon whom Parnok is modeled) in which Parnax describes Mandelstam as "the descendant of a long line of Courland jewelers" (III, 399).

38. See the discussion of Bergsonism in *On the Nature of the Word* (II, 241-42).

39. Mandelstam may have been aware that France's funeral so outraged a group of younger writers (Louis Aragon, Andre Breton, Paul Eluard, Philippe Soupalt) that they responded with one of the earliest Surrealist manifestos, "Un Cadavre" (October 1924)—a circumstance that suggests the appropriateness of the allusion to this ceremonial funeral in *The Egyptian Stamp*, a work that also attacks a literary Establishment. (See Herbert S. Gershman, *The Surrealist Revolution in France*, Ann Arbor: University of Michigan Press, 1969, p. 86, for a discussion of "Un Cadavre.")

40. Omry Ronen's *An Approach to Mandelstam* (Jerusalem: The Magnes Press, 1983), which contains many illuminating comments on Mandelstam's prose, glosses the lost "cold white substance" as another allusion to Ippolit; specifically, to the percussion cap missing from the young man's pistol in the Pavlovsk episode. (Ronen, p. 277)

41. Professor Taranovsky has pointed out to me that Parnok's reflections upon his ancestry contain a nonpolemical reference to a subtext from Pushkin. In the sentence "A kolležskie

asessory, kotorym 'mog Gospoď pribaviť uma i deneg'," the quotation is from *Mednyj vsadnik* and implies Parnok's literary descent from Pushkin's poor Evgenij.

42. L. N. Tolstoj, *Anna Karenina*, Part 7, ch. XXVI, in *Sobranie sočinenij v dvadcati tomax*, ed. N. N. Akopova, N. K. Gudzij, N. N. Gusev, and M. V. Xrapčenko (Moscow: Goslitizdat, 1960-65), vol. 9, p. 370.

43. Ibid., pp. 388-89.

44. On the connection of birds and baked bread with poetry, see Taranovsky, *Essays on Mandelstam*, p. 35 ff.

45. Omry Ronen, "Osip Mandeľstam: An Ode and an Elegy," Diss. Harvard 1976, p. 288.

46. In his notice for the rejected story "The Bassoonist," Mandelstam comments that "to a certain extent the device (*priem*) of *The Egyptian Stamp*—showing the epoch from a 'bird's-eye view' ("pokaz èpoxi skvoż 'ptičij glaz')—is repeated" (II, 497). The letter to Korobova mentioned in Note 2 characterizes *The Egyptian Stamp* as a work "consisting of fragments" "sosto-jaščej iz fragmentov" (II, 493).

47. See Taranovsky, *Essays on Mandeľstam*, p. 58, for examples of "Petersburg's frightening black and yellow coloration" from modern Russian poetry.

48. For a brief discussion of Gruzenberg's career, see S. L. Kucerov, "Evrej v russkoj advo-kature," *Kniga o russkom evrejstve*, vol. 1 pp. 429-37.

49. Examples of the textural analogy are found in lyrics No. 10, 12, 13, 15, 203-XI, 275-I, 275-II, and 371.

50. See No. 223, which bears the date "January 1931": "Pomogi, Gospoď, ètu noč prožiť:/ Ja za żizn' bojuś—za tvoju rabu—/V Peterburge żiť—slovno spať v grobu."

CHAPTER IV

1. "Fourth Prose" was written in the winter of 1929-30, before the Mandelstams left for Armenia. See Nadezhda Mandelstam, *Vospominanija*, pp. 288-89: "My uezžali v Armeniju, i mne ne zaxotelos' vezti s soboj edinstvennyj èkzempljar 'Četvertoj'"; *Vtoraja kniga*, p. 592: "Na službu v gazetu 'Moskovskij komsomolec' Mandelstam postupil osen'ju 29 goda. Dotjanul on tam do fevralja 30 goda. V dekabre pribliziteľno on načal diktovať 'Četvertuju prozu'."

2. Jane Gary Harris, "An Inquiry into the Use of Autobiography as a Stylistic Determinant of the Modernist Aspect of Osip Mandeľstam's Literary Prose," *American Contributions to the Eighth International Congress of Slavists*, vol. 2, ed. Victor Terras (Columbus: Slavica Publishers, 1978), p. 251.

3. Both episodes are described in Nadezhda Mandelstam's memoirs (see especially the chs. entitled "Ne ubij" and "Pereocenka cennostej" in *Vospominanija*), in Clarence Brown's *Mandelstam*, ch. 8, and in the introductory note to Professor Brown's translation of "Fourth Prose" in *Hudson Review*, 23, no. 1 (Spring 1970), pp. 49-66. Two of Mandelstam's personal letters, Nos. 52 and 53 (III, 260-62), together with two letters to the respective editors of *Večernjaja Moskva* and *Literaturnaja gazeta* (II, 477-80) throw light on his reaction to the Ulenspiegel affair.

4. Nadezhda Mandelstam, *Vospominanija*, p. 186.

5. Ibid., p. 185.

6. D. Segal, "Voprosy poètičeskoj organizacii . . . ," p. 351.

7. "Centraľnaja komissija ulučšenija byta učenyx," 'Central Commission for the Improvement of the Welfare of Scholars.'

8. As Mandelstam's "Pis'mo v redakciju 'Večernej Moskvy'" (see Note 3) indicates, references to the "literary overcoat" are first of all a response to Gornfeld's accusation that Mandelstam had stolen his overcoat, i.e., had plagiarized his translation. See Clarence Brown's discussion of this point in the introduction to his translation of "Fourth Prose."

9. A *konoval* is not a licensed veterinarian but someone who is self-taught or who carries on folk practices for treating horses. By extension *konoval* has come to mean 'quack,' i.e., an incompetent physician.

10. "Sluts and slobs": the Russian is *xaldy-baldy*, translated by Clarence Brown as "idiot-shmidiot," by Jane Gary Harris as "Higgledy-Piggledy," and by Sidney Monas (*Osip Mandelstam: Selected Essays* Austin: University of Texas Press, 1977) as "hack-shmack." The first element of this "nonsense phrase," as Professor Monas calls it, suggests the nominative plural of *xalda*, 'a vulgar, insolent woman' (in Ušakov the definition is "grubaja naglaja ženščina") or the Russian form of *Khalde*, the people of the Urartan state in the 14th-17th centuries B. C.; the second word sounds like the nominative plural of *balda*, a colloquialism for "fool."

11. Henry Gifford, "Mandelstam and the Journey," in *Osip Mandelstam, Journey to Armenia*, tr. Sidney Monas (San Francisco: George F. Ritchie, 1979), p. 13.

12. Carol Avins, *Border Crossings: The West and Russian Identity in Soviet Literature 1917-1934* (Berkeley: University of California Press, 1983), pp. 148-56.

13. On Dante's inferno as an analog for the Stalinist order and, more generally, on the Commedia as the master-text for Mandelstam in the period 1928-38, see Marina Glazova, "Mandel'stam and Dante," *Studies in Soviet Thought*, 28 (1984), pp. 281-335. On Mandelstam's use of Dante and Goethe in the "Journey," see Nancy Pollak, "The Obscure Way to Mandelstam's Armenia," diss. Yale University, 1984.

14. That Mandelstam is using his prose as a workshop for constructing a new outlook, as Nadezhda Mandelstam states, and that the implicit author of the "Journey" is, in effect, arguing with himself, is supported by an interesting claim made by Kuzin in his memoirs ("Ob O. M. Mandel'stame," *Vestnik russkogo xristijanskogo dviženija*, No. 140 [1983], pp. 99-129): Even after Armenia Mandelstam would have moods when a desire to champion the new order would come over him: "In particular, evidently there was for him a strong temptation to bring himself to believe in our official ideology, to accept all the horror for which it served as a screen, and to stand among the ranks of those actively fighting for the great ideas and for the splendid socialist future."

15. Mandelstam's lyric "K nemeckoj reči" (No. 266) is dedicated to Kuzin.

16. See Nadezhda Mandelstam, *Vtoraja kniga*, pp. 473-525.

17. In *Vospominanija*, pp. 232-34, Nadezhda Mandelstam uses the phrase "odin dobavočnyj den'" as a chapter title, to signify the period between Mandelstam's return from exile and his second arrest.

18. Sidney Monas, op. cit., p. 75.

19. A. Z. Ležnev, *Proza Puškina*, 2d ed. (Moscow: "Xudožestvennaja literatura," 1966), pp. 132-35.

20. A. S. Pushkin, "Putešestvie v Arzrum," *Polnoe sobranie sočinenij*, ed. V. D. Bonč-Bruevič (Moscow: Academia, 1937-50), VIII, 450.

21. The tendency toward an ornamental style does not rule out an occasional instance of sentence rhythms that bear some resemblance to Pushkin's. The last paragraph of "Journey to Armenia," for example, has a very different syntactic pattern than the opening paragraph:

> Legok son na kočev'jax. Telo, izmučennoe prostranstvom, tepleet, vyprjamljaetsja, pripominaet dlinu puti. Xrebtovye tropy begut murašami po pozvonočniku. Barxatnye luga otjagoščajut i ščekočut veki. Proležni ovragov vyxramyvajutsja v boka. Son murujet tebja, zamurovyvaet. Poslednjaja mysl': nužno ob'exat' kakuju-to grjadu" (II, 176).

The predominance of relatively brief phrases in this passage is associated with the narrator's weariness and with the equestrian tempo of his ascent; the resulting rhythmic structure also creates an effective final cadence for the narrative. However, if there is a Pushkinian echo in this and similar passages, it certainly does not extend to the semantic structure.

WORKS CITED

The most extensive compilation of bibliographic references to Mandelstam is to be found in Volumes 3 and 4 of the Struve-Filipoff *Sobranie sočinenij*. Nikita Struve's *Ossip Mandelstam* includes a short annotated bibliography.

Aleksandrova, V. "Evrej v sovetskoj literature," *Kniga o russkom evrejstve*, vol. 2. Ed. Ja. G. Frumkin, Gregor Aronson, and Alexis Goldenweiser. N. Y.: Sojuz russkix evreev, 1968.

Aronson, Gregor. "Jews in Russian Literary and Political Life," *Russian Jewry 1860-1917*. Ed. Jacob Frumkin, Gregor Aronson, and Alexis Goldenweiser, tr. Mirra Ginzburg. N. Y.: T. Yoseloff, 1966. The English translation of Aronson's article is a substantially reworked version of the Russian original that appeared in the first volume of *Kniga o russkom evrejstve*.

Belyj, Andrej. *Kotik Letaev*. Petrograd: "Èpoxa," 1922.

Berkovskij, N. "O proze Mandeľstama," *Tekuščaja literatura*. Moscow: "Federacija," 1930.

Broyde, Steven. *Osip Mandeľstam and his Age*, Harvard Slavic Monographs, No. 1. Cambridge: Harvard University Press, 1975.

Brown, Clarence, trans. "Fourth Prose," *Hudson Review*, no. 1 (1970).

――――, *Mandelstam*. Cambridge: Cambridge University Press, 1973.

――――, *The Prose of Osip Mandelstam*. Princeton: Princeton University Press, 1965.

Filipoff, Boris. "Proza Mandeľstama," *Osip Mandeľštam: Sobranie sočinenij*. Ed. G. P. Struve and B. A. Filipoff, 2d ed., vol. 2. N. Y. Inter-Language Literary Associates, 1971.

Gershman, Herbert S. *The Surrealist Revolution in France*. Ann Arbor: University of Michigan Press, 1969.

Gifford, Henry. "Mandelstam and the Journey," *Osip Mandelstam: Journey to Armenia*. Tr. Sidney Monas. San Francisco: George F. Ritchie, 1979.

Gillis, Donald C. "The Persephone Myth in Mandeľstam's *Tristia*," *California Slavic Studies*, no. 9. Ed. N. V. Riasanovskij, Gleb Struve, and Thomas Eekman. Berkeley: Univ. of California Press, 1976.

Ginzburg, Lidija. "Poètika Osipa Mandeľštama, *Izvestija Akademii nauk SSSR, Serija literatury i jazyka*, vol. 31, part 4 (1972).

Glazova, Marina. "Mandeľštam and Dante," *Studies in Soviet Thought*, 28 (1984).

Harris, Jane Gary. *Mandelstam: The Complete Critical Prose and Letters*. Ann Arbor: Ardis, 1979.

――――, "An Inquiry into the Use of Autobiography as a Stylistic Determinant of the Modernist Aspect of Osip Mandeľštam's Literary Prose," *American Contributions to the Eighth International Congress of Slavists*, Vol. 2. Ed. Victor Terras. Columbus: Slavica Publishers, 1978.

Isenberg, Charles. "Associative Chains in *Egipetskaja marka*," *Russian Literature*, July 1977.

Jakobson, Roman. "Concluding Statement: Linguistics and Poetics," *Style in Language*. Ed. Thomas A. Sebeok. N. Y.: MIT Press and John Wiley & Sons, 1960.

Koubourlis, Demetrius J. *A Concordance to the Poems of Osip Mandelstam*. Ithaca: Cornell University Press, 1974.

Kučerov, S. L. "Evrej v russkoj advokature," *Kniga o russkom evrejstve*, Vol. 1. N. Y.: Sojuz russkix evreev, 1960.

Kuzin, B. S. "Ob O. M. Mandeľštame," *Vestnik russkogo xristjanskogo dviženija*, No. 140 (1983).

Levin, Ju. I., Segal, D. M., Timenčik, R. D., Toporov, V. N., and Civjan, T. V. "Russkaja semantičeskaja poètika kak potencialʹnaja kulʹturnaja paradigma," *Russian Literature*, No. 7/8 (1974).

Ležnev. A. Z. *Proza Puškina*, 2d ed. Moscow: "Xudožestvennaja literatura," 1966.

Lukács, Georg. "The Ideology of Modernism, *Realism in Our Time*. Tr. John and Necke Mander. N.Y.: Harper and Row, 1971.

L'vov-Rogačevskij, V. *Russko-evrejskaja literatura*. Moscow: 1922.

Mandelstam, Nadezhda. *Vospominanija*, N.Y.: Chekhov Press, 1971.

———, *Vtoraja kniga*. Paris: YMCA Press, 1972.

Mandelstam, Osip. *Sobranie sočinenij*. Ed. G. P. Struve and B. A. Filipoff, 2d ed., 3 vols. N.Y.: Inter-Language Literary Associates, 1971; vol. 4. Paris: YMCA Press, 1981.

Merežkovskij, Dmitrij, ed. *Dafnis i Xloja. Drevne-grečeskaja povest' Longusa o ljubvi pastuška i pastuški na Ostrove Lezbose*. St. Pbg.: M. V. Pirožkov, 1904.

Monas, Sidney. *Osip Mandelstam: Selected Essays*. Austin: University of Texas Press, 1977.

———, "Translator's Notes," *Osip Mandelstam: Journey to Armenia*. San Francisco: George F. Ritchie, 1979.

Nilsson, Nils Åke. "Through the Wrong End of the Binoculars: An Introduction to Jurij Oleša." *Major Soviet Writers: Essays in Criticism*. Ed. Edward J. Brown. N. Y.: Oxford Univ. Press, 1973.

Pollak, Nancy. "The Obscure Way to Mandelstam's Armenia." Dissertation Yale University, 1984.

Puškin, A. S. "Putešestvie v Erzerum," *Polnoe sobranie sočinenij*, Vol. 8. Ed. V. D. Bonc-Bruevič. Moscow: Academia, 1937-50.

Ronen, Omry. *An Approach to Mandelstam*, Bibliotheca Slavica Hierosolymitana. Jerusalem: The Magnes Press, 1983.

———, "Leksičeskij povtor, podtekst i smysl v poètike Osipa Mandel'štama," *Slavic Poetics: Essays in Honor of Kiril Taranovsky*. Ed. Roman Jakobson, C. H. van Schooneveld, and Dean S. Worth. The Hague: Mouton Press, 1973.

———, "Osip Mandelstam: an Ode and an Elegy." Dissertation, Harvard University, 1976.

———, "Mandelshtam, Osip Emilyevich," *Encyclopedia Judaica Yearbook*, 1973.

Segal, D. M. "The Connection Between the Semantics and the Formal Structure of a Text," *Mythology*. Ed. Pierre Maranda. Middlesex, England: Penguin, 1972.

———, "Voprosy poètičeskoj organizacii semantiki v proze Mandel'štama," *Russian Poetics: Proceedings of the International Colloquium at UCLA, September 22-26, 1975*. Ed. Thomas Eekman and Dean Worth. Columbus: Slavica Publishers, 1983.

Sola, Agnes. "Mandel'štam, poéticien formaliste?", *Revue des Etudes Slaves*, 50, Fasc. 1 (1977).

Solov'ev, Vladimir S. "Buddistskoe nastroenie v poèzii," *Sobranie sočinenij*, Vol. 7. St. Pbg.: "Prosveščenie, 1907.

Struve, Nikita. *Ossip Mandelstam*. Paris: Institut d'Etudes Slaves, 1982.

Taranovsky, Kiril. *Essays on Mandelstam*. Harvard Slavic Studies, Vol. 6. Cambridge: Harvard Univ. Press, 1976.

Tolstoj, L. N. *Anna Karenina. Sobranie sočinenij v dvadcati tomax*, Vols. 8-9. Ed. N. N. Akopova, N. K. Gudzij, N. N. Gusev, and M. V. Xrapčenko. Moscow: Goslitizdat, 1960-65.

Vygotskij, Lev Semenovič. *Myšlenie i reč'*. 1934; reprinted Moscow: Izd. akad. pedagogičeskix nauk, 1956.

West, Daphne M. *Mandelstam: The Egyptian Stamp*. Birmingham Slavonic Monographs, No. 10. Birmingham, U. K.: Univ. of Birmingham, 1980.

Zholkovsky, A. K. "Invarianty i struktura teksta, II. Mandel'štam: 'Ja p'ju za voennye astry'," *Slavica Hierosolymitana*, No. 4 (1979).